Schiller to Derrida

Idealism in aesthetics

JULIET SYCHRAVA

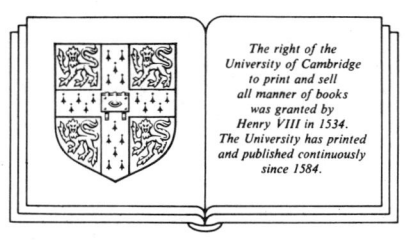

The right of the
University of Cambridge
to print and sell
all manner of books
was granted by
Henry VIII in 1534.
The University has printed
and published continuously
since 1584.

CAMBRIDGE UNIVERSITY PRESS

Cambridge
New York   New Rochelle
Melbourne   Sydney

Published by the Press Syndicate of the University of Cambridge
The Pitt Building, Trumpington Street, Cambridge CB2 1RP
32 East 57th Street, New York, NY 10022, USA
10 Stamford Road, Oakleigh, Melbourne 3166, Australia

First published 1989

Printed in Great Britain at
the University Press, Cambridge

British Library cataloguing in publication data
Sychrava, Juliet
Schiller to Derrida: idealism in
aesthetics.
1. Aesthetics
I. Title
111'.85

Library of Congress cataloguing in Publication data
Sychrava, Juliet.
Schiller to Derrida.
Bibliography.
1. Idealism in literature.   2. Schiller, Friedrich,
1759–1805 – Criticism and interpretation.   3. Romanticism.
4. Derrida, Jacques.   5. Clare, John, 1793–1864 –
Criticism and interpretation.   6. Structuralism
(Literary analysis) I. Title.
PN56.I4S93   1989   809.1'9145   88–35333

ISBN 0 521 36027 7

Schiller to Derrida

27.50

exhib stock

CONTENTS

INTRODUCTION

What made Wordsworth unique, one twentieth-century critic claimed, was

the peculiar method which he developed to draw the intellectual from the visual. His need to combine both these realms . . . is also what keeps Wordsworth from being what we commonly consider a 'landscape' poet . . . one who, like John Clare or Edward Thomas, keeps primarily to visual impression.[1]

The distinction made between a 'visual' descriptive poet, and an 'intellectual' expressive poet is well established in twentieth-century literary criticism, which typically favours the latter kind of poetry. This preference, and the distinction itself, can be traced back to an essay written by Friedrich Schiller at the end of the eighteenth century. The essay, *On the naive and sentimental in literature*[2] (1795–6), introduced an enormously influential distinction between 'naive' – broadly speaking 'realist' literature and 'sentimental' – broadly speaking 'idealist' literature. But although this distinction found favour, and lived on as a stylistic opposition of the kind illustrated above, that was not its original purpose.

The guiding principle of Schiller's essay, and all of his philosophical work, was the belief that art could re-unite man's divided psyche, bringing together the sensuous and the rational aspects of human nature which his great predecessor, Kant, had severed in his epistemology. The *Essay* develops this principle in the literary domain, arguing that the two aesthetic principles – the naive (or real and sensuous) principle and the sentimental (or ideal and rational) principle – had to be united in a new and higher synthesis.

1

However, Schiller himself was a fundamentally idealist or sentimental writer, indebted to and to some extent unable to escape the influence of Kant. In the first chapter of this book, I look at the way in which his allegiance to the subjective, idealist method and principle in aesthetics undermined Schiller's own endeavour; how despite himself he ended up widening the gap between this principle and its realist counterpart, between naive and sentimental literature.

This inevitable failure springs from the very method of the 'sentimental' or idealist writer, which relies on opposition for its dynamic.

If Schiller himself was acutely aware of the problems of his own 'sentimental' vantage-point, his successors were less cautious. The Romantic movement seized on Schiller's essay as a justification of the sentimental or subjective principle for art. His critical categories were transformed into the ubiquitous classical–romantic opposition, but whereas Schiller had aimed for a synthesis of the two, his successors focused on the particular virtues of the romantic, which – because it is underpinned by the dominant idealist epistemology – tends to overwhelm the classical alternative. Just as the former is identified with the subjective, idealist principle introduced by Kant, so the latter is identified with the discarded objective realism of the philosophers who preceded the Kantian revolution.

Coleridge passed the classical–Romantic distinction on – and his influence on practical criticism is felt in the tacit assumption by nineteenth- and twentieth-century critics that there is an intrinsic epistemological difference between the language of the Romantics and anything which preceded it. The notion of a peculiarly Romantic idiom is silently supported by the notion of an epistemological difference between Romantic art and earlier art which derives – ultimately – from Schiller's association of the naive with the realist, and the sentimental with the idealist, principle. Chapter 2 deals with the emergence of this belief in a privileged 'Romantic' idiom and style and the way in which it conceals the privileging of an idealist over a realist perspective. A philosophical difference is transformed into a stylistic difference – largely through a trick of organicist idiom.

The legacy of this distinction in the twentieth century is a preference for certain kinds of poetry over others – notably those

kinds which express idealist sentiments. In the third chapter I
look at the way in which the poet John Clare has been received as
'naive' and contrasted with major Romantics such as
Wordsworth. As the 'peasant poet' of an urbane society, Clare
received patronage which put him in the kind of relation to that
society in which Schiller's naive stood to the sentimental.
Contemporary and subsequent accounts of Clare's work insist he
is purely descriptive and simply imitated nature, while
Wordsworth is thought to transform what he saw by fusing
'objective' observation with 'subjective' spirit. The comparison
goes back to Schiller – though it is a much cruder version than the
original – and is again underpinned by the tacit distinction
between a realist (mimetic) aesthetic and an idealist (expressive)
aesthetic. I also look at the kinds of distinctions between 'literal'
and 'figurative' that such criticism implies, and I subject the
notion of 'objective' description to scrutiny.

The term 'descriptive' has a long history in aesthetics. Chapter
4 considers the emergence and persistence of the term through
eighteenth- and nineteenth-century criticism. Sustained in the
eighteenth century by a comparison of poetry with painting (the
'ut pictura poesis'), 'description' implies a particular understanding of visual art as a natural imitation and of verbal art as aspiring
to the visual.

While such views run contrary to the philosophical foundations of Romantic aesthetics, I suggest that Romantic critics cling
to the notion of descriptive writing – and the accompanying
assumptions about visual art – in order to set up an artificial
'naive' poetic principle against which an 'expressive' or truly
sentimental poetry can be defined. This tendency to retain a
rejected or historically superseded aesthetic as a 'naive' can again
be traced back to Schiller's essay, which, despite itself, retains
and patronizes the aesthetic of the pre-Kantians. The Romantics, I
argue, develop their own version of the pictorial analogy,
inconsistently retained alongside the eighteenth-century version
to illustrate the concept of an 'expressive' poetry. In this way, the
pictorial analogy is used to support two opposed and incompatible accounts of language.

However, in both cases visual art is construed as the 'naive'
counterpart of verbal art; it is more 'natural', less mediated, less
complex. In chapter 4, these eighteenth- and nineteenth-century

conceptions of the relationship between the arts are criticized and an alternative twentieth-century account of visual art and its relationship with verbal art is considered.

This is the account given by the pragmatic philosopher Nelson Goodman in his book, *Languages of art*.[3] Goodman offers an alternative to the neo-classical or idealist accounts of visual art, which can be used to argue against the tendency to conceive of visual art as a naive counterpart of verbal art. Goodman insists that visual art, like verbal art, makes use of a conventional and complex symbol system and is not more simple or naive than the latter. But the two are not the same: Goodman differentiates them in a new version of the pictorial analogy.

He argues that a painting and a poem are differently positioned with respect to the 'symbol systems' within which they occur. A painting occurs within what he calls a 'denser' symbol system: that is, one in which the individual terms which make up the system are less distinct and determinate than those in an 'articulate' symbol system, such as language. Here, the characters or terms are reasonably distinct, syntactically and semantically, whilst in a 'dense' system they run together. This means that whilst we can see how a poem − which occurs within the comparatively 'articulate' symbol system of poetic language − is governed by a set of rules, which we can distinguish from the poem itself, we cannot see what set of rules might similarly govern a painting. Whilst language is not semantically articulate, like music, it has a syntax which we cannot find in painting − a 'dense' symbol system.

This theory, which I explain in more detail, can be used to devise a new pictorial analogy. I suggest that the relation between the 'naive' and the 'sentimental' be reformulated as a 'dense'/'articulate' relation, following Goodman's terms. A poem will be 'dense' with respect to a particular critical system if we cannot formulate rules from it which conform to those of the system. Accordingly, a 'naive' poem will be 'dense' with respect to a sentimental critical system; it will fail to conform to that system. We will find no rationale, no system, in such a poem. A 'sentimental' poem, on the other hand, will be 'articulate' and will provide us with a set of suitable rules. These 'rules' may simply be a question of 'being about' the right kind of things. This allows us to reformulate naiveté not as an intrinsic characteristic of texts, but as a relative quality, both with respect to a critical system and with respect to other texts. 'Dense' and 'articulate' are comparative terms which depend on the way we construe texts within systems.

Chapter 4 thus puts forward an alternative explanation of what 'naiveté' might be, which avoids making any absolute or evaluative distinctions.

In chapter 5, I turn to the challenge offered by post-structuralist theory, arguing that this can be seen as a latter-day sentimentalism. Comparing Schiller's aesthetic with Derrida's, I trace a development from Schiller through the Romantics and Coleridge to post-structuralist thought: a 'sentimental' tendency whereby radical modernity articulates itself against a 'naive' which it sets up as a target for that purpose. Schiller contrasted the determinate, limited nature of the naive with the relativistic, open-endedness of the sentimental and this contrast is preserved in much (popular) post-structuralist thought, which upholds the myth of a determinate and limited interpretation of a text, just in order to reveal it as a myth. In both cases, the dynamic behind the argument is an opposition between the favoured contemporary aesthetic and a rejected aesthetic which is maintained and then dismantled by the sentimental critic.

Furthermore, much post-structuralist thought preserves the ambiguity between an account of *general* aesthetic experience in the subject, and an account of the *particular* art work as object, which was engendered by Schiller's transformation of Kant. This ambiguity was sustained in the Romantic concept of the poem as organism – something which is at once the process of living and its product. It survived into post-structuralism, which often favours a similarly ambiguous idiom. Critics talk of 'the text', as though it were a finished object, just in order to point out that there is nothing but the subjective process of reading or writing.

This is a sentimental device. Sentimental critics preserve the idea that the art work is 'naive' – a complete, bounded object – only in order to reveal that it is, in fact, 'sentimental' – an unfinished, subjective process. This device can be countered as follows:

Whereas it can be argued that every text depends on a context, and is accordingly *relative* (sentimental), it can also be argued that every context *determines* a text, which is accordingly determinate (naive). For this is just what systems or contexts do. We can just as well point out that a text is determined by, as that it is relative to, a system. We can reveal *process* in *product*,. as a sentimental aesthetic will, or we can determine the *product* from the *process*, as a naive aesthetic will. (Idealism does the former, realism the latter).

I argue that just such a double perspective – whereby we acknowledge not only how a text reveals its subjectivity, its relativism to a context or system, but also how it is read as determinate within the constraints of that context or system – can be found in Kant's third Critique. Kant's aesthetic allows for both 'reflective' and 'determinant' perspectives and thus permits the same thing to be seen in different ways. His insistence that, with respect to its 'outside' – the transcendental – the system is relative, reminds us that these are only ways of seeing. The system is determinate with respect to its 'inside' – what it determines – and reflective with respect to its 'outside' – what it is determined by. I suggest that this state is reversed in sentimentalism, which dissolves the internal distinctions of Kant's system in a wash of relativism while insisting on the absolute authority of that relativism. This philosophical alternative to sentimentalism can be dovetailed with my account of the naive as 'dense' with respect to a critical system.

In my final chapter, I put the alternative into practice. Taking up the account of Clare's poetry given by John Barrell in *The idea of landscape and the sense of place*,[4] I give my own reading of Clare as 'naive'. Barrell argues that Clare's work expresses a personal resistance to poetic convention, systematizing and philosophizing; and stresses the importance of communicating the particular instead. This reading of Clare as resisting the generalizing tendencies of a sentimental aesthetic accords with my own account of the naive poet as 'dense' with regard to a sentimental aesthetic. This is a question not only of what Clare chose to talk about, but also of his actual inarticulacy, recalcitrant grammar and idiom. In this chapter I look at the poetry included in Clare's anthology, *The midsummer cushion*[5] and show how it can be said both to articulate a 'dense' aesthetic and to achieve 'density' with respect to sentimental critical demands.

This is a reading of Clare as naive – not because he was unable to attain the heights of Romanticism, but because he subscribed to a different aesthetic and was interested in different things from his Romantic contemporaries. Criticism evaluated Clare as a naive poet because its requirements were sentimental and it construed non-conformity as inferiority.

This book shows how the philosophical idealism of the sentimental tradition underlies many apparently 'innocent' discriminations between literary texts. It is a tradition which persists in contemporary literary critisism and which nurtures philosophical contradictions in order to define modernity against the past. This is primarily achieved through the preservation of the notional 'naive'.

1

SCHILLER AND THE SENTIMENTAL TRADITION

'Sentimental' poetry, in Schiller's sense of the word, plays an incomparably greater part in the history of literature than 'naive' poetry. Even the idylls of Theocritus himself owe their existence not . . . to genuine roots in nature . . . but to a reflective feeling for nature and a romantic conception of the common folk.[1]

OVERVIEW

'An art that is to be *naive* . . . is a contradiction'. The point – made by Kant in the *Critique of judgment*[2] – is clear: 'naive' implies 'without artifice' while 'art' by definition involves artifice. Nonetheless, the concept of a naive poetry, and, hence, the contradiction Kant identified, are enshrined in the history of literary criticism since Schiller. The history of this contradiction constitutes what I call the 'sentimental' tradition.

Though Schiller himself did not belong to this tradition, it begins with his essay *On the naive and sentimental in literature* (hereafter 'the *Essay*') which gave the terms of its title currency in the vocabulary of nineteenth-century criticism (see Helen Watanabe-O'Kelly's introduction to the *Essay*, pp. 12–13). More importantly, it provided the seed for countless related and bastardized versions of the *Essay*'s original opposition between 'naive' and 'sentimental' – notably the familiar classical–romantic opposition.

In this chapter, I examine Schiller's essay and his aesthetic to show just what he meant by those terms and the way in which they were significant for subsequent literary theories. How exactly can literature be naive? How does this term function in

8

Schiller's aesthetic – and in the sentimental tradition of his followers? Before turning to these terms, however, the *Essay* must be placed in its philosophical context.

SCHILLER'S PLACE IN HISTORY

Schiller's *Essay* concentrates sufficiently on individual texts to read, at times, like a literary critical work. But its motivation and dynamic are best understood in the context of Schiller's philosophical endeavour and his more explicitly philosophical text, the *Aesthetic education*.[3]

This sets out Schiller's aesthetic theory, the reworking of Kant's aesthetic, which constituted a turning-point in the history of German idealist philosophy. Kant's system had provided the first full account of the aesthetic as an independent way of knowing the world, with its own governing principle, but this account of the aesthetic left it with a very restricted role in human experience and one with which Schiller, like other followers of Kant, was not satisfied.

Kant's exploration of human experience divides it into two distinct domains: the sensuous – which is conditioned by our necessary existence in the physical world – and the moral or rational, in which we are free by virtue of our self-determining moral activity. This dualism was something many of Kant's followers found unacceptable, and it was discussed by Schiller at length.

Nature deals no better with Man than with the rest of her works: she acts for him as long as he is as yet incapable of acting for himself as a free intelligence. But what makes him Man is precisely this: that he does not stop short at what Nature herself made of him, but has the power of retracing by means of Reason the steps she took on his behalf, of transforming the work of blind compulsion into a work of free choice, and of elevating physical necessity into moral necessity.

(*AE*, 3rd Letter, p. 11)

As this passage shows, Schiller recast the Kantian dualism as a *historical* progression from necessity to freedom and one which is extended from the configuration of the individual faculties discussed in Kant to the history of the human race. This revision of Kant's austere and structural account of human knowledge by a historical and psychological progression is typical of Schiller. It is a progression which must end in synthesis.

But how does this apply to aesthetics? In addressing the Kantian dualism of necessity and freedom, Schiller was also addressing himself to Kant's account of art, which he found inadequate. Like the rest of Kant's system, his account of art was formally couched in terms of the structure of the individual's faculties, not in terms of the living experience of the work of art – something Schiller wanted to remedy. Art, in Kant's system, is 'aesthetic judgment' and falls into the domain covered by his third Critique, the *Critique of judgment*. Judgment, in Kant's system, has an intermediate position between understanding – the faculty of knowledge and thus of sensuous man, and reason – the faculty of desire and thus of moral man, and is the means whereby the two are connected. This is because it is the faculty whereby we are able to bring particular sense data under general moral or rational laws.

Where does this leave art? Aesthetic judgment is one of two varieties of judgment – *aesthetic* and *teleological*. Both these kinds of judgment involve seeing an object as 'purposive', that is, judging it to be harmonious: in the first case with the external laws of nature, and in the second with its own internal laws. This is the place art has in Kant's system – as a way of judging an object to be inwardly purposive.

This gives art a very limited role in life. It has no real part to play in man's aspiration to moral truth, nor does Kant's system give any account of what the aesthetic experience means for the living individual and for culture and society.

These were the shortcomings Schiller attacked. In Kant's system, judgment was already the mediating or harmonizing faculty, midway between the two domains of necessity and freedom. Schiller reworked Kant so that aesthetic experience itself became the lived union of sense and reason, the harmonious experience in which man gained insight into moral truth. He reworked aesthetic judgment so that it was no longer an austere and formal way of apprehending an object but a moving and personal experience, the crucible in which man's two natures dissolved and were remade in a new unity.

So, in Schiller's work, the aesthetic becomes the very centre of human experience and the centre of philosophy. This is the reason why Schiller is so important to the history of aesthetics. His revision of Kant's epistemology to give an account of art as the high road to moral truth provided a justification for art as the most important activity in which man engages, and provided the impetus for a philosophical movement which took art as its model and ideal: post-Kantian idealism.

Leonard Wessel summarizes Schiller's importance in terms of his

attempt to resolve the dualism of Kantian philosophy on the basis of aesthetic categories. After Schiller, German philosophers felt obliged to integrate aesthetics into their metaphysical systems.[4]

This importance is acknowledged by Hegel, who points out that

It is *Schiller* [1759–1805] who must be given great credit for breaking through the Kantian subjectivity and abstraction of thinking and for venturing on an attempt to get beyond this by intellectually grasping the unity and reconciliation as the truth and by actualising them in artistic production.[5]

Not only Hegel, but Schelling, Fichte and Schopenhauer, take up Schiller's emphasis on art and the aesthetic. In his history of the period, Arnold Hauser points to the significance attributed to the work of art from Schiller onwards:

The harmonious structure of the work of art was transferred from the aesthetic sphere to the whole cosmos, and an artistic plan was ascribed to the creator of the universe . . . . That 'the beautiful is a manifestation of secret powers of nature' was asserted even by . . . Goethe, and the whole natural philosophy of the romantic movement revolved around this idea. Aesthetics became the basic discipline and the organ of metaphysics.[6]

Schiller's aesthetic was similarly important for the emerging discipline of literary theory and criticism. Rather than considering the aesthetic as a function within a formal philosophical system, he considered it as a practice and experience of the human subject, and thus opened the way for accounts of art as a creative activity, and for Romantic theories of the imagination. It is for this reason that Schiller is described by René Wellek as 'the fountainhead of all later German critical theory'.[7] David Simpson, in his overview of Schiller's successors, *German aesthetic and literary criticism* notes that in the transition from the *Critique of Judgment* to Hegel's *Aesthetics* one can trace already a move from rational philosophy to something approaching what we now recognize as 'literary criticism'.[8]

Schiller is the prime mover in that transition. Because he was less concerned with rational systematizing than with communicating the way art resolves the contradictions of life — he describes himself as 'little practised in the use of scholastic modes' (*AE*, 1st Letter, p. 3) — he can provide an account of art and of the creative imagination as the key to truth. This is why literary historians — notably M. H. Abrams — see him as the ultimate author of Romanticism, because he

inaugurates the concept of the cardinal role of art, and of the imaginative faculty which produces art, as the reconciling and unifying agencies in a disintegrating mental and social world of alien and warring fragments — a concept which came to be a central tenet of Romantic faith, manifested in various formulations by thinkers so diverse as Schelling, Novalis, Blake, Coleridge, Wordsworth and Shelley.[9]

Before Kant and Schiller, German theories of art and the aesthetic had been largely constrained by rationalism, which considered the aesthetic as a lesser form of knowledge rather than a subjective experience. Schiller has been seen by the literary historians as the first defector, pointing away from classical theories of art (which set out formal rules of composition) to more expressive theories of art as activity and process.[10]

It is not difficult to see why this was the case. Goethe himself identified Schiller's essay as the origin of the notion of Romanticism, and of the subjective principle for art. He remarks that

the concept of classical and romantic literature which is now spreading worldwide and is causing so many quarrels and divisions . . . emanated originally from Schiller and me. In literature I held to the principle of an objective procedure and only wanted to admit this as valid. Schiller, however, who worked quite subjectively, thought his way was the right one and in order to defend himself against me, he wrote the essay on naive and sentimental literature.   (*Essay*, Introduction, p. 13)

Goethe's words reveal exactly how Schiller's *Essay* came to be read by his successors. It was read primarily as a definition (and defence) of a particularly modern way of writing which came to be called Romantic and which was transmitted via Coleridge into twentieth-century aesthetic and literary criticism, where it still makes its presence felt. This is because, as Goethe indicates, it put forward a 'subjective' principle or rationale for literature to be set against the prevailing classical model – to which Goethe himself subscribed. This 'subjective' principle – the 'sentimental' of the *Essay* – underlies Romantic theories of literature.

What exactly is this sentimental principle? Schiller's aesthetic, as described briefly above, concentrates on the harmonious reconciliation of the Kantian dualism – sense and reason – in the aesthetic experience. In the *Essay*, the naive and the sentimental are two different aesthetic principles or kinds of literature loosely corresponding to this sense–reason dualism. Like sense and reason in the *Education*, they must ultimately be reconciled in a higher aesthetic principle. Throughout the essay, they are described in a number of different ways, but the sentimental – described as subjective, reflective and artificial – essentially corresponds to an idealist perspective, while the naive corresponds to a realist perspective. Watanabe-O'Kelly summarizes:

Schiller mentions Realism and Idealism as the two types of personality which correspond to the literary characteristics of the naive and the sentimental. The realist (or naive writer) thus bases his ideas on the real world around him, the idealist (or the sentimental writer) bases his on the ideal on what he imagines the world should be.

(Essay, Introduction, p. 13)

This is why, as Goethe points out, Schiller sees his own work as intrinsically and unavoidably sentimental. Schiller's own aesthetic was firmly based on Kant's.

As Goethe also points out, Schiller's work spawned an active debate over the respective merits of the naive and the sentimental or, as they became more widely known, the classical and the Romantic. But although Schiller considered his own writing to be governed by the subjective – or sentimental – principle, he was not himself an advocate of Romanticism or the Romantic cause. While the *Essay* contrasts the two aesthetic modes, naive and sentimental, it is driven by the belief that the two must be harmoniously reconciled in a higher synthesis. Schiller stresses the need for this union throughout the work and is frequently critical of the sentimental tendency in its wilder excesses.

But whatever Schiller intended, his *Essay* was used by many of his followers as the basis for what was to become – via

Romanticism – a sentimental tradition. Literary historians, such as René Wellek, describe how

In a changed form, his method continues in the writings of the two Schlegels, in Schelling, and in Solger; it comes to England through the mediation of Coleridge; and it culminates in Hegel, who in turn deeply influenced many 19th-century critics.[11]

M. H. Abrams illustrates in more detail some of the ways in which this happened.[12] As Wilkinson and Willoughby explain in their outline of the transmission of Schiller's thought (*AE*, Introduction, pp. cxxxiii–cxcvi) it is impossible, given the complex cross-fertilization of ideas in nineteenth-century aesthetic thought, to suggest a clear line of descent from Schiller through Romanticism to the twentieth century. They also point out how Schiller himself has been associated – often mistakenly – with a number of different aesthetic doctrines:

From the start his readers were a prey to the common human predilection for attending to the parts rather than to the whole. And once cut loose from their moorings within his own 'system' his individual concepts proved, not unnaturally, susceptible to some curious affiliations. As, in the course of the nineteenth century, they drifted to France and England, and . . . across the Atlantic and back again . . . as Romanticism turned into Symbolism and both became transformed into the doctrine of 'Art for Art's Sake', these ideas gradually began to reflect a temper of mind . . . alien to Schiller's own.
(*AE*, p. clxiv)

Wilkinson and Willoughby link Schiller with theories of aesthetic isolation or 'distance', 'significant form', 'art-for-art's sake' and organicism, among others (see *AE*, Introduction, pp. xlvii, clxiv).

It is in this vein that claims are made for the existence of an idealist tradition stretching into the twentieth century. Frank Lentricchia, in *After the new criticism*, points out how Kermode's influential work, *The Romantic image*, describes a line of descent from the Romantics through aestheticism and symbolism to Yeats and places

the New Criticism at the end of the line of neo-Coleridgean movements in poetics . . . all of which had affirmed the autonomous and autotelic nature of the single lonely poem.[13]

The Romantic account of a poem as an autonomous individual or system can be seen to originate from Kant's account of the aesthetic experience as set apart from ordinary knowledge and from Schiller's development of that account into a description of aesthetic experience as a harmonious whole in which sense and reason encounter one another. Similarly, modern conceptions of art as the gateway to freedom and self-determination have been traced back to Schiller: Frank Lentricchia's *After the new criticism*, for instance, claims that:

With Kant and Schiller is born the most visible philosophy of poetics down through Frye: aesthetic humanism. The 'consummation of his humanity', as Schiller puts it, depends on man's ability to free himself from all determinations.[14]

A connection has similarly been made between Schiller's account of the isolated aesthetic experience (midway between but distinct from either sense or reason) and organicist tendencies in twentieth-century criticism. Murray Krieger identifies the mood of twentieth-century criticism as post-Kantian and talks of 'the post-Kantian mood of our criticism of the last century and a half' as 'form-worship',[15] whilst Paul de Man mentions 'the line that links . . . the structural formalism of the New Critics to the "organic" imagination so dear to Coleridge'. 'The main critical approaches of the last decades', he said, 'were all founded on the implicit assumption that literature is an autonomous activity of the mind, a distinctive way of being in the world'.[16]

There is ample evidence, then, that Schiller transmitted an accessible version of Kantian aesthetics on to the twentieth century: he himself acknowledges in the *Aesthetic education* that his basic principles derive from Kant (*AE*, 1st Letter, p. 3). But if this Kantian strain underlies the increasingly subjectivist history of sentimental aesthetics, what are the alternatives? What aesthetic, for example, did Schiller contrast with the sentimental in his *Essay*? What might the naive aesthetic be?

A NAIVE TRADITION? AESTHETICS BEFORE KANT

When in the early 1790s Schiller began planning his work in aesthetics, the discipline was relatively new. Its emergence as a subject for serious philosophical consideration was due in part to the growing emphasis on sensibility or feeling which characterized eighteenth-century British philosophy. In marked contrast to the systematizing rationalists of the seventeenth century, these writers placed emphasis on the individual subject and on personal experience in their account of how we understand the world. Empiricism, which (to simplify) worked from observation of phenomena and psychological analysis towards laws rather than starting from pre-given laws, increasingly recognized the role of the particular experience and the feeling individual subject in knowledge. This recognition is similarly evident in the voluntarism of the contemporary moral philosophy, which stressed the individual will and the 'sensus communis' which replaced universal logic as the practical standard for human behaviour. This general movement from systematizing to sensibility opened the way for the study of aesthetics as a kind of knowledge based on feeling rather than reason. It was at this time, Ernest Tuveson says, writing on Shaftesbury and this age,

that the word and concept 'aesthetic' first appeared, and the isolation of sensibility from the process of knowing and of logical thinking made possible the romantic doctrine of the imagination.[17]

If modern aesthetics began with the British essayists of the eighteenth century,[18] that was only its beginning. The methodology of these writers was firmly tied to the empirical–psychological philosophy of the time. Most treatises of the period are 'scientific' in approach and draw conclusions based on observation or experience or on appeals to common sense, rather than establishing first principles for aesthetics. This empirical methodology means that eighteenth-century aesthetics is, as Walter Hipple summarizes in his study of the major writers, usually 'concerned with the response of the mind to the qualities and relations of objects in nature and in art',[19] and deals alternately with the psychological activity of the experiencing subject and the classification of the characteristics of the art object itself. Despite the movement towards subjectivity, no subjective principle was fully established before Kant's revolutionary abandonment of observed phenomena in favour of *a priori* principle. Instead, starting from 'scientific' observation, the writers of the eighteenth century frequently debated the possibility of establishing an *objective* principle, ground or *standard of taste* for art. This proved impossible, particularly in the face of the growing recognition that the subject had a central role in knowledge and in aesthetic experience in particular.[20]

It is easy to see why, looking back from the heights of idealism, the post-Kantian aestheticians might construe the aesthetics of the eighteenth century as naive. With their concentration on the particular, observed detail, their categories and accumulated generalizations, they fit Schiller's account of the naive, realist thinker, and all his criticisms of that thinker can be applied to their work.

KANT

German aesthetics before Kant was similarly constrained by the philosophical context in which it developed: rationalism. Baumgarten, often considered as the founder of modern aesthetics, defined the aesthetic as a kind of knowledge, but only as a lesser, confused version of ordinary knowledge.

It was only with the publication in 1781 of Kant's *Critique of pure reason* that aesthetics really came into its own. As Kant explains in the Preface to the second edition, his system completely reverses previous metaphysical systems:

Hitherto it has been assumed that all our knowledge must conform to objects. But all attempts to extend our knowledge of objects by establishing something in regard to them *a priori*, by means of concepts, have, on this assumption, ended in failure. We must therefore make trial whether we may not have more success in the tasks of metaphysics, if we suppose that objects must conform to our knowledge.[21]

This famous hypothesis and its development in the *Critique* is compared by Kant to the 'Copernican revolution' in that it overturned existing systems under which knowledge was derived from a lawful objective reality, in which it resided, independent of the knowing subject. The revolution, Ernst Cassirer explains,

rests on the fundamental idea that the relation between cognition and its object, generally accepted until then, must be radically modified. Instead of starting from the object, as the known and given, we must begin with the law of cognition, which alone is truly accessible and certain in a primary sense; instead of defining the universal qualities of *being*, like ontological metaphysics, we must, by an analysis of reason, ascertain the fundamental form of judgement.[22]

This shift in emphasis from *being* to *judgment* provides the opportunity for a change in the status of the aesthetic. The credibility of aesthetic knowledge or judgment had always been undermined by the belief that genuine aesthetic knowledge would have to involve establishing an objective ground for individual preference or experience. Otherwise, an aesthetic or judgmental apprehension would be inferior to a cognitive apprehension.

However, with Kant, all knowledge begins to be understood as something involving judgment. Knowledge is not the data we read off the world, but an activity we perform and philosophy can only talk about what falls within the limits of our own subjective experience of that activity and not about what is really out there. This means that Kant is not interested, as his predecessors were, in detailing the objective qualities of objects. Instead, he considers what kind of mental activity knowledge might be.

Because Kant's whole metaphysic focuses on the subject's experience of the world, aesthetic experience can be analysed as a particular way of experiencing or approaching the world, rather than as something defined by the class of aesthetic objects, or the psychological characteristics of the aesthetic experience. Kant is not at all concerned with beautiful objects, since, under his view, we are not entitled to say anything about things themselves, only our experience of them (see *CJ*, II, p. 38; III, p. 40; V, pp. 43–44; VIII, p. 49). He gives what Roger Scruton calls the first 'systematic account of aesthetic appreciation, without describing its material object, and without lapsing into Sentimentalism'.[23] And Osborne notes that Kant

made explicit and precise what had been implicit or partially glimpsed in his predecessors. Up to this time . . . works of art . . . had always been appraised for the pleasure they give, for their moral influence . . . their practical utility . . . because they embodied certain approved principles or conformed with certain rules. By rejecting all these grounds of judgment and showing that aesthetic judgments are differently based and form a class on their own Kant . . . laid the basis for aesthetics as a distinct branch of philosophy.[24]

I now turn to the way in which Kant established what was distinct about aesthetic judgments.

KANT'S THIRD CRITIQUE

The *Critique of judgment* is concerned with the faculty which mediates between understanding and reason in Kant's tripartite epistemology: the faculty of judgment. Kant sets out the aim of this third Critique in the Preface:

> Whether now the judgment, which in the order of our cognitive faculties forms a mediating link between understanding and reason, has also *a priori* principles for itself; whether these are constitutive or merely regulative (thus pointing out no special realm); and whether they give that rule *a priori* to the cognitive faculty and the faculty of desire (just as the understanding prescribes laws *a priori* to the first, reason to the second) – these are the questions with which the present *Critique of Judgment* is concerned. (*CJ*, Preface. p. 4)

Kant's aesthetic, then, is an inquiry into the nature and status of this faculty which does not create universal ideas (as reason does) and does not generate universal categories under which we subsume sense data (as understanding does), but is the general faculty whereby we bring the particular under the universal idea or category, judging it to be of a certain kind. Reason and understanding both have their own 'realm' – the realm of reason is freedom (in which realm we are moral beings) and the realm of understanding is nature (in which realm we are existential beings). By way of reason we apprehend things as free or self-determining and by way of understanding we apprehend things as necessary or determined. But judgment has no particular realm since its role is mediatory.

Nevertheless, Kant says:

> we have cause for supposing according to analogy that it may contain in itself . . . a special principle of its own to be sought according to laws, though merely subjective *a priori*.

The Critique must establish this subjective principle, which cannot be derived from external laws, but must originate from judgment itself. Kant goes on to divide judgment into two:

> Judgment in general is the faculty of thinking the particular as contained under the universal. If the universal (the rule, the principle, the law) be given, the judgment which subsumes the particular under it . . . is *determinant*. But if only the particular be given for which the universal has to be found, the judgment is merely *reflective*.
> (*CJ*, Introduction, IV, p. 15)

Both kinds of judgment concern the conformity of a particular to a universal, but in the *reflective* judgment this conformity, this adaptedness of a particular to a universal, is a principle derived from the particular itself. When we exercise the reflective judgment, we perceive a particular object as in itself adapted to our thought, or what Kant calls 'purposive'. This quality of purposiveness is a general quality, the general quality of being adapted to our thought or subsumable under concepts, and does not depend, as does the *determinant* judgment, on our actually judging the object under a specific concept. This is what we do in ordinary cognition, when we judge the particular object as, for example, a member of a species, bringing it under a pre-given concept of what it is to belong to that species. But in reflective judgment, we perceive the object not as a member of a species, but as a purposive entity. There are two kinds of reflective judgment: the aesthetic and the teleological. In the former, we apprehend the object as harmonious and purposive in itself and in the latter we apprehend it as purposive in its harmonious accordance with the laws of nature: it seems to have a purposive existence. I shall be concentrating in this book only on the aesthetic form of the reflective judgment. Kant tells us:

That which in the representation of an object is merely subjective, i.e. which decides its reference to the subject, not to the object, is its aesthetical character; but that which serves or can be used for the determination of the object (for cognition) is its logical validity.

(*CJ*, Introduction, VII, p. 25)

When we judge something to be aesthetic, we are only interested in certain characteristics of that object; we classify it according to certain, aesthetic criteria. We are not interested in, for example, how large the object is, or what species it belongs to. That is, we are not concerned with 'objective' qualities which locate that object in the empirical domain. Instead, we are concerned with 'subjective' qualities; how the object makes us feel. To summarize: when we judge something as aesthetic, we do not judge it to be one of a class, as we would in determinant judgment. We do not place it in the empirical world. Instead, we place it with respect to ourselves. In doing so, we apprehend the object not as belonging to a particular order or class of objects, but as belonging to, or fitting in with, our own faculties. The object thus seems to have as its own inner structure or order, a conformity to our own faculties; this is the order we are interested in. Kant calls this conformity 'subjective formal purposiveness'.

If pleasure is bound up with the mere apprehension . . . of the form of an object of intuition, without reference to a concept for a definite cognition, then the representation is thereby not referred to the object, but simply to the subject, and the pleasure can express nothing else than its harmony with the cognitive faculties which come into play in the reflective judgment, and so far as they are in play, and hence can only express a subjective formal purposiveness of the object.

(*CJ*, Introduction, VII, p. 26)

This subjective formal purposiveness is experienced with pleasure. Instead of actually *determining* what the object is (one of a class, for example), we simply *reflect* on the way it fits our faculties, and this gives us pleasure. Reflective judgment, then, is a suspended version of determinant judgment. In determinant judgment the imaginative faculty (whereby we apprehend sensible intuitions) is subsumed under the faculty of understanding (whereby we organize those intuitions under concepts) but in reflective, aesthetic judgments, the imagination and understanding simply interplay in the pleasure of the general adaptability of one to the other.

Such a judgment is an aesthetical judgment upon the purposiveness of the object, which does not base itself upon any present concept of the object, nor does it furnish any such. In the case of an object whose form . . . in the mere reflection upon it (without reference to any concept to be obtained of it), is judged as the ground of a pleasure in the representation of such an object, this pleasure is judged as bound up with the representation necessarily, and, consequently, not only for the subject which apprehends this form, but for every judging being in general. The object is then called beautiful, and the faculty of judging by means of such a pleasure (and consequently, with universal validity) is called taste.   (*CJ*, Introduction, VII, pp. 26–7)

Kant states that this harmony of the faculties in relating a representation to a subject, gives us a pleasure which we apprehend in the object represented, which we call beautiful. However, because this harmony is in our own faculties, it is common to all humanity. The mental structure of the aesthetic experience is always the same because we all have the same mental structure and so our aesthetic judgments are always universally valid: 'subjectively' universally valid. In other words, they are universally valid not with reference to any qualities in the objects themselves, but with reference to the subjective structure of the aesthetic experience.

From here, Kant leads into the *Analytic of the beautiful*, which develops this account of judgment. He thus provides an account of the beautiful in art and nature in terms of the way in which our faculties work when we judge something to be beautiful; and he supplies a new, *subjectively grounded* rationale for art.

SCHILLER'S RESPONSE TO KANT

Schiller's aesthetic is quite different in intention and method from that of Kant. Dieter Henrich describes the difference clearly in his essay 'Beauty and freedom: Schiller's struggle with Kant's aesthetics'.

> Schiller . . . was . . . certain of the necessity of progressing further along the tracks laid by Kant, and of comprehending the essence of beauty and of art even more profoundly than could the theory of the *Critique of Judgment* . . . Obviously, the point of view . . . with which Schiller approached Kant's aesthetics was quite different from Kant's own starting point. The problem of a transcendental theory of the possibility of knowledge carried no real weight. Schiller . . . was forced into philosophizing by the problem of human nature, the duality of its both sensuous and rational character, and by the problem of the moral standard of human action and the possibility of its perfection . . . Beauty had to be something more fundamental than a mere modification of a cognitive activity . . . the ground of the possibility of beauty had to be shown to lie in the innermost essence of man, that is, within his active, self-realizing essence.[25]

The view that Schiller (as an artist himself) was looking for an account of beauty, and especially artistic beauty, that would justify the practice of art on the highest moral level, is borne out by Schiller's own letters to Körner.[26] He was not trying to build up a metaphysical system, like Kant's, but to find an explanation of beauty that went beyond Kant's account of it as a subjective state in the experiencing subject, and demonstrated its moral significance for society and the education of man.

It is not difficult to see how Schiller could have found Kant's description of the beautiful rather lacking, although Eva Schaper argues that Schiller's reading of Kant is to blame.[27] What Schiller found especially difficult to accept was the section of the Critique which, classifying beauty as either 'free' or 'dependent' can be read as arguing that representational art must be excluded from the class of truly beautiful objects. If this was Schiller's reading of Kant, then it is not difficult to see why he found it limited. And looking at the Critique more broadly, it is clearly unsatisfying for anyone who wants to criticize or classify art, it fails to talk about art objects and it severely excludes anything other than an account of the way in which our faculties work in aesthetic experience. And Schiller, as an artist, believed that art actually brought about moral, social and political change and was a fundamental part of our development as individuals.

It is important to remember, when looking at Schiller's work on the naive and sentimental, how necessary it was to him to counteract what he saw as being the excessively subjective emphasis of Kant's work. This is clear from a letter he wrote to his friend Körner, in which he says that:

I think that I have discovered the objective idea of the Beautiful, which is qualified, *eo ipso*, to be the objective principle on which taste is founded, and which Kant tormented his brain about without success.[28]

This reveals Schiller's commitment to something which the pre-Kantians had also sought – a universal objective principle for beauty. The difficulties of his definition will become clear later. I begin by turning to the general thrust of Schiller's aesthetic.

THE *AESTHETIC EDUCATION*: AN INTRODUCTION

The motivation behind this work is, Schiller tells us, essentially moral and political, not epistemological. The spirit of philosophical inquiry is, he says,

being expressly challenged by present circumstances to concern itself with that most perfect of all the works to be achieved by the art of man: the construction of true political freedom.   (*AE*, 2nd Letter, p. 7)

It is with this search for freedom in mind that Schiller undertakes his revision of Kant. If man is ever to solve the problem of politics, he goes on,

he will have to approach it through the problem of the aesthetic, because it is only through Beauty that man makes his way to Freedom.

(*AE*, 2nd Letter, p. 9)

Starting from Kantian principles, the *Education* reworks Kant's two realms of necessity and freedom as two different psychological drives: the sense-drive and the form-drive. Schiller thus relocates Kant's system in the individual psyche, as befits his concern with the education of the individual towards freedom. Man, he tells us, is torn between these two drives, which make conflicting demands on his nature. There are, he says,

> two contrary challenges to man, the two fundamental laws of his sensuo-rational nature. The first insists upon absolute reality: he is to turn everything which is mere form into world, and make all his potentialities fully manifest. The second insists upon absolute formality: he is to destroy everything in himself which is mere world, and bring harmony into all his changes. In other words, he is to externalize all that is within him, and give form to all that is outside him. (*AE*, 11th Letter, p. 77)

The *Education* looks at the problem of man's divided nature as it manifests itself in society, the individual, and history. At the beginning of the work, Schiller defines the angst of modern man as the alienation of sense from form, or, to go back to more Kantian terms, of necessity and nature from freedom and reason. Modern society, Schiller tells us, is severed from the physical world, and instead of the organic harmony of the two that once existed we are left with two extremes: brute nature and over-abstracted and arid culture. This separation was a historical event – organic society is historically prior to modern civilization, and is superseded by it.

> It was civilisation itself which inflicted this wound upon modern man. Once the increase of empirical knowledge, and more exact modes of thought, made sharper divisions between the sciences inevitable, and once the increasingly complex machinery of State necessitated a more rigorous separation of ranks and occupations, then the inner unity of human nature was severed too, and a disastrous conflict set its harmonious powers at variance. (*AE*, 6th Letter, p. 33)

If the sophistication and consequent fragmentation of the sciences and arts was the reason for this severance, then its remedy must also be art. However much the whole has been dissected and dispersed, Schiller says,

> it must be open to us to restore by means of a higher Art the totality of our nature which the arts themselves have destroyed.
> (*AE*, 6th Letter, p. 43)

And, in an apocalyptic passage, he declares that

Truth lives on in the illusion of Art, and it is from this copy, or after-image, that the original image will once again be restored. Just as the nobility of Art survived the nobility of Nature, so now Art goes before her, a voice rousing from slumber and preparing the shape of things to come. Even before Truth's triumphant light can penetrate the recesses of the human heart, the poet's imagination will intercept its rays, and the peaks of humanity will be radiant while the dews of night still linger in the valley. (*AE*, 9th Letter, p. 57)

It is through art, then, that humanity is to be restored. But how is this to happen? Whereas, in Kant, judgment is the faculty that relates the two distinct faculties of reason and understanding, Schiller sets up a 'system', in which the aesthetic state, though it is still midway between the rational and the sensuous, is a state in which those two faculties or drives are actually reconciled. In the aesthetic state we recognize ourselves as not only rational but also sensuous and so we come to a full spiritual and moral understanding of ourselves as human. Whereas Kant only considers the formal relation of discrete faculties, Schiller brings the whole of rational man and the whole of sensuous man to a conscious reconciliation in the aesthetic state. In doing this he far exceeds the bounds of Kant's categories and programme.

Our psyche, Schiller says,

passes . . . from sensation to thought *via* a middle disposition in which sense and reason are both active at the same time. Precisely for this reason, however, they cancel each other out as determining forces, and bring about a negation by means of an opposition. This middle disposition, in which the psyche is subject neither to physical nor to moral constraint, and yet is active in both these ways, pre-eminently deserves to be called a free disposition; and if we are to call the condition of sensuous determination the physical, and the condition of rational determination the logical or moral, then we must call this condition of real and active determinability the aesthetic. (*AE*, 20th Letter, p. 141)

In this state of 'active determinability' our two natures conjoin, because we are at once passive and active, sensuous and reflective.

In the delight we take in beauty . . . no . . . succession of activity and passivity can be discerned; reflection is here so completely interfused with feeling that we imagine that the form is directly apprehended by sense. Beauty, then, is indeed an object for us, because reflection is the condition of our having any sensation of it; but it is at the same time a state of the perceiving subject, because feeling is a condition of our having any perception of it. Thus beauty is indeed form, because we contemplate it; but it is at the same time life, because we feel it. In a word: it is at once a state of our being and an activity we perform.

(*AE*, 25th Letter, p. 187)

This means, Schiller goes on to say, that because

an actual union and interchange between matter and form, passivity and activity, momentarily takes place, the compatibility of our two natures, the practicability of the infinite being realized in the finite, hence the possibility of sublimest humanity, is thereby actually proven.

(*AE*, 25th Letter, p. 189)

He never makes explicit exactly how this happens and, moreover, as is clear from the first passage above, never makes it clear whether he is talking about a psychic state in the experiencing subject – which would be easier to accept – or an encounter between the perceiving and experiencing subject and the beautiful object. 'Beauty', he says, 'is indeed an object for us' (see above), but how exactly does he make the transition from Kant's account of the subject's faculties, to his account of the beautiful object?

SCHILLER'S THEORY OF BEAUTY: LIVING FORM

We saw above how Schiller described beauty as 'freedom in appearance'. In the *Education*, he sets out his account of beauty in more detail, and talks of the beautiful not just as though it were a subjective experience, but as though it objectively existed in works of art.

When our two natures are joined in the experience of beauty, as described above, our two drives – the sense and the form drive which correspond to those two natures – are united in what Schiller calls the 'play-drive'. He goes on to say that:

The object of the sense-drive, expressed in a general concept, we call life . . . a concept designating all material being and all that is immediately present to the senses. The object of the form-drive, expressed in a general concept, we call form . . . a concept which includes all the formal qualities of things and all the relations of these to our thinking faculties.

The object of the play-drive . . . may therefore be called living form: a concept serving to designate all the aesthetic qualities of phencmena and, in a word, what in the widest sense of the term we call beauty.
(*AE*, 15th Letter, p. 101)

The matter–form distinction is Schiller's own remarkable exten- sion of the discrimination between the faculties of sense and reason in the individual to what is more like a discrimination between different aspects of objects. This is the source of much of the ambiguity of his aesthetic. Living form is Schiller's most explicit definition of beauty: the beautiful object is one in which form and content seem freely to determine one another, so that freedom and necessity are one and the same and the object seems to spring naturally from its own inner rationale. We perceive it as determining itself, or 'free in appearance'. This is an extension of Kant's account of the aesthetic as judging an object to be innerly purposive. For Schiller it is not just our experience of the object, it seems, but the object itself, which is purposive.

Schiller, unlike Kant, dwells on the objects of aesthetic experience. He places considerable emphasis on the artist's ability to conquer the natural resilience of his material (whether it is clay or ideas he is conquering is not made explicit) and to embue it with form.

This genial and aesthetically free handling of common reality is, wherever it may be found, the mark of a noble soul. In general we call noble any nature which possesses the gift of transforming, purely by its manner of handling it, even the most trifling occupation, or the most petty of objects, into something infinite . . . A noble nature is not content to be itself free; it must also set free everything around it, even the lifeless. Beauty, however, is the only way that freedom has of making itself manifest in appearance.   (*AE*, 23rd Letter, p. 167, n. 1)

This definition of beauty as 'freedom in appearance' implies an art object much more definitely than Kant's aesthetic ever could, even if it is only necessary for us to *see* the aesthetic object *as* free in appearance, rather than for it actually to *be* that way.

One of Schiller's main divergences from Kant is his emphasis on beauty as something which happens in an object. While Kant only talks about the subject's experience, Schiller insists that this experience is a way of seeing an object, something we must perceive as being in the nature of the object itself. Dieter Henrich tells us that

Schiller correctly sees that aesthetic enjoyment in the proper sense is absorbed in the object and that aesthetic consciousness is, as it were, wholly consumed by the object which it sees, although this holds only subjectively . . . . But this act of the subject is not experienced as subjective. Rather, an act of objectification is at work in this so-called play of the imagination. Its play is no longer the play of the subject with itself, occasioned by the intuition of an object; instead, in this act the subject plays itself entirely into the object.[29]

Schiller obviously had problems determining exactly how the object fitted into the subject's aesthetic experience, because he started from Kant, who didn't consider the object except as a function of the subject's experience. This is the problem that underlies Schiller's *Essay* too, where the subjective principle he starts from makes it very difficult for him to incorporate the objective principle for poetry he wants to include.

The result of the 'objectification' Henrich mentions is that Schiller ends up talking in parallel: on the one hand, like Kant, he talks about mental processes; on the other hand he seems simultaneously to be talking about art works. (This dual approach survives into contemporary theory and criticism: both the Romantic 'organism' and the twentieth-century 'text' are used as both subjective and objective terms.) It is noticeable that when Schiller talks about the creative process he emphasizes the artist's achievement in subduing subject-matter of a recalcitrant nature to form, implying a grappling which results in an art object that is a harmony of physical and mental, formal and material characteristics. Here he has come a long way from Kant's account of aesthetic experience.

The real problem with Schiller's aesthetic is that it seems to set up the notion of an autonomous art object whose formal harmony corresponds to the sense–reason harmony of the Kantian aesthetic experience. Whereas formal harmony in Kant was simply the interplay of our faculties, in Schiller it seems to have an independent existence as an art object. In his 22nd Letter, Schiller talks about each art conquering its medium and mastering its individual material (*AE*, p. 155). How exactly does Schiller conceive of the form which he says not only *embues* but actually seems to *subdue* the material of art? Critics have given different accounts of this 'form': Rose Egan, for example, describes it as 'the distinguishing spirit which gives life, unity and identity to inert and unorganized matter.'[30] But Schiller uses 'form' to mean both this shaping force and the formal harmony achieved by that force when it creates the aesthetic object. In a letter to Körner he says that

beauty manifests itself in its supreme glory when it conquers the logical nature of its object, and how could it conquer where there is no resistance? How could it bestow its form upon a completely nondescript matter? I at least am convinced that beauty is nothing but the form of a form, and that that which is called its matter must be formed matter.[31]

Here and elsewhere in the *Education*, Schiller suggests that the beautiful object is one that brings matter under the principle of form, and that what we appreciate about beautiful objects is this quality of having been composed, or designed.

In a truly successful work of art the contents should effect nothing, the form everything; for only through the form is the whole man affected, through the subject-matter by contrast, only one or other of his functions . . . it is only from form that true aesthetic freedom can be looked for.   (*AE*, 22nd Letter. p 155)

Schiller is not saying that we are only interested in art as a formal unity, but rather that we must apprehend all its other elements as resolved into a whole, as interrelated and interdependent. The argument seems similar to that put forward by Kant when he is talking about free and dependent beauty. We see a tree as beautiful when we see it as a perfect whole comprising all its other qualities, such as greenness and naturalness and so on. This is formal apprehension, but it can involve apprehension of a range of qualities, such as moral worth and intellectual value.

But the problem with Schiller's account of the beautiful object — and his divergence from Kant — remains. He places his own emphasis firmly on the encounter of experiencing subject and experienced object as it occurs *in* the aesthetic object. This seems to mean, working from the Kantian base, that the formal interplay of our faculties in purposiveness is somehow present in the object as structure as well as in the subject as experience. It seems to be a kind of emotional structure in the artwork itself. Schiller does talk of 'the inner lawfulness of the truly beautiful' (*AE*, 22nd Letter, p. 155), and this may be what he means when he insists on the primacy of form.

However, the problem then remains of how exactly that

subjective experience and that object do encounter each other – the problem which Kant had resolved by restricting his inquiry to the subject's experience.

Schiller remains vague on this critical point, at least where the epistemological details are concerned. He is quite definite inasmuch as he is making a political and moral point: aesthetic freedom is a state in which we are both necessary and free because we are at once absorbed in the experienced object (bound by necessity) and freely experiencing it as subjects. This is the high road to moral truth. What is less clear is exactly how Schiller moved from the Kantian epistemological framework which supports an account of aesthetic experience in the subject, to one which would support his new account of aesthetic experience as subject–object encounter. His failure to be explicit on this point leaves his work wide open to misinterpretation.

The consequences of this are evident in his own work, and in that of his successors. When he – or they – talk about the artwork itself, rather than the aesthetic experience, they run into difficulties; difficulties which are often concealed behind a conflation of aesthetic experience and artwork. This is inevitable: the Kantian epistemology is one in which the subject constructs the object of its experience and so provides no way for its followers to talk about 'the object' without slipping back into subjectivity.

PROBLEMS WITH THE *EDUCATION*

The ease with which Schiller slips from an intrinsically Kantian and formal account of the epistemological structure of experience to an account of experience which has a specifically political, cultural and historical flavour, is perhaps the source of all the confusion to which his aesthetic gave rise. In both the *Education* and the *Essay*, Schiller contrasts the sensuous and rational, the naive and sentimental, not only as constituents in the aesthetic experience, but as characteristics or types of individuals, and beyond that as historical epochs. Analysis of the conception of the sensuous and the rational given in the *Education*, makes it clear just how problematic that unacknowledged transition from Kantian foundation to Schillerian edifice can be.

We have already seen how, in his account of beauty, Schiller tacitly slips away from his stricter master in order to make beauty something more than the patterning of the faculties of the observing subject. The Kantian foundation, whereby the account of aesthetic experience is firmly located in the subject, is never philosophically refuted or rejected, nor is Schiller's emphasis on the play of the subject into the object given an explicit philosophical justification. In the same way, Schiller's account of the 'objective' or sensuous aspect of human nature diverges from Kant's in a fruitful but not a formally justifiable manner.

Kant's distinction between the two mental faculties or domains of understanding and reason is watertight. Schiller's distinction between sensuous and rational man is not: sense and reason are not just opposing faculties but are used to describe complete individuals, types, cultures and races. While this use of the opposition set up by Kant is both illuminating and convincing at a discursive level, on a formal philosophical level the unsealing of Kant's compartmentalized system means that a flood tide often threatens to overwhelm Schiller's system completely, as all barriers and divisions are submerged.

The analysis of Schiller's account of beauty suggests that the problem with his aesthetic lies with his attempt to realize beauty as sensuous and objective, and not just subjective. Similarly, when he is talking about the sensuous and the rational in a more general way, the problem lies with his conception of sensuous man.

The final goal of the *Education* is, as discussed above, to restore to man his lost natural and sensuous state, but in a new harmony with his later cultural awakening and sophistication. Schiller's aesthetic relies for its philosophical structure and rationale on the distinction between these two states, which are then to be reconciled. But just as the 'objective principle of beauty on which he relies never fully emerges from the Kantian subjectivity, so it can be argued that Schiller's conception of sensuous man never fully escapes from Schiller's fundamental Kantian understanding of man. It is perfectly possible to argue that this ambiguity is deliberate, and that Schiller's whole endeavour is a picture drawn inside a Kantian frame – but that means looking backwards to Kant rather than forwards to Hegel's dialectic, located in real history.

The contrast Schiller draws between man in nature and man in culture seems clear enough at first sight. The transition from the one to the other is the transition from physical necessity to moral freedom. What makes man human is his ability to master his natural self:

> the power of retracing by means of Reason the steps she (Nature) took on his behalf, of transforming the work of blind compulsion into a work of free choice, and of elevating physical necessity into moral necessity.
> (AE, 3rd Letter, p. 13)

How does this transition take place? Schiller has made Kant's synchronic opposition into a historical transformation of a fairly dramatic kind – but we are not told how this is possible. Is the natural state simply physical necessity? Schiller talks at times as if it were:

> This Natural State (as we may term any political body whose organization derives originally from forces and not from laws) is, it is true, at variance with man as moral being.   (AE, 3rd Letter, p. 13)

But unless Schiller is actually talking about a sub-human, savage state, he is not likely to deny man's rational aspect; and it is clear from a Kantian point of view that man must be both sensuous and rational at once. Even Schiller's savage, he implies, 'despises civilisation and acknowledges nature as his sovereign mistress' (4th Letter, p. 21) in a conscious and considered way.

Schiller goes on to describe natural humanity in his own age which, while it is later contrasted with the classical as an age of culture as opposed to nature, is here portrayed as divided between two far from admirable exemplifications of nature and culture. The lower classes in their depraved indulgence of their animal instincts are an example of savage, or natural man, and the upper classes in their lethargy an example of cultivated man – and both are equally sick (AE, 5th Letter, pp. 25–27). We are already a long way from Kant's formal opposition of necessity and freedom as mental domains.

Schiller proceeds to a comparison of modern and classical society:

> Closer attention to the character of our age will, however, reveal an astonishing contrast between contemporary forms of humanity and earlier ones, especially the Greek. The reputation for culture and refinement, on which we otherwise rightly pride ourselves vis-à-vis humanity in its merely natural state, can avail us nothing against the

natural humanity of the Greeks. For they were wedded to all the delights of art and all the dignity of wisdom, without however, like us, falling a prey to their seduction. The Greeks put us to shame not only by a simplicity to which our age is a stranger; they are at the same time our rivals, indeed often our models, in those very excellences with which we are wont to console ourselves for the unnaturalness of our manners.

(*AE*, 6th Letter, p. 31)

What exactly is the 'natural humanity' Schiller ascribes to the Greeks? He can't mean the naturalness of the savage compared with civilized man, given the existence of Greek civilization. Rather, he seems to mean by 'natural humanity' a lack of artifice and sophistication in the derogatory sense of those words. But he has no real foundation for claiming that Greek society was natural in this way, other than his own personal value judgment, which reflects a rather idealized view of Greek art and society. There is little here to provide a substantial basis for a philosophical distinction between the sensuous and the rational.

In fact, Schiller's lament for Greek society is very akin to the Romantic yearning for the agrarian idyll – something he himself acknowledges to be characteristic of the sentimental modern. When man passes from the state of nature, he says, he attempts to

retrieve by means of a fiction the childhood of the race: he conceives, as idea, a state of nature, a state not indeed given to him by any experience, but a necessary result of what Reason destined him to be; attributes to himself in this idealized natural state a purpose of which in his actual natural state he was entirely ignorant, and a power of free choice of which he was at that time wholly incapable. (*AE*, 3rd Letter, p. 11)

Here, the state of nature is described as something more like an unconscious and unwilled state and is therefore something to which civilized modern man only has access through imaginative fiction. This is sick sentimentalism for Schiller – it is the sentimentalism later typified by Romantic longing for an idealized organic society – but it is not so removed from Schiller's own conception of the Greek culture and society. His account of natural society is organicist: all the parts are integrated with the whole, which has a solid, concrete feel about it. By contrast, in our modern society, we have abstract speculation on the one hand and brute necessity on the other: hence his drive for a new union of the two.

This new union is, as we have seen, to be achieved through art, which provides the model for abstract conception and concrete realization in perfect harmony. But while this is a seductive and convincing concept, the fundamental problem inherited from Kant remains. If sensuous man is simply a savage, then rational man has no access to him except through his own cultural fictions. If the objective aspect of beauty is simply the physical material, then how is it fused with the subjective spirit except in the subjective consciousness of the individual? And if natural man is not just a savage, but an idealized or non-artificial civilized man, then the distinction between him and civilized man loosens. Similarly, if the objective aspect of beauty is in some way also subjective, then it can never really be distinguished from that subjective.

Schiller's emphasis on the concrete individuation of the Idea as the ideal towards which we should be striving is firm. But he is essentially talking about a kind of society, or culture, which differs from the modern not in any rigid structural sense, which can be supported by epistemological differences, but simply in tastes and preferences. When we turn to the *Essay*, this becomes even clearer.

ON THE NAIVE AND SENTIMENTAL IN LITERATURE

Like the *Education*, the *Essay* contrasts two ways of being in the world which correspond, albeit loosely, to the sensuous and rational states described in the former text. Like the *Education*, the *Essay* has the moral purpose of showing how the two can be united, and describes the aesthetic experience as the whole in which they harmonize. Just as, in the former, Schiller said that 'an actual union and interchange between matter and form, passivity and activity, momentarily takes place' (*AE*, 25th Letter, p. 189), so in the latter he says that 'the poetic mood is an independent whole in which all differences and all deficiencies vanish' (*NS*, p. 80). Driving deeper into aesthetic territory, the *Essay* looks at this union in the specific realm of poetry, following very similar lines of argument to the *Education* and using its central opposition in a similarly shifting manner. While all poetry is seen as harmonious it is always more or less naive or sentimental. The goal of the *Essay* is the perfect balance of the two in a new poetry. In this balance:

the naive character would combine with the sentimental in such a way that each would preserve the other from its extreme and while the naive protected the spirit from exaggeration, the sentimental would keep it safe from insipidity. For we must finally admit that neither the naive nor the sentimental character, regarded alone, can quite exhaust the ideal of noble humanity which can only emerge from the close combination of both.   (*NS*, p. 80)

Again, there is no account of how exactly this is to be achieved in poetry. Nor is the distinction between the two modes so rigid that each cannot achieve its own kind of balance.

Like the *Education*, the *Essay* applies its central opposition to historical epochs, human types and temperaments, authors and literary works, and shifts between the atemporal Kantian analysis of structure and a teleological, historical focus on individual cultures and works. It is, among other things, an attempt to provide an aesthetic rationale for modern literature comparable to and rivalling the prevailing classical model. Arthur Lovejoy's account of the dominant aesthetic of Schiller's time describes

a doctrine characterized by an insistence upon 'objective' aesthetic standards, by a conviction of the priority of 'form' over 'content', of unity over expressiveness in art, and by a belief in the superiority of ancient art, as the most adequate realization of these standards.[32]

This sort of aesthetic, which we associate not only with classical literature but the neo-classical works of the eighteenth century, was felt by Schiller to be at odds with what he was himself trying to achieve as a writer. Writing to Wilhelm von Humboldt, he asks:

Given my distance from the spirit of Greek literature, to what extent can I still be a poet and indeed a better poet than the extent of that distance seems to allow?[33]

His essay can accordingly be read not just as a part of his philosophical programme and his revision of Kant, but also as the search for a personal aesthetic which is specific to his own place and time. It must be remembered that Schiller saw himself as a sentimental poet in a sentimental age, and that naive literature is in his view closer to the literature of the classical age. His attitude towards it is similar to the vexed relationship which modern man in the *Education* has with the Greek culture: he looks longingly but impossibly back at it from the vantage point of his own sophistication.

Although the main body of the text is a discussion of literary texts (and this is an important divergence from Kant, who never focuses on individual works of art) the *Essay* begins with a more general account of the naive and sentimental as human types or tendencies, which can easily be linked with those discussed in the *Education*. Similar questions also arise, particularly with respect to the naive.

Schiller's account of the naive is convoluted and often ambiguous. He begins by saying that when we apprehend something – notably a natural phenomenon or a child – as innocent and simple in contrast with our own sophistication, then we apprehend it as naive. In such experiences, the naive object is revealed to be infinitely purer and better than our artful watching selves, and we find the experience both revelatory and salutary. Wordsworth's numerous astonished encounters with childish innocence in an adult world – and indeed Schiller's own vision of Greek culture – fall into this category of experience.

> This sensitivity to nature is called forth especially strongly by those objects, for example children and childlike races, which stand in close connection with us and which encourage us to look at ourselves and what is *unnatural* in us.   (*NS*, p. 23)

Innocence, of course, is necessarily a concept that the innocent don't possess about themselves, any more than the unselfconscious know that they are. It is sophistication that looks on in wonder and labels what it sees 'innocence'.

Schiller expands the notion of naiveté to embrace the 'naive way of thinking' (p. 26). When someone, consciously or unconsciously, lapses from sophistication into simplicity, then we perceive that person as naive, and experience the astonishment described above at a simplicity where it wasn't expected. Just as in the *Education* he used both the idea of the 'noble savage' and the idea of the civilized Greek to represent what it was to be natural man, here he uses both the idea of the child or natural phenomenon which is truly unselfconscious, and the adult who can be *both* sophisticated and simple. In fact, he goes on to suggest that it doesn't count as being naive for a flower to be natural and innocent, since it is unconscious and therefore there is nothing remarkable in its natural innocence: the concepts are even inapplicable. To be naive you must yourself be sophisticated.

The naive is a childlike quality where it is no longer expected, and cannot therefore be attributed in the strictest sense to real childhood.
(NS, p. 24)

And, he goes on:

The naiveté of surprise can only come to man and to man alone in so far as he is no longer in that moment a pure and innocent nature. It presupposes a will which is not in harmony with what nature does on its own account. (NS, p. 25)

The naiveté of surprise occurs when someone deliberately lapses into being naive; the naiveté of disposition is unwilled, but equally is not something that is simply given by nature:

The naiveté of disposition can, strictly speaking, only be attributed to man as a being not absolutely subject to nature, although only in so far as pure nature really still acts in him. (NS, p. 31)

Schiller is thus at pains to distinguish naiveté from the state of nature. His naiveté consists of the capacity in a sophisticated human to be like a simple child – but how or why this happens is not considered. And the naiveté itself is an elusive if not illusory quality, which is mainly characterized by the sentimental frame that is placed round it. To be naive is to stop being sentimental; to be natural is to stop being cultured – but the naiveté and the naturalness are only ever viewed from a sophisticated vantage point. In Schiller's own philosophy, naiveté is framed by sentimentalism, so that they give each other definition. And again, it is to the Greeks that he looks back:

When one remembers the beauties of nature which surrounded the ancient Greeks; when one considers how intimately this people could live under its happy sky with free nature, how much nearer its way of imagining things, its way of feeling, its customs lay to simple nature and what a true impression of it its literary works are, then one is unpleasantly surprised to notice that one meets with so few signs of the *sentimental* interests with which we moderns cling to natural scenes and natural characters. (NS, pp. 32–3)

Schiller criticizes modern society for sentimentalizing nature, as in the *Education* he criticizes the artificial fiction of a natural state created by modern society. But what of his own conception of the naive, and of the Greeks? He could hardly idealize Greek society more. And what he pinpoints as naive – the unthinking and practical proximity to nature – is something that is only appealing to the modern for whom the utilitarian life of the peasant can acquire from far off the patina of charming simplicity.

However, the *Essay* does not advocate a return to the naive. It insists that we move forward, to recover through art the identity with nature we have lost, and to join it to our own sensibility. And, in his discussion of literature, Schiller is explicitly critical of the sentimental tendency, even if he can be seen as falling prey to it himself.

Naive and sentimental literature correspond, on one level, to the classical and modern cultures compared in the *Education*. But more often, Schiller distinguishes two mentalities associated respectively with a simple, unreflecting society, and a complex, reflective society like his own. These two mentalities are compared across history and often cut across the historical sequence from classical to modern, since some ancients are sentimental, and some moderns naive, and more importantly, all poets are to some extent both because every individual is both sensuous and rational. Because Schiller is always at once synchronic and diachronic, his definitions are infinitely flexible. The process from naive to sentimental is one that can be experienced by every poet just as it was experienced in history:

The path on which the modern poets are moving is . . . the same one on which man individually and mankind as a whole must travel. Nature makes him one with himself, art separates and divides him, through the ideal he returns to that unity.   (*NS*, p. 40)

In general, then, the sentimental state follows the naive, and is characterized by an alienation from, and idealization of, nature. It is followed – theoretically – by an ideal in which the two are unified, though Schiller says himself that this ideal can never be fully realized.

The ideal is clearly distinguished from sentimental idealization of the naive. Talking about the idyll, a typically sentimental genre, Schiller describes the way in which it looks back to the pastoral state:

The poetic representation of innocent and happy humanity is the general intention of this kind of writing. Because this innocence and this

happiness seem incompatible with the artificial circumstances of society
as a whole . . . the poets have removed the scene of the idyll . . . to the
simple pastoral state and have assigned it a place before the beginning of
culture in the childlike age of man . . .

But such a state is not just to be found before the beginning of culture
but is also what culture, if it is only to have one definite trend, intends as
its ultimate goal.   (*NS*, p. 62)

The nostalgic retrospection of the idyll, Schiller says, holds out no
hope for the future, and is thus inadequate to the true task of
poetry. Unfortunately, he says, these poets

place behind us the goal towards which they should be leading us and
thus can only inspire in us the sad feeling of loss, not the cheerful feeling
of hope.   (*NS*, p. 63)

It is plain that, while he may himself have tended towards
sentimentalization, Schiller's philosophical and poetic aspiration
was directed towards a new ideal. Again, how this is to be
achieved is not made explicit. While Schiller is always looking
towards a synthesis of naive and sentimental, they are said to be
most successful as poetic modes when sticking to what they do
best, as he says of the idyll:

Thus here too . . . as in all poetic genres, one must choose once and for all
between the individual and the ideal; for to want to satisfy both
demands at the same time is the surest way, as long as one has not
reached the goal of perfection, to miss both together.   (*NS*, p. 65)

With this in mind, the reconciliation of individuation and
idealization, naive and sentimental, is even more difficult to
grasp. Individuation – if perfect – is ideal, and the ideal – if
perfectly individuated – is perfect.

So far, we have little idea of what exactly it is for a poet to be
naive. How does Schiller translate his account of the naive state of
mind – so similar to the sensuous or natural state – into an account
of naive poetry? In fact, it is when Schiller goes on to describe
individual poets as naive or sentimental that the breach between
the philosophical basis of his argument and its application in
practical criticism becomes apparent. Underlying this breach is
the problem of how Kant's critique can – or can't – be transformed
from an epistemological system into a way of describing individual works of art.

It has become clear that the naive, as a general temperament, is as difficult to separate from the sentimental as the sensuous was difficult to separate from the rational man. Either naiveté is a completely unselfconscious condition which can only be appreciated within sentimental culture, or it is really not so different from the sentimental after all — as the example of the Greeks suggests. When it comes to describing texts as naive or sentimental, a similar problem arises. Schiller's account of naive poetry is essentially a description of how the naive poet sees and is in the world. He constructs a model of the kind of way of looking at the world naive poetry communicates.

The naive poet, Schiller says, is typified by the lack of attention he pays to describing his own emotions and responses — a stance which parallels natural man's unthinking and immediate response to the world around him. He uses as example a scene from Ariosto and one from Homer. While the former is emotive, he says, Homer is very matter-of-fact, and sticks to describing external events or things. This is where Schiller draws the line between naive and sentimental.

Since the naive poet only follows simple nature and simple emotions and restricts himself solely to the imitation of nature, so he can only have a single relationship with his subject-matter and in this regard he has no choice in his treatment of the material . . . Things are quite different with the sentimental poet. He reflects on the impression which objects make on him, and the emotion into which he himself is transposed and into which he transposes us is based only on that reflection . . . The sentimental poet therefore is constantly dealing with two opposing concepts and emotions, with reality as boundary and with his idea as the infinite.   (*NS*, p. 42)

It is not difficult to see how this account of the naive poet's difference from the sentimental could begin to give way under Romantic pressure. For it can be read in several ways. Schiller may be saying that the naive poet really can't help himself. He writes almost involuntarily, and takes his cue from the natural objects around him — a view that was fairly current, as we shall see, in eighteenth-century British aesthetics. Or, he may be saying that the naive poet chooses to write about the way things look rather than the way he feels — in which case the distinction between him and the sentimental poet would be a matter either of changing historical and literary convention, or deliberate choice. Thus classical poets might be said to have been less interested in describing the private feelings of the individual than were the Romantics – due to a cultural change towards individualism.

Aesthetics since Kant has focused on the way in which we subjectively participate in and construct our own experience. The poetry and philosophy of the Romantics reveal an intense preoccupation with this issue – a preoccupation characteristic of the sentimental frame of mind. Attention is focused in particular on perception and the way in which the individual apprehends the perceived world. Although intimations of the Kantian perspective were, of course, emerging in Hume and – as we shall see – in the British aestheticians of the eighteenth century, to say that pre-Kantian philosophy focused more on the object rather than the subject–object relationship would not be unfair. Schiller's account of the sentimental poet who 'reflects on the impression which objects make on him' and the naive poet who 'only follows simple nature' cannot but bring this historical transition from pre- to post-Kantian epistemology to mind. Moreover, we cannot but see how very post-Kantian Schiller's own perspective on the pre-Kantian, or naive, is. It is a perspective that survives in many ways. If a post-Impressionist culture looks back at the art of a neo-classical age, it may find the absence of its own fascination with perception both charmingly simple and naively simplistic. The question is – what exactly is the difference between the two, and how right would we be to use the term 'naive' – implying as it does that the earlier epoch was not articulate about its own perception – *did not, in other words, possess a theoretical aesthetic*?

I argue that the distinction Schiller makes between the naive and the sentimental is largely founded on the distinction between a pre- and a post-Kantian philosophical perspective. One of the difficulties with Schiller's work is that he does not always make it clear whether his naive and sentimental poets consciously choose to express different philosophical perspectives of this kind or whether they are simply the products of different cultures who must, willy nilly, see things as their age and education dictate. Thus naive literature could either be a genuinely primitive and simple literature, the product of a culture or the work of an individual acting naturally and impulsively, unable to give a theoretical articulation for its work. Schiller often suggests that this is the case in his descriptions of the naive poet as a child of nature. Alternatively, naive literature might simply be the literature of an age with different values and theories, judged by the modern, in retrospect, to be naive.

This suggests that the naive is only naive in that it is not interesting to the sentimental and that it is interested in different things – the community rather than the individual, for example. Schiller himself acknowledges that the sentimental age is not very interested in naive poets, who are 'no longer really in place in an artificial era' (*NS*, p. 38). And elsewhere he remarks of the naive poet that:

> The dry truth with which he treats his subject often appears insensitive. The subject possesses him utterly, his heart does not lie like base metal just under the surface but needs like gold to be sought for in the depths. As the godhead stands behind the edifice of the world, so does he stand behind his creation, he is the creation and the creation is he.
>
> (*NS*, p. 35)

What Schiller may simply be saying is that because the naive poet doesn't discuss internal events, they have to be extrapolated from his accounts of external events, rather as a deconstructionist reading of an apparently straightforward description seems to excavate a subjectivity that was at first not apparent.

But this is not how his account of naiveté in poetry was taken up. Rather, Romanticism polarized naive and sentimental, to the detriment of the former. ('Descriptive writing' often has – in twentieth-century practical criticism – a negative connotation and, more importantly, practical criticism itself is often taken to task for not being sufficiently explicit about its theoretical position. When post-structuralism does this to 'naive' practical criticism, it is betraying its own sentimental and Romantic origins.)

Schiller gives many varying accounts of what it is to be a naive poet. Talking about Shakespeare, who he considers naive, he explains how Shakespeare is never explicit about his own feelings:

> Misled by my acquaintance with more modern poets to look first of all in the work for the author, to encounter his heart, to reflect on his subject-matter together with him, in short to look for the subject-matter in the person, it was unbearable to me that here the poet could nowhere be grasped, was nowhere answerable to me.   (*NS*, p. 36)

The naive poet is too close to his subject-matter, Schiller suggests, to reflect upon it. 'The poet, as I have said, either is nature or he will seek it. The former constitutes the naive, the second the sentimental poet' (p. 38). The ability to seek involves the alienation from nature already mentioned – the naive poet is thus assumed to be in an almost unreflecting proximity to nature. Naive poetry is thus the poetry of limitation, of the real and not the ideal.

Here again, we are being asked to draw on the poet's relationship with the natural world as the source of explanations for the poetry. Naive poetry springs from a particular way of being in the world (or from the choice to adopt that stance) – a way of being in the world which is either involuntarily or voluntarily limited to the practical and has no access to the theoretical.

So what is the naive? It seems that to be naive is to stand in a particular relationship to the sentimental. Historically anterior, the naive is an art which is constructed as naive by the sentimental, which defines itself against that naive. Schiller identifies characteristics of classical literature he calls naive – lack of explicit consideration of the subject's inner life, for example – but there is nothing intrinsically naive about this.

CHARACTERISTICS OF THE SENTIMENTAL AESTHETIC

I suggest that the naive–sentimental is simply a relationship constructed by Schiller's aesthetic as a means of defining the Romantic present against the neo-classical past. That is, rather than corresponding to identifiable characteristics of texts – such as subject-matter – the two terms of his essay correspond to philosophical or critical stances or ways of reading. However, Schiller slips from talking about different philosophical stances to talking about texts as though they embodied those stances – as though the structure of the text was an embodiment of a particular philosophical consciousness. This tendency, which we know better in Romanticism as organicism, survives into modern structuralism which reorganizes conflicts in theoretical aesthetics as opposing and contrasting pieces of scaffolding in the structure of the work of art. The ambiguity generated by the origins of this doctrine in Kant's formalism persists through Romanticism as an account of the text as an autonomous entity which is in some way an interface with the subjective consciousness, a 'product' in which 'process' can always be revealed, as the movement of a shuttle is implicit in a woven cloth.

One of the characteristics of this kind of sentimental aesthetic is its tendency to universalize, to shape and generalize particular and historical details into universal relations. Kant had argued that aesthetic judgment was based on the 'subjective universal validity' of beauty: the structure of the beautiful experience is the same for every individual, whatever the work of art is like. It is the formal *design*, or interrelation of parts that constitutes the beautiful for Kant: if we see a tree as beautiful we see how its branches, leaves and blossom form a united whole, rather than noticing that it is a cherry tree and is twenty feet tall. It is this formality that Schiller actually seems to have disliked about Kant's account of art, and yet his own work did little to dislodge it.

Sentimental criticism, then, is disposed towards the formal, shaping, creating, processual aspects of literature, not the specific or local meaning for an individual reader in a particular place and time. Sentimental criticism unearths in texts its own universal model of the creative or critical process, rather than talking about what that text means – or meant to a particular individual or community. This is noticeable in twentieth-century structuralist and much post-structuralist theory which sets aside the biographical and historical to look at the text as a free-floating, autonomous structure.

CONCLUSION

Schiller's aesthetic has as its mainspring an opposition between two modes, which Schiller ultimately aimed to unite in a higher harmony. But it is this opposition which drives his essay, in which the naive is essentially the creation and object of the sentimental mentality, which distinguishes itself historically by articulating the naive. The natural consequence of this aesthetic is the subordination of the naive, for it must reveal the formal, subjective, critical principle everywhere and neglect the specific and objective. Everything that seems simple and objective is revealed as being complex and subjective – an outcome Schiller himself did not intend, for he wanted, reciprocally, everything complex and subjective to also be revealed as simple and objective. (Thus a neo-classical and a post-Impressionist tree would, presumably, both be at once embodiments of a subjective consciousness and descriptions of real trees, the two being inseparable just as the tree is a tree just because it is a mass of moving atoms.)

Sentimental aesthetics does not generate or even tolerate what we can call 'naive' readings of literature: that is, readings which are specific, local, or historical. Such readings pick out and place an individual work in space and time; an example would be a reading of John Clare's poetry which discussed the effect of the enclosure of the fenlands on his writing. Sentimental aesthetics is similarly uninterested in the way writing communicates, the way it achieves significance or reference in a particular context. This is because it always considers literature as a subjective process, not an objective product. It generates structural readings, which emphasize the design and subjective origin of literature. and which can be applied equally to all literature. The common sentimental use of analogy goes back to Kant's own 'subjective universal validity'.

Sentimentalism is an often unacknowledged legislator of the way we classify and appreciate poetry. Recent preferences for 'self-consuming' or 'self-referential' readings illustrate sentimentalism's lack of interest in the fact that a text refers and communicates – as well as being a process. The next chapter will show how Romanticism furthered the sentimental tendency, and the exclusion of what it understood as 'naive' writers from the canon.

2

MYTHS OF ROMANTICISM

OVERVIEW

If Schiller stood sceptically back from unadulterated sentimentalism, his successors in the Romantic school had fewer reservations. It is their aesthetic, as Jerome McGann has persuasively argued in *The Romantic ideology*[1] which pervades twentieth-century criticism. Many of the critical texts which inform twentieth-century appreciation of the canonical nineteenth-century poets like Wordsworth and Coleridge (and similarly, inform opinion about non-canonical poets) are themselves 'sentimental' in approach, because they derive their first principles and their manner of speaking from the Romantics.

If Schiller tended to find the subjective principle he inherited from Kant pervading his work and undermining his attempt to establish a new marriage of the objective and subjective, the Romantics were even more spellbound by the subjective, sentimental principle. Unlike Schiller, his successors were scarcely critical of sentimentalism and their work extends the sentimental principle from modern poetry to what they called *all* true poetry. However, in a typical sentimental gambit, writers like Schlegel retain the naive principle to provide a contrast and a foil for this true sentimentalism. This is, of course, illogical, because it involves sustaining two contrasting aesthetic principles – the realist and idealist, or pre- and post-Kantian, within one theory as though they were characteristic of different kinds of poetry rather than different philosophical perspectives.

This is possible just because of the Romantic ambiguity – again inherited from Schiller – between philosophical theory and poetic practice. Romantic writers tend to talk about poems as though they were structural embodiments of theoretical beliefs, as though philosophical principle were almost physically realized in the form of a text. Thus 'naive' or classical texts are described as though they embodied the epistemological structure of pre-Kantian aesthetics in which a subject receives sense data from an object, and 'sentimental' or Romantic texts are described as though they embodied the epistemological structure of post-Kantian aesthetics, in which the subject 'constructs' an object-for-the-subject. This tendency is sustained by Coleridge and his successors, and results in a well-established habit of talking about what a poem is about (what it says) as though it were what the poem actually embodied (what it is).

This is exacerbated by the Romantic penetration of the linguistic domain. Romanticism draws a contrast between naive and sentimental poetic *language* which is based on a distinction between literal and figurative language, and which underlies the descriptive/expressive contrast mentioned in the introduction. The contrast is as difficult to establish as the original naive–sentimental opposition, just because the prevailing philosophy of language had – as we shall see – long since established the importance of the subjective or figurative element in *all* language.

However, much twentieth-century criticism of nineteenth-century poetry still relies on the distinction, and claims that truly Romantic language – like that of Coleridge – has a special figurative quality, structured like post-Kantian epistemology, in which the subject creates the objects of its knowledge, or at least transforms them. If this were a theory of language extended to all poetry it would be fine – but the concept of a naive, literal, descriptive language, which simply records what is out there, is sustained at the same time. This is despite the fact that no post-Kantian theory of language ever justified a hard-and-fast distinction of this kind with success, and contemporary theories of language have long since stopped making easy discriminations between the literal and the figurative. However, the literary critics maintain the opposition between descriptive and expressive, and the poetic canon has been structured accordingly.

ROMANTIC PROBLEMS

In my last chapter I showed how Schiller tended to find the sentimental or subjective principle pervading his account of both naive and sentimental art, despite his intention of differentiating and then uniting the two. This was almost inevitable, given that the sentimental principle loosely approximated to the idealist perspective he inherited from Kant and never escaped. In the work of Friedrich Schlegel, who actually supplied the term 'Romantic' for the sentimental, this subjective tendency is exaggerated. Schlegel identifies the Romantic principle with the essence of poetry itself. At the same time, he sets it against the classical principle. He does not intend to reconcile the two, as Schiller would have done.

Just as Schiller was unhappy with Kant's sense–reason dualism, so Schlegel is dissatisfied with Schiller's opposition, in literature, of the naive and the sentimental. This already fluid opposition becomes even more fluid in Schlegel's work, as Kathleen Wheeler explains in her work on *German aesthetic and literary criticism*:

> The difference between disparate literary forms could not be one of fundamental aesthetic principle, as Schiller seemed at least to suggest by his dualism, but merely a matter of emphasis, or of degree rather than kind. Friedrich Schlegel then transformed the original meaning of his term 'romantic' to signify the characteristic synthesis of these pairs of opposites common to all great art, where before 'romantic' had been used merely as a historical term in relation to modern literature.[2]

In his essay 'The antinomic structure of Friedrich Schlegel's "Romanticism"', Leonard Wessel (who argues elsewhere for the essentially contradictory nature of Romanticism as it develops from Schiller's aesthetic)[3] contends that Schiller's thought is, despite its attempts to overcome the Kantian dualism, just as divided as Kant's. Naive and sentimental divide just as sense and reason did in Kant's metaphysics, and:

> The ineluctable antithesis of the sentimental and the naive, and the correlative need for reconciliation, are the psychological equivalents to Kant's antinomy of pure reason.[4]

Thus Schlegel inherits a dichotomy, and his literary history

> must be seen as an attempt to unite these two antagonistic aesthetics, to find a synthesis of the antique and the modern.[5]

This distinction, which is also found in Friedrich Schlegel's brother August Wilhelm's writing on dramatic art and literature, is initially one between the (historically) classical and modern. Thus August Wilhelm Schlegel says that

> the poetry of the ancients was the poetry of enjoyment, and ours that of desire: the former has its foundation in the scene that is present, while the latter hovers between recollection and hope . . . The feeling of the moderns is, upon the whole, more inward, their fancy more incorporeal, and their thoughts more contemplative . . . The Grecian ideal of human nature was perfect unison and proportion between all the powers – a natural harmony. The moderns, on the contrary, have arrived at the consciousness of an internal discord which renders such an ideal impossible; and hence the endeavour of their poetry is to reconcile these two words between which we find ourselves divided, and to blend them indissolubly together.[6]

In this passage, A. W. Schlegel slips almost indiscernibly from the traditional contrast between the classical and the modern (or romantic) to an account of modern poetry as embracing classical poetry and reconciling it with itself. Thus romantic poetry becomes the poetry that 'delights in indissoluble mixtures; all contrarieties: nature and art, poetry and prose, seriousness and mirth, recollection and anticipation, spirituality and sensuality'.[7]

This is exactly the same slippage that we noticed in Schiller, as the sentimental category begins to absorb the naive, but here it is articulated explicitly, and all distinction vanishes. The problematic opposition – initially historical – of two aesthetics is itself taken into and absorbed by one of those aesthetics, which reshapes itself to encompass the rejected aesthetic. What was an irreconcilable opposition in history is transformed into synchronic, aesthetic harmony. Schlegel characterizes Romantic art as the productive opposition of the classical and the romantic, simultaneously extending the Romantic principle to become that which underlies all art. For him,

> the Romantic is not so much a literary genre as an element of poetry which may be more or less dominant or recessive, but never entirely absent . . . all poetry should be Romantic.

And:

> The Romantic genre of poetry is the only one which is more than a genre, and which is, as it were, poetry itself: for in a certain sense all poetry is or should be Romantic.[8]

Problems inevitably arise from this absorption of the problematic naive–sentimental opposition into a new aesthetic formula. For

> once Schlegel broadened the application of his term *romantic* in this way, it was inevitable that he should lose control over it. Soon he began to discover all sorts of 'romantic' traits in even the most classical writers.[9]

Tzvetan Todorov draws attention to this difficulty in his work on romantic theories of the symbol:

> If romanticism is defined by the resolution of all contraries, sooner or later it is bound to encounter the classic–romantic pair: if it absorbs the opposition, it achieves one of those paradoxes . . . in which a whole comes to figure as an element within itself. Such absorptive capacity . . . rules out any separation between classical and romantic, and in effect it robs the term 'romantic' itself of all meaning. This transformation of the concept is particularly striking in Friedrich Schlegel. In the *Dialogue on Poetry* . . . he defines 'the ultimate goal of all literature' as 'the harmony of the classical with the romantic' (p. 112), and . . . declares, in what is both the affirmation of the supremacy of romanticism and of its dissolution, that 'all poetry should be Romantic' (p. 101).[10]

The Schlegels, like Schiller, wanted to apply idealist aesthetic principles to specific works of art and literature. But because a subjective idealist aesthetic gives an account of art as an experience in the subject, it is essentially incompatible with a classification of artworks as if they had objective properties. This problem was experienced in embryo by Kant's eighteenth-century predecessors, whose accounts of aesthetic experience in the *subject*, and aesthetic qualities in the *object*, were deeply divided. Kant himself only resolved the contradiction between the two by introducing the object-for-the-subject.[11] He did, however, limit himself to talking about the aesthetic object as experienced by the subject, not as it is in itself. But Kant cannot be accused of lapsing into indiscriminate, sloppy sentimentalism, in which generalizations overwhelm any specific classification. He sustains objective/subjective distinctions within the framework of a subjective aesthetic with a rigour the later idealists were unable to match.

For Kant's epistemology is just that: it makes no claim to talk about or classify art and the theory of art that the third Critique provides is very much a part of a wider, carefully circumscribed and orchestrated theory of knowledge. It is Schiller who introduces a theory of genre and talks specifically about literary texts and the Schlegels, even though their romantic principle is really an account of aesthetic experience, also use it ambiguously as a means of classifying literature. We noticed the problems Schiller encountered in reconciling his scenic classification with his Kantian foundation and these problems were intensified in the work of his Romantic followers. For it was then that the very problem of aesthetics, the relationship between subject and object – or aesthetic process and product – becomes the central concern of aesthetic theory.

The Romantics formulated the concept of the text as a 'system', or internally coherent and autonomous 'organism'. Consequently, they not only established an important ambiguity between the verbal and the existential, even the biological, domains; but also fostered an increasingly apparent discrepancy between the subjectivist account of poetry as aesthetic experience in the subject and an account of poetry or the poem as an objective entity.

Romantic aesthetics sustains a double perspective on to poetry. It is at once a *process* ('Romantic poetry is a progressive universal poetry . . . it is always becoming . . . it can never be completed')[12] and a *product*, an organic whole ('an object of nature that wants to become an object of art').[13] This is how an account of poetry as subjective experience – creative or critical – was combined with an account of the poem as object. This object is structured like the subjective, experiencing consciousness – it is an *objectification* of the experience. This 'objectification', whereby the critical process is also the structure of the artwork, brings about the coincidence of criticism – or theory – and poetry – or practice so desired by the post-Kantian movement. As Cassirer says in *The philosophy of the Enlightenment*:

A correlation is now sought between the content of philosophy and that of art; and an affinity is maintained which appears at first to be too dimly felt for expression in precise and definite concepts . . . This unity of demand and act, of artistic form and reflective contemplation . . . results directly from the dynamic interplay of . . . fundamental formative forces.[14]

Accounts of poetry as ironic or self-critical consciousness arose from this contrived coincidence of theory and practice. The ironic principle as 'a principle essential to all art'[15] was transmitted into twentieth-century literary theory as the doctrine of the poem as self-critical or self-consuming. Via Coleridge, who maintained this 'double view, alternately capable of dwelling on a poem as a poem, and on a poem as a process of mind',[16] twentieth-century criticism came to define poetry according to a sentimental principle. For Coleridge, as Paul Hamilton says, inherited an idealist tradition, and

could participate in a defence of poetry based on poetry's awareness of its own aesthetic status. It is this tradition which is felt most strongly in literary theory today. The English Romantics' poetic affirmation of the importance of poetry could be seen to point to self-consciousness as an essential constituent of poetry and the key to its philosophical consequence.[17]

What we have to remember is that this account of a poem as self-conscious is a function of the Romantic 'objectification' of the creative or critical process as a 'system', and hence as an autonomous entity. It is an account of poetry which claims on the one hand that the poem is an 'object', and on the other that that object is nothing more than subjective process.

COLERIDGE

Coleridge's critical theory is similarly ambivalent. As Wellek says:

Coleridge does not always recognize the distinction between the poet and his poetry . . . In the wake of Schiller, the Schlegels, and Schelling Coleridge sometimes extends the term 'poetry' to all the arts and even to all human creativity.[18]

Like Friedrich Schlegel, who extended the poetic principle to all arts, and indeed to science, insofar as it was creative:

The whole history of modern poetry is a continuous commentary to the short text of philosophy: every art should become science, and every science should become art; poetry and philosophy should be unified;[19]

Coleridge also wishes to identify what the essence of poetry is. And this means insisting that poetry is different from other arts and disciplines. Thus, just as Schlegel suggests elsewhere that poetry and science cannot have anything in common; because 'strictly speaking, the idea of a scientific poem is probably as nonsensical as that of a poetic science';[20] so Coleridge also attempts both to show how poetry is a universal principle (as creativity), and also how it is different from other arts or activities. At times he seems to side with Schelling, who understands the creative or imaginative faculty as productive not only of art, but of the natural world, and thus as a pervasive force in our experience. At other times, in line with Kant, he insists that poetry is quite distinct from any other experience. As Mary Warnock says in *Imagination*:

In the *System of Transcendental Idealism* Schelling distinguishes between the 'productive intuition' and the 'poetic faculty'. The existence of nature is deduced from the productive faculty of the absolute I; and . . . what was an *active* function, constituting the world-as-it-appears-to-us, in Kant becomes, in Schelling, a properly *creative* function constituting the world as it really is. All the concrete forms of nature itself are actually made by the productive intuition. How far did Coleridge go with Schelling against Kant? It may be said that he is not completely committed . . . to idealism . . . Perhaps we must be content to say that there is no clear answer to the question whether, in Coleridge's view, the imagination does or does not create the world.[21]

The question of where Coleridge places the limits of imagination and of how he defines poetry is complex and is discussed by Paul Hamilton in his book. What is certain is that Coleridge contradicts himself or at least shifts his ground, here asserting the autonomy of the poetic imagination, there its participation in all apprehension. This obviously affects the way in which poetry relates to science or to philosophy and criticism. In the *Biographia literaria* and in his Shakespearean criticism, Coleridge tries to distinguish poetry from science and the other arts.

A poem is that species of composition which is opposed to works of science, by proposing for its *immediate* object pleasure, not truth; and from all other species (having *this* object in common with it) it is discriminated by proposing to itself such delight from the *whole*, as is compatible with a distinct gratification from each component *part*.[22]

Here we have the old problem of aesthetics. If art is distinct from science, then it runs the risk of being non-cognitive, having no access to truth, being simply decorative. And if it is not distinct, then why is it art? The introduction of the concept of art as somehow holistic and circular or organic, rather than atomistic and linear, a special kind of synthetic knowledge which we receive all at once, and which is diffused through the artistic whole, is a Romantic solution to the problem. But Coleridge, like the other Romantics, also wants to claim that poetry is the underlying truth in every discipline, and says that:

All the fine arts are different species of poetry. The same spirit speaks to the mind through different senses by manifestations of itself, appropriate to each. They admit therefore of a natural division into poetry of language (poetry in the emphatic sense, because less subject to the accidents and limitations of time and space); poetry of the ear, or music, and poetry of the eye.[23]

Here, Coleridge tries to have it both ways: poetry is at once all arts, and specifically the art of language. And where philosophy is concerned, as Paul Hamilton argues, he tries simultaneously to sustain the distinction and to bypass it: whilst insisting that philosophy is a kind of science, and thus distinct, he 'wants to be able to show the relevance of poetry to philosophy without collapsing one into the other'.[24]

This is exactly the sentimental critic's problem: trying at once to maintain and to overcome an opposition. The sentimental or subjective creative principle seems to apply everywhere, yet it must also be asserted to be the special principle of the sentimental, which must distinguish itself from the naive that it establishes.

The problem of what exactly counts as poetic also arises within the poetic domain itself. Not only does Coleridge try and, according to Wellek, fail to distinguish poetry from prose or science in his criticism (and his Shakespearean criticism certainly reveals the difficulties he encounters),[25] but he also tries to set up a distinction between a true and a lesser kind of poetry. The discrimination of two different faculties involved in poetry – the mechanical 'Fancy' and the organic 'Imagination' – allows him to set up a distinction between two correspondingly different kinds of poetry. As M. H. Abrams says:

Again and again, Coleridge uses his bifocal lens to discriminate and appraise two modes of poetry. One of these can be adequately accounted for in mechanical terms. It has its source in the particulars of sense and the images of memory, and its production involves only the lower faculties of fancy, 'understanding,' and empirical 'choice.' . . . The other and greater class of poetry is organic. It has its souce in living 'ideas,' and its production involves the higher faculties of imagination, 'reason,' and the 'will.' Hence it is the work of genius.[26]

It will be remarked that the 'mechanical' account of poetry is similar to that accepted by eighteenth-century critics, and in my fourth chapter I will argue that the retention of a rejected aesthetic as 'naive' partner to a sentimental category is typical of sentimentalism.

Coleridge's aesthetic corresponds closely to Schiller's, setting up similar literary categories. As Wellek says:

> he draws a distinction similar to that drawn by Schiller between naive and sentimental, when he said that the poetry of the ancients reflects the world without, while the allegorizing fancy of a modern poet . . . is striving to project the inward.[27]

This distinction, Wellek notes, is articulated by Coleridge as the difference between a 'pictorial' and a 'musical' poet.[28]

In many different ways, Coleridge insists upon this naive/sentimental distinction. In particular, there is a contrast drawn between a poetry which transcribes and perhaps combines images from nature, and a poetry which actually transforms nature. The former just gives us an 'objective' picture while the latter fuses the poetic subjectivity with the appearance of nature:

> It has been observed that images, however beautiful, though faithfully copied from nature, and as accurately represented in words, do not themselves characterize the poet. They become proofs of original genius only insofar as they are modified by a predominant passion; or by associated thoughts or images awakened by that passion; or when they have the effect of reducing multitude to unity, or succession to an instant, or lastly, when a human and intellectual life is transferred to them from the poet's own spirit.[29]

In suggesting that there is a simply 'objective' poetry in which the creative subject does not participate, Coleridge sets up as the contrast for true poetry a 'naive' counterpart which could never really exist. In many ways, he is simply selecting certain aspects of poetry for praise and others for criticism. He accuses Wordsworth of 'laborious minuteness and fidelity in the representation of objects',[30] and insists that true poetry 'avoids and excludes all *accident*'.[31] Whatever is material, referential or specific is not poetic, for poetry is the universal, shaping process.

For in all that truly merits the name of *Poetry* . . . there is a necessary predominance of the Ideas (i.e. of that which originates in the artist himself), and a comparative indifference of the materials.[32]

This insistence on the essentially spiritual and universal (or sentimental) character of poetry is typically sentimental. Like Schiller, Coleridge distinguishes between 'classical' and 'romantic' art,[33] and 'like Schiller, he assumes that the modern aesthetic consciousness is irretrievably sentimental and literary'.[34] His own work bears his theory out.

Professing the Romantic desire for 'the fine balance of observing, with the imaginative faculty in modifying the objects observed';[35] Coleridge is committed in theory to the 'translucence of the Special in the Individual or of the General in the Especial'.[36] However, in practice he reinforces the distinction between a 'descriptive' and an 'expressive' poetry; where the former is criticized for its 'minute accuracy in the painting of local imagery',[37] the latter is praised for its holistic grandeur. In his Shakespearean criticism, he constantly emphasizes the importance of the poem as a *whole* and the lesser significance of visual detail: 'the grandest efforts of poetry are where the imagination is called forth, not to produce a distinct form, but a strong working of the mind'.[38]

In line with Burke and the 'sublime' school, Coleridge considers whatever is particular, distinct or limited to be inferior to that which is universal, obscure and boundless.

This opposition between aspects – or kinds – of poetry, which makes claims to being philosophically grounded, is in fact completely without foundation. It is an objective–subjective distinction which cannot be used to categorize literary texts or aspects of texts. It goes against Kant's recognition that *all* aesthetic judgment is subjective; all apprehension, indeed. I will argue that this kind of classification is little more than a classification of literature according to subject-matter, which isolates as 'inferior' whatever is insufficiently idealist and philosophical in its concerns.

Hazlitt, who makes similar distinctions to those of Coleridge, sides with him in attacking 'descriptive' poetry: Crabbe is dismissed as overly-detailed and 'Dutch' in his pictorial approach:

the adept in Dutch interiors . . . and pig-styes must find in Mr. Crabbe a man after his own heart. He is the very thing itself; he paints in words, instead of colours: there is no other difference.[39]

Displaying the Romantic tendency 'to consider concrete expression a decadence',[40] Coleridge and Hazlitt are in fact reacting against the subject-matter and concerns of the previous generation of poets. But Coleridge couches this revolt in organicist language: writing of this 'concrete' or atomistic kind, he says,

seems to be like taking the pieces of a dissected map out of its box. We first look at one part, and then at another, then join and dove-tail them . . .[41]

We must not look to parts merely, but to the whole, and to the effect of that whole.[42]

Organic poetry is not simply aggregative and imitative, but creative, participating in what it represents. The kind of poetry which simply 'copies' scene after scene is associated with a certain kind of painting; painting was, for these nineteenth-century critics, generally discussed as if it were, unlike poetry, naturally representational and imitative. (I shall give a full critique of this discrimination between the visual and verbal and of the notion that painting as pictorial representation can be 'accurate', in chapter 4.)

Thus Coleridge's aesthetic encourages a distinction between two kinds of poetry, partly in an attempt to isolate qualities specific to 'true' Romantic poetry. I shall show in my next chapter how this belief in a special Romantic idiom has governed readings of Wordsworth's poetry. And yet Wordsworth himself is far from truly Romantic.

WORDSWORTH

René Wellek tells us that Wordsworth holds a position in the history of literary criticism which must be called ambiguous or transitional. He inherits from neoclassicism a theory of the imitation of nature to which he gives, however, a specific social twist; he inherits from the eighteenth century a view of poetry as passion and emotion which he again modifies by his description of the poetic process as 'recollection in tranquillity' . . . he also adopts . . . a theory of poetry in which imagination holds the central place as a power of unification and ultimate insight into the unity of the world.[43]

M. H. Abrams describes Wordsworth as 'more thoroughly immersed in certain currents of eighteenth-century thinking than any of his important contemporaries',[44] and, noting the absence of post-Kantian terminology in his criticism, points out that he 'remained within a well-defined tradition in the general pattern of his criticism'.[45] Wordsworth appeals to norms, to common sense and to basic human standards, rather than to first principles, as do the German aestheticians. Thus, Abrams concludes,

Wordsworth adopts and elaborates the old antithesis between nature and art and, like the aesthetic primitivists of the preceding age, declares himself for nature.[46]

This seems to suggest that Wordsworth's own aesthetic leans towards the 'naive,' just as my reading of Clare's aesthetic will suggest that he was less 'naive' himself than he appeared to be. Paul Hamilton similarly links Wordsworth's thought with that of the previous century: he is not, it seems, with Coleridge and Schiller in defining himself *against* the conservative naiveté of the past.

Wordsworth's reluctance to consider the poet as anything other than a faithful transcriber partly arises from the eighteenth-century cast of his thoughts. Passages of the 1802 'Preface' are reminiscent of Kames' idea that the excellence of a poetic representation is measured by its success in placing the reader in the position of spectator.[47]

In the 'Preface' and elsewhere, Wordsworth adheres to the notion of a natural and universal standard to which poetry must aspire, sloughing off artifice. And in many ways his own stated aims do not seem so very different from those expressed by Clare:

The principal object, then, proposed in these Poems was to choose incidents and situations from common life, and to relate or describe them, throughout . . . in a selection of language really used by men.[48]

For Clare, this is not such a conscious effort, but is simply a question of class and situation. However, Wordsworth *is* ambiguous and one can see how easily he can be collapsed into a Coleridgean aesthetic, especially if one concentrates on the 1815 'Preface' and 'Essay Supplementary' which deal more specifically with the crafting, conscious processes of art. However, it is important to note that Wordsworth's aesthetic is far less idealist than it has been painted, in particular by those critics whose readings of Wordsworth's psyche through the poetry (see chapter 3 below) are intensely idealist.

The opening sentence of Wordsworth's 'Preface to the Edition of 1815' reveals an ambivalent attitude to description in poetry, typical of the criticism of the previous century (see chapter 4 below). Beginning with an emphasis on 'objective' description:

The powers requisite for the production of poetry are: first, those of Observation and Description, – i.e., the ability to observe with accuracy things as they are in themselves, and with fidelity to describe them unmodified by any passion or feeling existing in the describer.

Wordsworth goes on to insist that:

This power, though indispensable to a Poet, is one which he employs only in submission to necessity, and never for a continuance of time: as its exercise supposes all the higher qualities of the mind to be passive, and in a state of subjection to external objects.[49]

Separating out the capacity whereby the poet records the visible object – which may dominate and subdue his ability – from the imaginative poetic sensibility which transforms nature, Wordsworth goes on to suggest that poems could be classed according to the kind and degree of imagination at work ('Preface, 1815', p. 29). Imagination proper, he tells us, is nothing to do with ordinary representation: it

has no reference to images that are merely a faithful copy, existing in the mind, of absent external objects: but is a word of higher import, denoting operations of the mind upon those objects, and processes of creation or composition, governed by certain fixed laws.

('Preface, 1815', pp. 30–1)

It is in this passage that we have an account of the way in which 'the conferring, the abstracting, and the modifying powers of the Imagination' ('Preface, 1815', p. 33) transform the appearances of nature: a view which, whilst consonant with Coleridge's account of the Imagination as creative to some extent, owes much to eighteenth-century descriptions of the poetic process as selective and combinatory – enhancing rather than completely remaking nature.

However, if Wordsworth owes a debt to the critics of the previous century, it is a debt owed not only to Addison (in his explanation of imaginative processes) but to the 'sublime' school of aesthetics. This last influence, in conjunction with a more clearly Romantic, Rousseauesque view of language and poetry, ensures that Wordsworth places firm emphasis on the role of passion in poetry. The Appendix to the 'Preface to the Lyrical Ballads' offers just such a Rousseauesque account of how:

The earliest poets of our nations generally wrote from passion excited by real events; they wrote naturally, and as men: feeling powerfully as they did, their language was daring and figurative.[50]

Wordsworth's own insistence on the return to nature and to the language of men in their most natural state is well known and described in the 'Preface' in detail. In particular, he reacts against the 'artificial' diction of the eighteenth-century poets, contrasting the 'low state' to which 'knowledge of the most obvious and important phenomena had sunk' over that century and the artifices of Dryden and Pope[51] with true poetry, which is characterized *both* by genuine observation of nature, *and* by imaginative power. For though he criticizes the previous century (notably in the 'Essay Supplementary to the Preface of 1815') for failing to observe and being cut adrift from true nature, he also insists that:

The appropriate business of poetry . . . is to treat of things not as they *are*, but as they *appear*; not as they exist in themselves, but as they *seem* to exist to the *senses*, and to the passions.

('Essay Supplementary', p. 63)

Passion and simplicity go hand-in-hand in their naturalness ('Essay Supplementary', p. 64), and can be contrasted with the artificial state in which poetic diction is simply a 'dress' for meaning:

If words be not . . . an incarnation of the thought, but only a clothing for it, then surely will they prove an ill gift . . . Language, if it do not uphold, and feed, and leave in quiet, like the power of gravitation or the air we breathe, is a counter-spirit, unremittingly and noiselessly at work to derange, to subvert, to lay waste, to vitiate, and to dissolve.[52]

The force of Wordsworth's aesthetic is directed not against description but against artifice and so is not aligned with that of Coleridge, who was particularly concerned with the distinction between poetry and prose. Wordsworth's quarrel with Coleridge over this issue, and his insistence that the language of Prose may yet be well adapted to Poetry . . . a large portion of the language of every good poem can in no respect differ from that of good Prose . . . They both speak by and to the same organs . . . their affections are kindred, and almost identical, not necessarily differing even in degree; Poetry sheds no tears 'such as Angels weep', but natural and human tears; she can boast of no celestial ichor that distinguishes her vital juices from those of prose; the same human blood circulates through the veins of them both;

('Preface to Lyrical Ballads, 1850', p. 135)

contrast with an apparent endorsement of the distinction between 'literal' and 'figurative' language in the 'Preface to the Edition of 1815', where the notion of Imagination as a modifying power depends on a distinction between a 'literal' use of – for instance – the word 'hang' (Wordsworth's example, 'Preface, 1815', p. 31) and a figurative use. Coleridge, I argue, relies heavily on such a distinction in order to isolate poetry from prose or other arts and sciences – though this is a distinction (although widely accepted) which can be easily attacked.

Wordsworth's emphasis on the 'natural' as opposed to the 'artificial' and his concomitant refusal to separate poetry from ordinary language should militate against 'literal'/'figurative' oppositions when they are used to separate prose and poetry. It should thus militate against distinctions between kinds of poetry based on that opposition of the kind which Coleridge encourages when he opposes Fancy and Imagination: the 'objective' descriptive poetry, and the 'subjective' expressive poetry. But in fact, Wordsworth is more often read as anti-descriptive, subjective and idealist, like Coleridge and the German idealists. It is the aesthetic of the latter that has survived.

Accepting this aesthetic means accepting the distinction between 'descriptive' and 'expressive' poetry which has already been shown to rest on rather unstable ground. I now turn to another important failing of that much-used critical opposition.

DESCRIPTIVE POETRY AND PICTORIAL AESTHETICS

The term 'description' in so far as it referred to a type of poetry written in the eighteenth century reflected an absence of that moral conflict which Shairp identified with 'good' nature poetry. The misinterpretation of 'description' as a definition of what Thomson, for example, was doing, is prevalent in other modern uses which define 'description' as 'discourse whose object is to present a picture' or a use of language which is formal and rhetorical rather than iconic – Leavis' distinction between 'description' and 'enactment.'[53]

Ralph Cohen's authoritative account of the uses and misuses of the term 'description' in the history of criticism and in particular the way in which it has been used to distinguish eighteenth- from nineteenth-century poetry points out how what has subsequently been construed as a stylistic or structural difference can in fact be explained in ideological terms. Cohen makes the point that prejudice against a poet like Thomson not only has a lot to do with a dislike of his subject-matter and moral or social attitudes, but also, and more importantly, has a lot to do with a rejection of the eighteenth-century aesthetics with which he was associated.

Modern critics who reject the eighteenth-century view usually reject, too, the poetry to which it refers . . . In this respect, the pejorative uses of 'description' continue to propagate misapprehensions, identifying preferred values such as moral strife and complexity with 'interpretation,' 'enactment' – and distasteful values, though far from accurately defined, with 'description'.[54]

It is certainly the case that critics, as I shall show, do discriminate against pre-Romantic poetry, often on the basis of a Romantic distinction between 'descriptive' and 'symbolic' or 'expressive' poetry. Although this distinction implies stylistic or idiomatic differences, its similarity to the distinction between eighteenth-century and nineteenth-century accounts of poetry suggests that it is in fact simply a Romantic transformation of a prejudice against an unfashionable aesthetic, into a more authoritative distinction between texts.

Cohen's history of the use of the term 'descriptive' in criticism traces the late eighteenth-century movement from a primarily visual and mimetic aesthetic, which drew heavily on analogies with painting in its account of poetry, to an aesthetic which was founded on an account of the imagination as an internal faculty, directed less at the evocation in the mind's eye of natural scenes, and more at the expression of poetic subjectivity, and feeling.

The history of descriptive criticism moved from the localization of problems in the visual presentation of external nature to the description of the landscape of the mind, from sight to insight.[55]

Eighteenth-century aesthetics, taking the lead from the dominant empirical philosophy, employed a firmly visual idiom, understanding imagination as a kind of perception and poetry as the vivid or lively recall of nature to the reader's inner eye by way of images. Locke's epistemology, for instance, worked on a perceptual model:

To ask, at what *time* a man has at first any ideas, is to ask, when he begins to perceive: − *having ideas*, and *perception*, being the same thing.[56]

Following the philosophers, the literary critics of the time also describe imagination as a primarily visual activity. Addison, whose essays on the Imagination were so influential, explains how sight

furnishes the imagination with its ideas; so that by the pleasures of the imagination of fancy . . . I here mean such as arise from visible objects . . . We cannot indeed have a single object in the fancy that did not make its first entrance through the sight.[57]

Accordingly, the focus of eighteenth-century aesthetics was on the visual arts which set the pattern for the other arts. Thus the 'limited' and 'decaying' language of poetry was compared with the assumed universal and unchanging language of painting.[58] It was in this way that the 'ut pictura; poesis' doctrine that enjoyed such popularity at the time came to be central. As Lee McKay Johnson summarizes from Hagstrum's book, *The sister arts*,

the implication is that in attempting to imitate or mirror nature, the writer can learn from the painter how to add *energeia* to his depiction . . . the locus classicus of the 'sister arts' tradition is found in Horace's offhand comment 'ut pictura; poesis' . . . elevated to a kind of command that the writer imitate the painter.[59]

Although, as Roy Park points out in *Hazlitt and the spirit of the age*,[60] the transition from this attitude to the arts and that which prevailed in the nineteenth century cannot be construed as a smooth changeover from a visually-based to an internalized aesthetic, it is generally accepted that aesthetics began to move in that direction towards the end of the eighteenth century. In an essay on the 'sister arts', Elizabeth Abel argues:

The ideal of *ut pictura poesis* is rarely voiced in the criticism of the Romantic period; on the contrary, the imitation of painting in poetry serves often as an instance of what is to be avoided. Coleridge and Hazlitt both insist that the poet must evoke an imaginative or emotional response rather than simply depict concrete visual imagery.[61]

Hegel seems to adopt this anti-pictorial stance when he describes

the most spiritual presentation of romantic art . . . the universal art of
the spirit which has become free in itself and which is not tied down for
its realisation to external sensuous material.[62]

This transition naturally affected attitudes to 'descriptive'
poetry. A theory that valued accuracy and vividness in the
depiction of nature would encourage poetry to build relationships
with painting, both by direct reference, and through 'literary
pictorialism' or describing nature as if it had been painted. A
theory that no longer values, but actively discourages pictorialism, will reject topographical poetry of the kind previously
popular. Thus:

In his lecture on 'Didactic and Descriptive Poetry' (1783) Hugh Blair was
able to say that it was in descriptive poetry that 'the highest exertions of
genius may be displayed' . . . But ten years later the *Monthly Review*
was protesting – 'More descriptive poetry! Have we not enough!'[63]

This change in the favoured account of poetry and the close
association of eighteenth-century landscape and topographical
poetry with pictorial accuracy of description (like the close
association of nineteenth-century poetry with symbolic transformation of landscape) is not explicable in terms of a change in
the poetry itself. It is difficult to claim that Thomson is any more
'accurate' or 'pictorial' than Wordsworth, for instance, and
indeed, the whole association of 'pictorial' and 'accurate' is itself
merely conventional. The same is true of the concept of
'descriptive' poetry. And yet Romantic and subsequent literary
theories, whilst they discard much of previous aesthetic theories'
assumptions about the way language works, often retain as a
naive shibboleth a concept of a poetry which works through a
kind of picture language which bears no analysis.

It is undoubtedly true that Thomson differs from Wordsworth.
His concerns, subject-matter and vocabulary are different. His
views on painting and poetry are different. His metre, rhythm
and rhyme scheme are different. But this substantial explanation
for his difference from Wordsworth should not be couched in
terms of the difference between an eighteenth-century and a
nineteenth-century 'language', particularly not when such an
approach carries with it inherent disapproval of the earlier poetic
idiom, whilst using it to distinguish the more recent one as

valuable and special. I will return to eighteenth- and nineteenth-century aesthetics in my fourth chapter.

TWENTIETH-CENTURY CRITICAL APPROACHES TO EIGHTEENTH- AND NINETEENTH-CENTURY POETRY

One of the most significant ways in which eighteenth- and nineteenth-century poetry have been differentiated by twentieth-century critics from M. H. Abrams to Isobel Armstrong is in terms of an epistemological shift, identified in poetry by a changed relationship between the subject and the object. This shift is believed to correspond to the shift in philosophy from a pre- to a post-Kantian account of subject–object relations: that is, to a constructivist theory of knowledge. Following a Romantic lead, many critics talk as if there were some kind of unmediated relationship between this philosophical theory, the poetic consciousness and the structure of the poem, not to mention readerly consciousness and access, positing some kind of structural analogy which takes no account of the complex ways in which texts are written and understood within language or ideology or society. Moreover, this subject–object relationship is conceived as a structural characteristic of the poem, which is understood not as a piece of referential language, but as an organic entity. This is the sentimental model, which creates structural analogies that span isolated consciousnesses, neglecting historical or social processes.

Thus, for example, Earl Wasserman, in a heavily-loaded comparison of eighteenth- and nineteenth-century poetry, remarks that the whole organization and structure of the former is inadequate.

The bulk of eighteenth century descriptive poetry . . . is . . . trivial, and most of it betrays an uncertain or ineffectual conception of how one experiences the external nature which is its subject matter . . . the problem of the transaction between the perceiving mind and the perceived world was either evaded or left uneasily indecisive in descriptive verse.[64]

I would argue, for a start, that most eighteenth-century descriptive poetry is not remotely uneasy or indecisive about subject–object relations. It simply does not discuss them, and to suggest that it must is mere sentimental prejudice. Wasserman goes on to describe this poetry in terms intended to be derogatory, though in fact his definition neatly covers Wordsworth's *Lyrical Ballads*, for instance.

This lack of any significant epistemology can be taken as typical of the hundreds of eighteenth-century meditative-descriptive poems. When the poet is not merely organizing sense-data into some picturesque, sublime, or beautiful distribution, he usually devotes himself to humanizing the external scene by associating it with some emotion, moral theme, historical episode, moving narration, or autobiographical experience . . . Such tenuous, inorganic bonds between inner man and outer world betray the impotence of later eighteenth-century poetic epistemology.[65]

This passage begs many questions. It seems to be talking about the relationship of the poet to the subject-matter ('he . . . devotes himself to humanizing the external scene') rather than the topics with which the poem deals. What Wasserman seems to suggest is that the eighteenth-century poet relates in a limited way to his subject-matter, which is something that remains separate from him and which he cannot fully engage with or transform. Quite how it is possible to make these assumptions from the reading of a poem is not clear. Wasserman suggests, without even considering how our own reading might affect the issue, that we apprehend in the eighteenth-century text a mimetic relationship between poet and nature, rather like that which Schiller imagined obtaining between the naive and the environment.

The unresolved dualism of the poets and aestheticians results in a dualistic poetry; the scene is perceived and then felt or associated or thought, but seldom, if ever, apprehended *in* the perception. It is therefore a poetry of hobbling simile, rather than symbol.[66]

Here Wasserman suggests a simple correlation between the aesthetic or epistemological theories of the eighteenth century and the kind of poetry poets were able to produce. The logic seems to be: because post-Kantian epistemological theories had not yet been formulated, poets were only able to relate mimetically to their subject-matter. Now, even supposing that such a thing as a simple mimetic relationship – that is, a completely innocent, unideological perspective onto things as they really are – were possible, this would not be very acceptable as an argument. And moreover, mimesis is an aesthetic, theoretical label, and not a poetic act. How 'the scene' is separated from the poet writing it is again hard to visualize. What Wasserman is really getting at is the fact that the poets he is discussing are interested in, or write about, something different from the later poets with whom his sympathies more obviously lie. That is, the earlier poets, like Schiller's naive, at least seem *to be about* different kinds of relations between man and nature than the later poets. This is not the same as saying that they are epistemologically or structurally different, and certainly not the same as saying that one is better than the other. In this chapter, I am arguing that the difference between an eighteenth- and a nineteenth-century poet can quite adequately be explained in terms of what their respective work is *about*, and that our habitual distinctions on the grounds of structural differences cannot be justified. M. H. Abrams, in 'Structure and style in the greater Romantic lyric', makes just such a (sentimental) distinction between poems on structural grounds, when the difference involved could easily be explained as a difference in reference, or subject-matter.[67]

Abrams begins with a comment on the eighteenth-century loco-descriptive poem, whose organization 'was soon reduced mainly to the procedure of setting up parallels between landscape and moral commonplaces' (*GRL*, p. 537). This mode, he goes on, was anathema to the Romantic poets:

> To the Romantic sensibility such a universe could not be endured, and the central enterprise common to many post-Kantian German philosophers and poets, as well as to Coleridge and Wordsworth was to join together the 'subject' and 'object' that modern intellection had put asunder. (*GRL*, p. 546)

Here we have the link between the aesthetic and philosophical endeavour of the Romantics, and what their poetry is supposed to have achieved.

> The shift in Coleridge's theory of descriptive poetry corresponded with a change in his practice of the form . . . we can observe him in the process of converting the conjunction of parts, in which nature stays on one side and thought on the other, into the Romantic interfusion of subject and object. (*GRL*, p. 550)

Even assuming that Coleridge, or anyone, could have this kind of control over language (for this is a very Romantic view of the willing poetic force moulding language into shape); and even if it were possible to make sense of the idea of a poetic form in which nature is on one side (one side of what?) and thought on the other, this structural model would only conceivably work as a description offered by Coleridge of how subjects relate to objects, not as a description of some miraculous linguistic alchemy taking place in his poetic laboratory. It is certainly true that Coleridge does describe and talk about what could be called post-Kantian epistemological models, but this is not surprising given his aesthetic theories.

'In the fully developed Romantic lyric', says Abrams, 'the description is structurally subordinate to the meditation' (GRL, p. 552). Again, this is hard to disentangle. *Structurally*, it is quite impossible to separate description and meditation. Would the line 'The sounding cataract / Haunted me like a passion' ('Tintern Abbey') count as description or meditation? And description of what? Of nature? Of metaphysics? What Abrams seems to be saying is in fact that the Romantic lyric is more *about* the personal significance of an experience in the context of an individual philosophy than it is about the way the view looks from the top of Grongar Hill through a Claude-glass.[68] I would argue that, like many Wordsworth and Coleridge critics, Abrams translates into a structural and stylistic difference what is in fact simply a difference in what the respective poetries *talk about*, and that this uneconomical account reflects a sentimental bias, begging many organicist questions about the text as an autonomous, self-organizing entity.

As Jerome McGann remarks in *The Romantic ideology*, 'the scholarship and criticism of Romanticism and its work are dominated by a Romantic ideology'.[69] Much accumulated prejudice against descriptive poetry in general, not just the eighteenth-century poetry against which Romanticism must assert itself, rests on this sentimental foundation. I shall go on to look at the ways in which Wordsworth criticism is often dominated by an idealist epistemological model and by the accompanying sentimental methodology which works by opposing naive and sentimental. But first I want to look at one of the tenets most central to criticism of Romantic poetry: the claim that there is an identifiable Romantic idiom that distinguishes Romantic poetry from other poetry. Much criticism of Romantic poetry concentrates in some way on this concept of a special Romantic language, which embodies the new epistemology and parallels that epistemology's synthesis of subject and object in the act of perception. Whilst I do not quarrel with the view that Romantic poetry may be read as preoccupied with new philosophical ideas about the individual's relationship with nature, I question the frequent construction of complex structural accounts of Romantic poetic idiom intended to explain this new preoccupation. This, I argue, is sentimental practice.

THE ROMANTIC IDIOM

The main interpretative effort of English and American historians of romanticism has focused on the transition that leads from eighteenth-century to romantic nature poetry.[70]

Paul de Man, in 'The rhetoric of temporality', describes the way in which many commentators 'define the romantic image as a relationship between mind and nature', and, as he points out, one of the problems of this kind of account is that it can also be applied to eighteenth-century landscape poets 'who constantly mix descriptions of nature with abstract moralizings'. However, he concludes, 'commentators tend to agree . . . that the relationship between mind and nature becomes much more intimate towards the end of the century. Wimsatt was the first to show convincingly . . . that . . . a fundamental change in substance and in tone separated the two texts'.[71] (I shall go on to consider Wimsatt's argument later.)

In a 1960 essay, de Man himself endorses this view, arguing that a distinct change in poetic language occurred with the advent of Romanticism. He himself points out that this supposed change in poetic diction is coterminous with a change in the vocabulary of criticism:

The most recent change . . . takes place towards the end of the eighteenth century and coincides with the advent of romanticism . . . the term *imagination* steadily grows in importance and complexity, in the critical as well as the poetic texts of the period. This evolution in poetic terminology – of which parallel instances could easily be found in France and in Germany – corresponds to a profound change in the texture of poetic diction.[72]

In this essay, de Man argues for a specifically Romantic idiom, when it is apparent that what he is in fact identifying is a change in beliefs or theories about poetry, to which he himself is heir. For, just like Coleridge and his German forerunners, de Man sets up a sentimental opposition between the 'literal' and 'mimetic', and the 'figurative' and 'symbolic', only to argue that the two are brought together in Romantic language. Romantically, he argues that Romantic poetry – rather than *being about* or discussing aesthetic problems of the subject–object relationship, *actually manifests those problems in the structure of its language*: in

the inherent tension that resides in the metaphorical language itself. At times, romantic thought and romantic poetry seem to come so close to giving in completely to the nostalgia for the object that it becomes difficult to distinguish between object and image, between imagination and perception, between an expressive or constitutive and a mimetic or literal language.[73]

Here, de Man himself seems to yield to a nostalgia for the object, suggesting that language can – like something bodily – contain tension and can manifest the strain of subject–object relations. It cannot: it is only words. It can, of course, refer to them and be about them. This passage illustrates de Man's begging of the literal/figurative question. Why should we ever be able to distinguish what is literal, and what figurative, what is denotative, and what connotative? I would argue that the very conclusion of Romantic theories of language is that we cannot *ever* distinguish the two, and I will return to this question in chapter 4. It is perhaps surprising that de Man does not express the more post-structuralist belief that figurative language is omnipresent and inescapable. But whilst he admits the presence of the figural, it is always as something to be revealed, at critical moments, behind or beyond the literal: the distinction between the two readings remains. This belief in a changed relationship between mind and nature, or subject and object, expressed in a new poetic language which somehow fuses the two, is pervasive.

The poetry's 'idiom' says E. D. Hirsch, 'especially the idiom of "Tintern Abbey" was different in mind from that of any previous English poetry'.[74] Wordsworth is often taken as the archetype of this new poetry. Edward Bostetter speaks more ambiguously of 'the formulation of a new cosmic syntax' which the Romantics 'not only utilized . . . successfully in their art but triumphantly justified . . . as a philosophy of life'.[75] And Isobel Armstrong, in her detailed study of the language of nineteenth-century poetry, explains that

In deriving an account of the language of nineteenth-century poetry from the structure of Romantic epistemology, and in calling this idealist language, I mean that this language discloses a concern with the relationship of subject and object and with the nature of reality.[76]

Rather than saying that Romantic poetry is *about* the relationship of subject and object, Armstrong says that *the language discloses* a concern with that relationship. Her tendency to attribute active powers to language, which 'struggles with the problem of relationship itself' and 'restructures its own elements'[77] is, I suggest, a very sentimental one. She is suggesting that the language somehow *embodies* something, or *does* something, as though it were some kind of dynamic, working model which we could watch, rather than words which form part of a shared language practice. She talks about poetic language in structural, even organicist terms, aiming

to consider a structure of poetic language and how it behaves in relation to an epistemology concerned with the structure of consciousness.[78]

In drawing this analogy between the structure of poetry and that of consciousness, Armstrong follows an idealist model and her construal of nineteenth-century poetic interest in, and discussion of, subject–object relations as a structure disclosed in the language itself is similarly idealist and sentimental. She adopts the position which we have just seen both Abrams and Paul de Man take up, according to which the Romantic poets actually transform the structure of the language by way of a special metaphor. This special metaphorical process is identified by Armstrong as that

with which Wimsatt has familiarized us, in which tenor and vehicle are wrought in parallel process out of the same material; so much so as to make the distinction between tenor and vehicle virtually superfluous in that it is not possible to make it.[79]

Before moving on to Wimsatt's classic statement about the Romantic idiom, it is worth noting that Armstrong seems to identify many characteristic concerns and habits of the nineteenth-century poets and there need be no quarrel with her here. It is her account of what might just be differences in subject-matter as if they were differences in the intrinsic structure of Romantic language that must be scrutinized. For example, when she says that

Romantic syntax is fluid, coalescing, a syntax of transition, because it restructures its own elements and discovers ambiguous relationships as it forms[80]

she adopts the sentimental terminology whereby it is the poem, or language as a diffused consciousness, that acts on itself. This seems remote from any practical understanding of how we use language, although the basic point, which is that Romantic poetry is often deliberately ambiguous, need not be dismissed but can be explained in terms of a changed view of what poetry should be like and be about.

In his influential essay, 'The structure of Romantic nature imagery', W. K. Wimsatt begins by asking

whether romantic poetry . . . exhibits any imaginative *structure* which may be considered a special counterpart of the subject, the philosophy, the sensibility and the theory[81]

of Romanticism. He then goes on to argue that such a structure does exist, and that it develops with the Coleridgean aesthetic. Before the emergence of this aesthetic and this new, poetic structure, he suggests, poetic language is inadequate to the burgeoning sensibility of the writer. Accordingly, in the mid-century poets

one may feel . . . a new sensibility, but at the same time one may lament an absence of poetic quality – that is of a poetic structure adequate to embody or objectify the new feeling.[82]

How we are able to apprehend this sensibility through the inadequate language which expresses it is not clear: Wimsatt suggests that we can separate the feeling of the poem from the language in which it is expressed, and judge the latter inadequate to it. What he is really saying is that he judges the eighteenth-century poets by Romantic standards and finds them lacking. But this is not a question of 'imaginative structure', as he implies.

Through an analysis and comparison of a Bowles sonnet and one by Coleridge (Bowles, 'To the River Itchin' with Coleridge's

'To the River Otter'), Wimsatt argues that in the latter subject and object, the how and the what of description, are inextricably bound together as they are not in the former. In other words, he uses a Coleridgean account of how poetry works – by combining subjectivity with nature – to read both poets, and reads that aesthetic into the language of Coleridge's poem *as structure*. To do this, he uses I. A. Richards' famous tenor–vehicle account of metaphor, whereby metaphor is treated as a structure with two parts, the 'tenor' and 'vehicle' or, as Richards puts it, 'the tenor, as I am calling it – the underlying idea or principle subject which the vehicle or figure means'.[83]

If we are to accept Wimsatt's reading, we have to accept Richards' account of metaphor, and I go on to question this. Wimsatt uses this account to argue that there is a special relationship between tenor and vehicle in Romantic metaphor, not found elsewhere, for

Both tenor and vehicle . . . are wrought in a parallel process out of the same material. The river landscape is both the occasion of reminiscence and the source of the metaphors by which reminiscence is described.[84]

What Wimsatt – fairly – says is that Romantic poetry is about nature and also uses natural metaphors to illustrate its topic, whereas in eighteenth-century poetry we might find different, more 'artificial' metaphors. Thus:

The tenor of such a similitude is likely to be subjective – reminiscence or sorrow or beguilement – not an object distinct from the vehicle, as lovers or their souls are distinct from twin compasses. Hence . . . Wordsworth's 'ennobling interchange of action from within and from without'.[85]

From making the point that most Romantic comparisons are drawn from nature, and are thus more ambiguously close to what they describe and less obviously contrived and artificial, Wimsatt jumps to the conclusion that Romantic language is structured like an 'interchange', a concept which, once again, he derives from the aesthetics of the Romantics themselves, and according to which he reads the poetry. But ambiguity of this kind is not a Romantic prerogative, nor need it be explained in terms of this subject–object model of idealist consciousness, as though subject and object exchanged and interacted *in* language. The 'rich ground of meaning in Coleridge's sonnet beyond what is clearly stated'[86] is a complicated notion, derived from the fact that Coleridge is more ambiguous than Bowles, more syntactically complex (more subordinate clauses, enjambment and so forth). What is this 'rich ground', and how do we have access to it, if not through language?

We have two characteristically sentimental tendencies here. The first is the analogy between epistemological models of consciousness (subject–object relations) and language as a working model. The second is the assumption that there is a basic literal meaning which language in poetry works on and transforms and that we can thus have access to meaning in this literal, as well as in a figurative, way. Literal meaning is set up as a naive, to be worked on and transformed by poetic process in sentimental poetry, on a subject–object–synthesis model, analogous to that of idealist philosophy. Wimsatt relies on an account of language and of metaphor which is similarly sentimental: I. A. Richards' account, to which I now turn.

In *The philosophy of rhetoric*, I. A. Richards compares eighteenth-century theories of metaphor, which hold that

figures are a mere embellishment or added beauty and that the plain meaning, the tenor, is what alone really matters   (Richards, p. 100)

with Romantic, Coleridgean views, according to which the symbol is 'a translucent instance, which while it enunciates the whole, abides itself as a living part of that unity of which it is the representative' (Richards, p. 109).[87]

Like Coleridge, I. A. Richards recognizes the inadequacy of the eighteenth-century distinction between literal and figurative language and the notion of a 'plain meaning' which can be extrapolated from language. But, also like Coleridge, he preserves the distinction in his own theory. In the first quotation above, we see how his 'tenor' is a 'plain meaning', which exists before its transformation by the 'vehicle', even though he acknowledges elsewhere that 'the boundary between literal and metaphorical uses is not quite fixed or constant' (Richards, p. 120), and that 'Literal language is rare outside the central parts of the sciences' (Richards, p. 120) and; 'Our practice to do without metaphor is never more than a bluff waiting to be called' (Richards, p. 92). This reminds us of Coleridge's attempt to distinguish poetry from science, whilst wanting to admit that language is always creative of what it says. But Richards' tenor–vehicle 'model of metaphor' is atomistic in its conception of language as interacting particles which can be discretely identified. This model which preserves the literal/figurative distinction is typically sentimental in that it makes that distinction in order to argue that, in metaphor (Romantic metaphor), the distinction is undermined and overcome.

A detailed account of Richards' theory of metaphor has been given by David Leppard in his thesis, 'An investigation into the theory and structure of metaphor', which defines Richards' 'interaction' model for metaphor:

Under the interaction model, the identity of the underlying thing (substance) is irrecoverable, altered beyond recognition by the chemical-like process of interaction between tenor and vehicle, metaphorical language and underlying idea. This model of semantic change and radical interpenetration is designed to put the received distinction between form and content into crisis.[88]

This shows just how Richards' view has to imply, or set up, an opposition between form and content, just in order to 'put it into crisis'. We have a pre-existing, underlying idea and in the tenor–vehicle opposition, discrete parts of meaning which act on one another to produce another kind of meaning. This simplistic working model of how language works, of metaphor as an organic, bivalvular entity, is unacceptable to any sophisticated theory of language as spoken and understood. It is a sentimental, structural model, setting up a naive and working on it.

There are many arguments against this kind of literal/figurative opposition – which is so clearly non-viable in any absolute sense that it is surprising that it has persisted in literary criticism to such a degree. A persuasive article by Stanley Fish reminds us that our attempts to characterize literary language as special are wasted, in that

ordinary language is extraordinary because at its heart is precisely that realm of values, intentions and purposes which is often assumed to be the exclusive property of literature. What characterizes literature then is not formal properties, but an attitude . . . towards properties that belong by constitutive right to language.[89]

The Romantic attempt to isolate the aesthetic has always failed and there has never been any successful account of how figurative language differs from literal, when ordinary language is so saturated with metaphor.

Many critics who recognize this at one level continue to employ the old distinction and thus sustain the persistent belief in the Romantic idiom. Keith Hinchcliffe, for instance, notes that nineteenth-century poetry develops the eighteenth-century use of abstract words: Wordsworth can be characterized as using 'a limited number of special terms involved in the mediation between physical and mental realities'.[90] Hinchcliffe suggests that Wordsworth's use of words like 'impress', 'fasten' or 'circumfuse' – ambivalently suggesting mental or physical activity – derives from the diction of the previous century, which is 'hardly explicable in terms of tenors and vehicles . . . derives from the restrained or tactful use of dry, prosaic or neutral terms'.[91] Wordsworth, he says, seems to be 'trying to take the eighteenth-century "generalizing habit" to its limit'.[92] This view, softening the boundary between centuries, seems a fair account of the kind of uncomplicated language Wordsworth uses. It would be quite compatible with an understanding of Wordsworth as more concerned with metaphysics than his predecessors. But Hinchcliffe also brings in the tenor–vehicle machinery:

Wordsworth's entire philosophy depended on such a confounding of tenor/vehicle distinctions, such a working of mental and physical distinctions 'out of the same material' as Wimsatt describes.[93]

Wimsatt certainly describes Coleridgean aesthetics in his essay. Whether he describes Wordsworth's poetry is a different matter. As I have said, to some extent, Wordsworth himself (and certainly Coleridge) seems to endorse the idealist or sentimental account, arguing that

processes of imagination are carried on either by conferring additional properties upon an object, or abstracting from it some of those which it actually possesses, and thus enabling it to re-act upon the mind which hath performed the process, like a new existence.[94]

It is not hard to trace the origins of Wimsatt's theory.

A typically sentimental reading of Wordsworth, which exploits the 'interaction' theory of metaphor, is Herbert Lindenberger's discussion of imagery in The Prelude. 'It is difficult', he says, to distinguish between the literal and metaphorical level in Wordsworth, for the literal becomes figurative and then literal again. Distinctions between tenor and vehicle, crucial as they are to the understanding of Renaissance and metaphysical verse, are of little avail in this type of poetry. Wordsworth's use of imagery stands at an opposite extreme, one might say, from that of a Shakespearean play . . . . We could conceivably cut the metaphorical element out of *Hamlet* and still have a substantial drama, though certainly impoverished drama. But to rob *The Prelude* of its images is to rob it of its whole plot and continuity.[95]

Lindenberger makes the usual literal/figurative distinction. and on this unstable foundation constructs his reading of the poem as a dissolution of that distinction. Adopting the conventional belief that Wordsworth is less straightforwardly narrative, more 'poetic' than Shakespeare, for instance, he cannot justify *why* we could more easily cut the metaphor out of the latter. This is simply not true. He assumes that the critical tenor–vehicle tool is somehow necessary to the text, to the extent that Renaissance verse could not be understood before I. A. Richards. He thus begs all the questions about the kind of emphasis placed on Wordsworth and Romanticism by the critical tradition.

CONCLUSION

This overview of twentieth-century perspectives on to nineteenth-century poetry reveals just how dependent on a sentimental, and more specifically, a Romantic aesthetic contemporary criticism is. Reading by the light of the Romantic lamp, we have cast a shadow over those poets whose subject-matter – and articulated aesthetic or metaphysic – does not conform to the standard. What could be explained in terms of this kind of difference, as well as in terms of simple changes in linguistic conventions, has been dramatized as an absolute difference between two individually structured idioms.

This opposition contrasts Wordsworth's 'deliberate blurring of tenor and vehicle, his insistence on fusing the literal level of things with their larger symbolic meanings',[96] with pre-Wordsworthian poetry which, it suggests, simply adds decorative figure to a pre-existing, literal meaning. Thus the theory of the Romantic idiom is really nothing more than the comparison of a post-Kantian with a pre-Kantian aesthetic perspective introduced by post-Kantian aesthetics. Post-Kantian sentimental idealism begs the question of whether pre- and post-Kantian, literal or figurative, can be neatly divided in the first place. It makes an absolute distinction between two eras and idioms for critical purposes without considering that one might shade into the other. The responsibility for keeping the two separate weighs heavily on the sentimental critic.

3

CRITICS OF CLARE AND
WORDSWORTH

OVERVIEW

In the essay discussed in the last chapter, Herbert Lindenberger makes a statement that takes us into the heart of this book:

Again, what makes Wordsworth's poetry unique is not the fact that he combined the sense-impressions of nature with more complex ideas, but the peculiar method which he developed to draw the intellectual from the visual. His need to combine both these realms in his poetry . . . is also what keeps Wordsworth from being what we commonly consider a 'landscape' poet. The true landscape poet is one who, like John Clare or Edward Thomas, keeps primarily to visual impressions and only incidentally, if at all, to the more complex ideas toward which these might lead.[1]

Lindenberger distinguishes between a poetry of visual impressions and a poetry that goes beyond the merely visual to the intellectual. He assumes that the visual and the intellectual can be distinguished without difficulty: an assumption which I query in my next chapter. In this chapter I give an overview of the critical reception of the two poets Lindenberger categorizes above, Clare and Wordsworth, and show how, like Lindenberger, the majority of critics have constructed them according to a naive/sentimental opposition between the simply 'descriptive' and the expressive; between the sensuously mimetic, and the thoughtfully intellectual. As usual, such sentimental criticism often ends up by perceiving Wordsworth, the sentimental poet, as embracing and resolving the contradiction between the two approaches.

Looking at Clare and Wordsworth's respective accounts of their own poetry, I argue that their own aesthetic theories are more ambiguous than critical history suggests. I conclude that the existing sentimental model dominates Clare and Wordsworth criticism, and must be reconsidered and revised.

JOHN CLARE AS NAIVE: THE NINETEENTH-CENTURY VIEW

An overview of Clare criticism in the nineteenth century reveals a relationship between Clare and the critical establishment which coincides remarkably accurately with the model of sentimental appreciation of the naive set out so far. Sentimental and patronizing in both senses of those words, much of this criticism is devoted to the construction of Clare as a naive genius, in the established manner of the pastoral patronization of rural life. Clare's agricultural background makes him an obvious candidate for this treatment; he is Schiller's 'badly brought-up son of nature' who 'can never emerge as part of society' (*NS*, p. 38). Standing in an eighteenth-century tradition of peasant poets

he was typecast from the first. His publisher, John Taylor, had earlier been involved with the successful publication of Robert Bloomfield, another rural poet, and was convinced that he had now acquired a Robert Bloomfield of his very own.[2]

Given this vogue, and the nineteenth century's growing Romantic taste for the primitive genius, it is not surprising that Taylor should have presented Clare's poems less on their intrinsic merit than on the unusual situation of their author, 'the genuine productions of a young peasant, a day-labourer in husbandry, who has had no advantages of education'.[3] That, as Mark Storey says 'it was the phenomenon of Clare, the Northamptonshire Peasant Poet, which was attractive, rather than the poetry itself',[4] is substantiated in reviews of the time, which, as a critic has noted this century, 'tended to stress his simplicity, to find charm in a kind of rural naiveté'.[5]

A natural corollary of this biographical focus is an understanding of Clare's poetry as different in rationale and technique from that of his more urbane contemporaries. Because, like Schiller's naive, Clare is in immediate contact with nature and because he has not received any formal education and is not conventionally articulate, it is assumed that the *process* by which he composes poetry – not just the subject-matter – must be essentially different from that used by, for example, Wordsworth. The theory generally held is that Clare possesses the opportunity and capacity for close observation of nature, together with an unsophisticated appreciation of its charms and that this natural 'eye' is translated into accurate transcriptions of the countryside, so accurate that a reader can 'see' it in all its true detail. Clare is accordingly a transcriber of nature. In 1835 a contemporary said that he was

an observer the most acute – an admirer the most passionate – a painter the most graphic of the beauties of nature, – his poetry is a beautiful scene laid before us of woodland, copse, field, meadow and roadside . . . there is not perhaps a single verse in all Clare's descriptive poetry which is not as distinct and perfect a picture as the most finished delineator of nature might give . . . he has described things as they exist, with the fidelity to the original, that we cannot separate the reality from the description.[6]

Notions of accuracy and fidelity arising from an eighteenth-century critical trend, prevail in early nineteenth-century criticism of Clare, with its understanding of the poetic eye as a transparent mirror-reflection of the natural world. Clare's is truly believed to be an innocent eye.

Another contemporary of his, writing in the *Eclectic Review*, claimed in 1822 that:

These poems breathe of Nature in every line. They are . . . not studies from Nature, but transcripts of her works: his cattle, his birds, his trees and bushes are all portraits. There is a literal fidelity in the sketches, which only true genius could keep from sinking into vulgarity.[7]

It was Clare's misfortune that not all critics felt he avoided that vulgarity and, as has already been noted, when the critical tide turned away from commendation of accuracy, and the pictorial or visual analogies that accompanied such praise, Clare's poetry lost favour. Clare was castigated for his failure to be explicitly 'sentimental', to draw moral or philosophical conclusions from Nature. Thus John Taylor relayed Keats' suggestion to Clare that he should cut down on 'description':

I think he wishes to say to you that your Images from Nature are too much introduced without being called for by a particular sentiment . . . his Remark is only applicable now & then when he feels as if the Description overlaid & stifled that which ought to be the prevailing Idea.[8]

A shift in critical vocabulary away from the pictorial analogy that pervaded eighteenth-century criticism, towards an emphasis on individual sensitivity and subjectivity resulted in a fall from favour of the 'descriptive' poetry which had previously enjoyed such popularity. As Mark Storey notes:

The problem was not peculiar to Clare: as detail in poetry increased, as nature poetry became more tied to the countryside as it really was, the balance between description and imagination became more important for the theorists . . . Even John Aikin warned against Dutchification: Crabbe became the butt of Wordsworth, Coleridge and Hazlitt.[9]

Clare was initially praised for the 'artless description of Nature's works . . . the result of very close observation',[10] and later criticized because critics: 'do not conceive that occasional sweetness of expression, or accurate delineations of mere exterior objects, can atone for a general deficiency of poetical language'.[11] He was in either case subjected to the assumption that his poetry was little more than transcription, to be valued for its accuracy or dismissed for its objectivity and lack of personal feeling. But this assumption must be called into question.

TWENTIETH-CENTURY VIEWS

As Romantic critical values began to establish themselves and the old criteria of vividness or accuracy were diminishing in importance, Clare's poetry was increasingly subjected to objections of the kind described above. Throughout the twentieth century it was to face comparison with the explicitly metaphysical poetry of the now canonical Romantic poets, whose connections with the dominant aesthetic were of course very close. Whilst there are clearly important differences between Clare and, for example, Wordsworth, it is by no means necessary that these should be formulated in the way that the prevailing sentimental aesthetic has formulated them: in terms of an intrinsic difference in method and idiom which is moreover translated into a qualitative difference in sensibility or imagination.

Arthur Symons' assessment in 1908 that

the impulse and the subject-matter are alike his own, and are taken directly from what was about him. There is no closer attention to nature than in Clare's poems; but the observation begins by being literal;

nature a part of his home rather than his home a part of nature. The things about him are the whole of his material, he does not choose them by preference out of others equally available . . . His danger is to be too deliberate, unconscious that there can be choice in descriptive poetry[12]

is an accurate echo of Schiller's point that

the naive poet only follows simple nature and simple emotions and restricts himself solely to the imitation of nature . . . he can only have a single relationship with his subject-matter and in *this* regard he has no choice in his treatment of the material.   (*NS*, p. 42)

From Symons onwards, this sentimental conception of Clare is preserved, and the underlying assumptions about description are not questioned. Clare 'wrote down what he felt, and felt what he wrote'; there was 'a simplicity, freshness and charm in [his] vivid transcripts from Nature'[13] in 1920 as in 1820. In 1921, Harold Massingham asked in a review, whether

the body of his work translated or transliterated its material; whether, in Coleridge's words, it trusted more to the memory than the imagination; whether it observes or creates, describes or sees; whether a radical defect in imaginative will confused truth to nature with truth to poetry.[14]

Massingham comes down on Clare's side with some reservations, but the terms within which he formulates the contrast between the major poet and the minor poet are essentially sentimental and beg the usual questions. What is the 'material' that exists before its treatment? There is the same belief in an objective reality which the poet then gets to work on, and, if his imagination is up to it, successfully transforms.

With John Middleton Murry's work on Clare, an explicit comparison with other Romantics is made.

As a poet of nature Clare was truer, more thoroughly subdued to that in which he worked than Wordsworth. Wordsworth called upon the poet to keep his eye upon the object; but his eye was hardly so penetrating and keen as Clare's. Yet Wordsworth was a great poet . . . and Clare was not . . . Wordsworth belongs to another sphere than Clare in virtue of the range of his imaginative apprehension . . . In one respect Clare was a finer artist than Wordsworth, he had a truer ear and a more exquisite instinct for the visualizing word; but he had nothing of the principle of inward growth which gives to Wordsworth's most careless work a place within the unity of a great scheme.[15]

Here again, the accordance with Schiller's allocation of space to naive and sentimental poets is exact. Schiller's naive is 'subdued to that in which he worked' – 'The subject possesses him utterly . . . *he* is the creation and the creation is *he*' (*NS*, p. 35) and his strength is visual – 'A work for the eye finds its perfection only in limitation. A work for the imagination can attain it also by means of the infinite' (*NS*, p. 41), whilst that of the sentimental poet is visionary. But it is this visual/visionary opposition, now firmly entrenched, that must be subjected to close scrutiny. When Wordsworth talks about keeping one's eye on the object, is he separating observation from imagination, sense from intellect, as Murry suggests? Examples of this polarization are plentiful. Robert Lynd, in a 1921 review says of Clare that his poetry

is a mirror of things rather than a window of the imagination. It belongs to a borderland where naturalism and literature meet . . . He brings things seen before our eyes: the record of his senses is more important than the record of his imagination or his thoughts.[16]

Edmund Gosse attacks Clare violently in 1924, saying that his poetry is 'unreflecting observation' and that Clare 'was a camera, not a mind',[17] while John Speirs in 1935 makes the by now familiar comparison with Wordsworth:

He is a nature-poet as Wordsworth is not, for Wordsworth is a psychologist interested fundamentally in the workings of his mind. What Clare's poetry evidences is a complete absorption with that other life, not felt as another life. It consists of perceptions . . . crystallized richly and presented with a particularity and correctness which warrant of their absolute authenticity. Yet Clare has no hard core of individuality compelling his perceptions to serve an inner purpose. He has no inner purpose. He is scarcely even conscious of himself.[18]

A similar comparison is made by Rayner Unwin in *The Rural Muse* (1954), when he says of Clare that anything that he wrote

was firmly based on the reality of the physical world around him. He lacked the vision of Wordsworth, who used nature as a medium of interpretation to plumb the deeper mysteries of beyond.[19]

This comparison is reminiscent of Fichte's remark in the *Wissenschaftslehre* that there are

two major types of man. Some, who have not yet raised themselves to full consciousness of their freedom and absolute independence, find themselves only in the presentation of things; they have only that dispersed self-consciousness which attached to objects, and has to be gleaned from their multiplicity. Their image is reflected back at them by things, as by a mirror; if these were taken from them, their self would be lost as well; for the sake of their self they cannot give up the belief in the independence of things, for they themselves exist only if things do.[20]

Whilst Schiller had made the point that the naive poet was absorbed in his material, his essay nowhere goes so far as to assume the utter unselfconsciousness that this and similar readings imply. Middleton Murry is another critic who understands Clare as unselfconscious:

the quality in Clare which most enthrals us . . . is one which we can only describe as a kind of naivety – an abiding sense of a quite simple fraternity with all the creatures of the world save self-conscious man.[21]

Other critics defend Clare in a more complex way and, in the second half of the century, less obviously 'sentimental' readings of Clare occur. Robert Pinsky, in 1970, attacks the fallacy (perpetrated by Tibble in editing Clare) of imagism, the idea that Clare 'can communicate his emotion by describing the objects which aroused it'.[22] Comparing Clare's 'Badger' with Roethke's 'Orchids', Pinsky argues against an account of Clare as simply 'descriptive'. Whilst the symbolist 'Orchids' 'takes the fusion of emotion with the natural object as an accepted starting point', Clare's 'Badger' 'takes the fusion of emotion with the natural object as an eventual goal'. The poem is, Pinsky suggests, 'a sustained effort to establish a powerful sense of irresistible, necessary connection between sense and feeling – exactly that sense of connection which the modern convention takes almost for granted'.[23] Pinsky, who does Clare more credit than most of the critics considered so far, nevertheless sustains the distinction between *sense* and *feeling*. Clare's poetry is the struggle of human subject to establish a bond with the objective world of nature – Pinsky thus explains it by giving a model of poetic consciousness rather than by talking about the different culture and views that inform 'Badger' and 'Orchids', which are *about* different things.

In an article in 1971, Thomas Frosch attacks the same question of Clare as 'descriptive'. Putting forward the view that Clare is preoccupied with the location of natural objects in space and time, Frosch claims that even when he seems to be giving us description for its own sake . . . in his moments of apparently 'pure' description his stylistic manners, his way of describing, are the gestures of a dramatic situation.[24]

Tracing a development from Clare's early to his late poetry, Frosch resists the critical tendency to schematize that development as a movement 'away from the particulars of nature into a radically internalized poetic mode', suggesting instead that Clare is consistently interested in the location or structure of an event or object, and moves simply from 'a primarily spatial orientation . . . to a temporal scheme'. There is, says Frosch,

a change from a landscape of mental abstraction to one of direct perception, in that an interest in the typical structure of an event is replaced by an interest in the experience of an event as singular.[25]

Frosch thus recognizes that the 'description' of Clare's poetry is never 'objective', but can be interpreted in this way as strategic. He counters the tendency to view Clare as moving *away* from the particular or suggesting – like Barrell – that he is increasingly concerned with capturing the particular. Frosch, however, continues to depend on a notion of Clare's relationship with nature and traces what is essentially a naive/sentimental progression in his poetry, lending him significance by revealing complexities in his description as it moves from the fixed to the fluctuant, from the objective to the subjective. He sees Clare's poetic process centring on the desire to *fix*, whether by giving a full and exhaustive account of a scene, or by concentrating on a single instant as the focus of a shifting drama of perceptual relations. Moreover, Frosch sees in Clare's 'early urge towards a thoroughness of precise description . . . an encyclopedic procedure that removes the object from immediate experience, giving us a version of it that will generally hold true'.[26] The implication that more detail means more objectivity also needs to be questioned.

Richard Lessa, whilst he recognizes that an account of Clare as simply 'pictorial' is inadequate, and says that 'Clare's descriptive art would be more accurately characterized as narrative', still says that Clare's is a 'clear, steady voice . . . completely dedicated to the truth of nature'[27] and speaks of his 'direct objective representation of a rural world he knew and loved'.[28] Lessa is not able to explain how this 'objectivity' is more than just pictorial description: he gives us the rather lame statement that Clare's poetic voice is one that 'manages to convey simultaneously a strong sense of objectivity and paradoxically one of subjectivity'.[29]

Set against the 'objective description' approach to Clare, is that which reads his development as progress from the naive and objective to the sentimental and subjective, and Harold Bloom falls into this category. 'Clare's dialectic', he says in *The visionary company* (1961)

> begins like Wordsworth's, passes into a creative opposition resembling that in Coleridge's *Dejection: An Ode*, and climaxes, in a handful of great poems, remarkably close to Blake's.[30]

Bloom's Romantic idiom − 'creative opposition', 'dialectic' and 'climax' − reveals his own origins and it is this extremely sentimental position which leads him to the conclusion that Clare's work is 'a postscript to Wordsworth'.[31]

Timothy Brownlow's (1983) study of Clare, *John Clare and picturesque landscape*, takes up this Schylla and Charybdis of Clare criticism:

> I have tried to steer a course between what I see as two critical pitfalls: treating Clare either as a Peasant Poet or as a failed Blake. The former patronizing attitude was the habit of many critics until recently. The latter danger is more in evidence in the approach to Clare typified by Harold Bloom. His attempt to ascribe great Romantic qualities to Clare has the effect of proving how much greater Blake's and Wordsworth's Romantic qualities are.[32]

Brownlow's interpretation of Clare, which takes off from John Barrell's influential study, *The idea of landscape and the sense of place 1730–1840* − of which more later − begins with a critique of the kinds of approach to Clare outlined above. Viewing Clare in the historical context of the picturesque tradition, Brownlow, following Barrell, is concerned to understand Clare 'on his own terms', to construct an aesthetic which credits him with an evolving response to his specific poetic needs, and the ability to work within and transform the poetic tradition in which he stood.

> My aim is to show how Clare absorbed and modified the eighteenth-century tradition in a unique way, so that he is misjudged if he is seen either as the culmination of a worn-out mode or as a lesser star in the Romantic galaxy.   (Brownlow, p. 3)

Whilst Brownlow's book rightly attacks critical precedent where Clare is concerned and explores the picturesque tradition in detail, it also preserves many of those fallacies that have been highlighted above.

> To create his own system, like Blake, was beyond him . . . and he had no particular relish or gift for metaphorical or symbolic profundities. His gift was for description and his subject matter was the landscape.
>
> (Brownlow, p. 67)

Without ever analysing exactly what is meant by 'descriptive' poetry, Brownlow continues to contrast it with 'metaphorical' poetry and whilst acknowledging that Clare is not simply descriptive (pp. 84, 93), he retains the critical idiom of imagism and its associated fallacies:

> Clare crystallizes his descriptions into whole experiences. He does this by sensuous vitality, by co-operation with the forces of nature, and by keeping himself moving through the landscape. We have seen how Clare's relationship with external phenomena is a continuously active one, a process heightened by his habit of walking. By such means, Clare brings his verbal picture alive.   (Brownlow, p. 96)

Here, the assumedly unmediated relationship between Clare's own habits and the structure of his poetry does not take into consideration any of the complexities of writing or reading, and the contexts in which those procedures take place. The 'sensuous vitality' and 'verbal pictures' echo earlier critics. Much of what is less sentimental in Brownlow's work – the study of picturesque conventions and syntactical structuring – have their origin in John Barrell's earlier book.

Whilst many critics have construed Clare in terms of this opposition between the 'real' natural world and symbolic representations of subjectivity and imagination, critics such as L. J. Swingle have recognized that his descriptions of birds, for example, involve a subjective and emotive charge, *without* becoming something else. In Clare

> the bird does not transfigure into mystery. It remains stubbornly bird-like . . . If anything, in fact, Clare's birds become more humanly comprehensible than we might ordinarily conceive a bird to be . . . for Clare the human and the non-human worlds both participate in the same perilous existence.[33]

It seems that, however, a sense of poetic language as the transformation of everyday reality remains, and the Romantic and specifically Coleridgean distinction between prose and poetry, literal and figurative, still makes its presence felt, giving true poetry its special transformative status. If we accept that a bird can be a bird and still be subjectively charged without ceasing to be a bird and becoming a symbol, then the distinction between Clare's ordinary bird and the Romantic skylark vanishes.

John Barrell's study of Clare is outstanding in providing a full theoretical aesthetic for Clare and in its recognition that representation or reference to specifics need not stand in opposition to the expression of subjectivity. Although he does not make this principle explicit, he applies it to the poetry of Clare, recognizing that it is in and through the 'description' or reference to places in their particularity that Clare expresses his subjectivity and that it would be impossible for things to be otherwise. Barrell does this by explicitly linking Clare's detailing of locality with his personal commitments and investment of emotion, formulating a theory which understands description as an act of commitment and self-expression.

> Clare's writing after 1821 or so is increasingly preoccupied with being 'local,' and . . . he is concerned with one place, Helpston, not as it is typical of other places, but as it is individual.   (Barrell, p. 120)

Whereas, Barrell points out, critics have constantly suggested that Clare excludes sentiment by being descriptive, it is through description that he expresses sentiment:

> Ever since the publication of Clare's first volume, the charge has been made against his poetry that it is *too* descriptive; that is, that it is descriptive at the expense of sentiment, of ideas, of (it is suggested) content . . . But Clare's purely descriptive poems do have content, I want to suggest . . . The content . . . is precisely the accuracy of the description, the richness and the completeness of it, understood in this particular way, that it is a body of knowledge, a set of details, that Clare has arrived at in this particular place, and not elsewhere. The content of the poem thus becomes the sense of place that the imagery and the language . . . together express.   (Barrell, pp. 129–31)

Barrell's thesis thus dismantles the habitual sentimental opposition of description and sentiment by constructing a description–location–sentiment chain of identification. Schiller pointed out that naive poetry was often unappealing because of its lack of obvious subjectivity. But he also suggests that the subjectivity is of course there, but it is 'buried' in the presentation of the objective 'reality'.

> The subject possesses him utterly, his heart does not lie like a base metal just under the surface but needs like gold to be sought for in the depths . . . Misled by my acquaintance with more modern poets to look first of all in the work for the author, to encounter *his* heart, to reflect on his subject-matter together *with him* . . . it was unbearable to me that here the poet could nowhere be grasped.   (*NS*, pp. 35–6)

This seems to provide an account of the usual response to Clare. Because he is not explicitly sentimental, he is dismissed as being 'insensitive' (*NS*, p. 35).

What exactly, then, distinguishes the explicitly sentimental poet from the naive counterpart? Barrell's account concentrates on the different way in which Clare handled the picturesque traditions which he, like Wordsworth, inherited. Because Barrell proposes an interpretation which places emphasis on locality, hypothesizing that the expression of locality is Clare's prime preoccupation, he argues that the highly formalized conventions of landscape poetry inherited from the picturesque traditions of the eighteenth century were inappropriate for Clare and that he therefore had to discover a new method.

> Clare understood his own idea of landscape very much in eighteenth-century terms – as a descriptive poet no less than as a pastoral poet he thought of himself primarily as continuing the eighteenth-century tradition. At the same time he realised that his idea of landscape did not satisfy any of the principles of eighteenth-century taste. The desire to describe things as particular, therefore, he understood as a tendency towards disorder, because a thing could make itself felt to be particular in an eighteenth-century landscape only at the expense of the composition, or the rule of order. The desire to represent the multiplicity of things in a landscape he understood also as a tendency towards disorder; and out of these two desires he developed a whole aesthetic of disorder.   (Barrell, p. 152)

This thesis is supported by a close analysis of Clare's syntax, and the structure of his poetry, which is contrasted with the formalized structure of eighteenth-century picturesque poetry:

> The objects Clare introduces into his descriptions of landscape obliterate by their particularity whatever traces remain . . . of correct eighteenth-century descriptive procedure . . . no sooner does on object enter the

poem than it is pushed aside by the next; so that we have the sense that always outside the poem are hundreds of images hammering to be admitted. (Barrell, p. 151)

Again, it is worth noting one of Schiller's criticisms of Kleist:

Detail after detail changes quickly and abundantly but without becoming concentrated enough to form an individual. (*NS*, p. 53)

This effect can be limiting, Schiller says, in the way that the naive limits, and criticisms along these lines have been made of Clare. But for Barrell this disorder can be given a rationale. The multiplicity of images, each given weight and the lack of syntactical subordination or composition have their purpose.

I want to suggest . . . that while Clare has suppressed as far as he can the sense that one clause is subordinate to another, one image more important than another, he makes, nevertheless, the particular connections he does make between the images, to reveal them all as parts not so much of a continuum of successive impressions as of one complex manifold of simultaneous impressions. (p. 157)

This rationale is the 'aesthetic of disorder', Clare's desire to convey, without formalizing or reorganizing, the richness and immediacy of landscape and place: an aesthetic reinforced by his informal use of punctuation.

Barrell formulates this distinction between Clare and Wordsworth by saying that

Wordsworth's idea of nature was always more or less platonic, and the 'spirit' of a place was something, for him, to be found by looking *through* the place itself . . . The idea that Clare entertained of his 'knowledge,' on the other hand, at once the place he knew and everything he knew, means that the sense of place he communicates in his poems becomes their entire content, from which no other more abstract knowledge could be deduced. (Barrell, p. 182)

Here, Barrell does not assume that the movement 'through' is the essence of poetry but that it expresses a particular ideological position and that in talking about nature in a Platonic way, Wordsworth is talking about something different from Clare, but not in any sense accordingly producing a qualitatively different poetry. The poems are interested in different things, perhaps, but from there it is a question of preference or received wisdom that decides which survives.

Bearing in mind what Barrell says about the 'aesthetic of disorder' in Clare, and what, for example, a critic of post-Kantian critical directions like Murray Krieger has to say about its 'aesthetic of order', which

destroys the subjective freedom of the random, of the unstructured, of the indeterminate, in its service of the formal impulse[34]

Barrell's study of Clare can be seen as a significant movement away from the holistic and teleological assumptions of sentimental criticism, which traces progress from real and disorderly to ideal and harmonious.

'I FOUND THE POEMS IN THE FIELDS': CLARE'S AESTHETIC[35]

In line with popular preference, Clare's publishers and other critics, such as Keats, suggested that he should elevate the tone of his poetry by including more explicitly philosophical and sentimental material. Charles Hessey, Clare's publisher with John Taylor, wrote to Clare in 1824 that

the great fault with the whole of them [Clare's poems] is that they abound to much in mere description and are deficient in Sentiment & Feeling & human Interest.[36]

Similarly, John Taylor told Clare that he should 'speak of the Appearances of Nature each Month more philosophically . . . they have too much of the language of common every Day Description'.[37] But as Brownlow – who, like Barrell, provides a full account of this issue – says:

Clare . . . feels almost as uneasy with the constant need for elevation of sentiment in Wordsworth and Keats as he does with the ambiguities of the topographical tradition. Clare's reaction to Keats is that 'behind every rose bush he looks for a Venus & under every laural a thrumming Appollo;'[38]

and as his prose, letters and poems show, he resists artifice or poetic diction, as he sees it, vigorously. Closely identifying poetry with nature, he criticized the fashionable pastoral for its conventional language and its failure to communicate a real understanding of nature in its particularity:

Pastoral poems are full of nothing but the old thread bare epithets of 'sweet singing cuckoo' 'love lorn nightinggale' 'fond turtles' 'sparkling brooks' 'green meadow 'leafy woods' etc these make up the creation of Pastoral and descriptive poesy and every thing else is reckond low and vulgar in fact they are too rustic for the fashionable or prevailing system of ryhme till some bold inovating genius rises with a real love for nature and then they will no doubt be considered as great beautys which they really are.[39]

He rejects this 'armchair' nature poetry, placing emphasis on his own close contact with, and observation of, the natural world. Just one of many letters making this point illustrates how closely he associates, in the idiom of both his prose and poetry, the written word with the living nature it describes:

I coud soon daub pictures anew for the Descriptive – there is a thing or two in Spring that I am pleasd with I know the thought is new & hope it is general & true to nature tis the description . . . [of] the landrail or landrake – I dont think you know these names but you know the bird its a little thing heard about the grass & wheat in summer & one of the most poetical images in rural nature.[40]

This is the account of Clare's poetry that critics have adopted. Because of its proximity to nature, its successful imitation of nature, Clare tells us in the idiom of much eighteenth-century critical theory (see chapter 4 below), poetry will appeal widely and be preserved for posterity. He tells us that poetry expresses

universal feelings . . . it is the echo [of] what has been or may be . . . nature is the same everywhere . . . nature gives every one a natural simplicity of heart to read her language tho the grosser interferences of the world adulterate them like the bee the flower and deaden the heart with ignorance.[41]

This sentiment, reminiscent of Wordsworth's statements in the 'Preface to the Lyrical Ballads', is nothing out of the ordinary in its emphasis on universal standards and conformity to nature's truth: a neo-classical doctrine. Similar to Wordsworth too in his idealization of childhood, Clare tells us that:

There is nothing but poetry about the existence of childhood real simple soul moving poetry the laughter and joy of poetry and not its philosophy and there is nothing of poetry about manhood but the reflection and the remembrance of what has been nothing more.[42]

It is in accordance with this emphasis on simplicity, and on (naive) spontaneity, that Clare's account of his own processes of production presents his creativity as unconstrained and impromptu:

I used to drop down behind a hedge bush or dyke and write down my things upon the crown of my hat . . . I always wrote my poems in great haste and generaly finished them at once wether long or short for if I did not they generaly were left unfinishd what corrections I made I always made them while writing the poem and never coud do anything with them after wards.[43]

Writing to Taylor in 1820, he asked him to

recoolect the subjects are roughly sketch in the fields at all seasons with a pencil I catch . . . nature in every dress she puts on so when I begin to ryhme & polish up I have little to do in studying description I am like the boy that gets his book alphebet by heart & then can say his lesson with his eyes as well shut as open,[44]

and this presentation of his own creativity as an instinctive response to the natural world was adopted widely by the critical establishment; partly as a result of Taylor's account of Clare as a rustic genius:

He loves the fields, the flowers, 'the common air, the sun, the skies;' and therefore, he writes about them. He is happier in the presence of Nature than elsewhere. He looks as anxiously on her face as if she were a living friend . . . Most of his poems were composed under the immediate impression of this feeling, in the fields or on the road-sides.[45]

Thus Taylor described Clare in his introduction to *Poems descriptive of rural life and scenery* (1820).

This view is endorsed in Clare's own poetry. Describing his compositional methods in 'The Progress of Rhyme' (*MC*, p. 224), he claims that

> My harp though simple was my own
> When I was in the fields alone
> With none to help & none to hear
> To bid me either hope or fear
> The bird & bee its chords would sound
> The air hummed melodys around
> I caught with eager ear the strain
> & sung the music oer again
> Or love or instinct flowing strong

> Fields were the essence of the song
> & fields & woods are still as mine
> Real teachers that are all divine

Clare's alluring picture of his own naiveté is so resonant that it is easy to forget that it is artful, that he is writing poetry about his own poetry and thus denying the spontaneity insisted upon in that poetry. Similarly, when he claims that

> I never feared the critic's pen
> To live by my renown
> I found the poems in the fields
> And only wrote them down
> ('Sighing for Retirement')

his claim should not be accepted as a straight statement of fact, particularly in the context of his real response to criticism, complaints about public opinion and authorship of such poems as 'Fame'.[46] It is the seductive simplicity of Clare's rhymes and rhythms that make his presentation of his own simplicity so convincing, and familiarity with his background makes the scenario doubly compelling, as our knowledge of Wordsworth's precludes our construing the *Lyrical Ballads* as naive poetry. Whether or not there is any correlation between Clare's real, and his poetic, persona is something that cannot be ascertained. It is at least necessary that Clare be given the credit for constructing that persona, as a Yeats or Wordsworth might do, rather than assuming that he speaks from the heart, as so many critics have chosen to do. Inheriting a sentimental tradition, there is no reason why Clare should not have, to some extent, constructed his own naiveté, much as Wordsworth constructed his childhood in *The Prelude*, and in the context of fiction, whether poetry or prose, that naiveté is necessarily a construction.

It is easy to read Clare's poetry as expressing a mimetic aesthetic. In 'Shadows of Taste' (*MC*, pp. 131–2) for example, he talks of

> The singing bird the brook that laugh along
> There ceaseless sing and never thirst for song
> A pleasing image to its page conferred
> In living character and breathing word
> Becomes a landscape heard and felt and seen
> . . . Thus truth to nature as the true sublime
> Stands a mount atlas overpeering time.

Similarly, 'Pastoral Poesy' (*MC*, p. 291) and 'The Autumn Robin' (*MC*, p. 122) present the poet accommodating himself to the natural world in order to secure truth and posterity.

The majority of critics, like Clare himself, offer an account of his poetry as a window onto the natural world and accordingly concentrate less on rhetorical strategy, or unconscious revelation, than on an apparently obvious 'content', the visual appearance of nature. It is rare that criticism takes the form of speculations about the way in which Clare, consciously or unconsciously, located himself in language. Because his vocabulary is not obviously philosophical or moralistic, because he is known not to have been articulate or educated in the conventional sense, readings of his poems that devised complex descriptions of his consciousness, as so much Wordsworth criticism has done, would perhaps seem far-fetched. And yet, from a post-structuralist perspective, neither intentions nor context should affect the possibility of such schemes discovered in the text.

TWO VOICES: AN OVERVIEW OF WORDSWORTH CRITICISM

Since the naive poet only follows simple nature and simple emotions and restricts himself solely to the imitation of nature, so he can only have a single relationship with his subject-matter. . . . Things are quite different with the sentimental poet. He *reflects* on the impression which objects make on him, and the emotion into which he transposes us is based only on that reflection. The object is related here to an idea and his poetic strength rests only on this relationship. The sentimental poet therefore is constantly dealing with two opposing concepts and emotions, with reality as boundary and with his idea as the infinite, and the mixed feeling which he excites will always bear witness to this double source.   (*NS*, p. 42)

If Clare criticism almost exclusively constructs a 'naive' Clare, with a singular, mimetic relationship to nature, Wordsworth criticism correspondingly follows the 'sentimental' line, as described by Schiller. Wordsworth's relationship to nature has (at least in this century) been constructed as 'double' or vexed, in the way that Schiller suggests, and criticism has accordingly been divided in its emphasis – some critics selecting the 'naive' or 'simple' Wordsworth; others the 'complex' version.

M. H. Abrams, in an introductory overview of Wordsworthian studies, describes the history of this ambivalent approach

The first critic of Wordsworth's poetry was Wordsworth himself, and in his criticism, as in his poetry, he speaks with two distinct voices.[47]

From the beginning, two views were established:

Wordsworth as primarily the simple, affirmative poet of elementary feelings, essential humanity, and vital joy, and Wordsworth as primarily the complex poet of strangeness, paradox, equivocality . . . these diverse views . . . were established as persistent alternative ways to the poet by Matthew Arnold and by A. C. Bradley.[48]

In other words, Wordsworth can be either 'naive', understood in the way that Clare has been understood, or 'sentimental', and this equivocality springs from Wordsworth's own divided position, rather as Clare's may be seen to originate in his own single-minded critical naiveté.

Bypassing nineteenth-century approaches to Wordsworth, given the volume of criticism that could be taken into account, and moving on to this century, it is clear that even those critics who have emphasized Wordsworth's relationship to simple nature take some account of possible fissures in that bond.

In *Wordsworth's poetry 1787–1814*, Geoffrey Hartman, stating his own 'sentimental' position with respect to Wordsworth's poetry, points out that many readers

have felt that Wordsworth's poetry honors and even worships nature . . . Scholarship, luckily, tempers the affections, and the majority of readers have emphasized the poet's progression from nature worship or even pantheism to a highly qualified form of natural religion, with increasing awareness of the 'ennobling interchange' between mind and nature and a late yielding of primacy to the activity of the mind or of the idealizing power of imagination.[49]

This understanding of Wordsworth as divided in his loyalties between direct and absorbed worship of nature and the recognition of the powers of the human imagination and will sets the scene for later critical studies. In 1936, Joseph Warren Beach pointed out that:

In several of the romantic poets there is to be traced a distinct conflict between the naturalistic and the 'transcendental' elements, and an appreciable progress from the more naturalistic to the more transcendental phase during the period of their writing. Wordsworth and

Shelley tried to be naturalistic and succeeded but indifferently in keeping to the position with which they started.[50]

and drew attention to an earlier study by Professor Gingerich,

who shows how the poets' concern with 'the human mind, its self-contained and constituent energies, its active, transcendental powers' gained ground over their interest in 'external nature and sensation and the language of the sense'.[51]

That there is a contradiction or opposition in Wordsworth between response to external nature and emphasis on the imagination is a theory developed early in the century and subsequently modified. In 1950, Frederick Pottle, taking up Wordsworth's own statements in the Preface: 'Poetry takes its origin from emotion recollected in tranquillity' and 'I have at all times endeavoured to look steadily at my subject'[52] wrestles with the critical problem of combining 'descriptive' and 'interpretative' accounts of Wordsworth:

At first sight they appear to be hopelessly contradictory. The natural image that rises in one's mind as one reads the statement 'I have at all times endeavoured to look steadily at my subject' is that of an artist painting from a model or an actual landscape . . . But if poetry takes its rise from 'emotion recollected in tranquillity', it is hard to see how this can happen.[53]

Because his understanding of the imaginative process derives from Coleridge, Pottle divides the 'raw matter' of poetry from the transformative process. He tells us that the 'true matter consisted of certain perceptions, visual, auditory, tactile, which Wordsworth and his sister had on that windy April morning'.
    Reconstructing the composition of 'Daffodils', he says:

In Dorothy's entry this raw matter has already been grasped and shaped by a powerful imagination, and it has been verbalized. The entry is not a poem, because it contains a good deal of true but inconsequential statement.[54]

Pottle goes on to explain the poetic process, 'to reshape this world of common perception in the direction of a unity that shall be even more satisfactory and meaningful'.[55] He insists, rather desperately, on the distinction between what he calls 'literal, positivistic, "scientific" fact' and poetry, so that whilst, 'In a literal, physiological sense, Wordsworth did look steadily at the natural objects that appear in his poetry', nevertheless, the subject he is talking about in the sentence in the Preface is not an object in external nature; and the eye that looks steadily is not the physical eye. The subject is a mental image, and the eye is that inward eye which is the bliss of solitude . . . He starts with the mental image of a concrete natural object . . . As he looks steadily at it, he simplifies it, and as he simplifies it, he sees what it means . . . It is a great mistake to consider Wordsworth a descriptive poet.[56]

Thus, whereas a poet like Clare simply looks, Wordsworth first looks, then modifies the natural object; which is first received pure and simple by the visual eye, then imaged to the mind. Pottle's account of the creative process is not so different from that 'vivid' imaging ascribed to Clare by his critics, but it is sophisticated by the notion of a recollecting, transforming act.

Subsequent criticism has similarly concentrated on the relationship between 'description' or observation and 'expression' or contemplation in Wordsworth and even those critics, who like John Danby choose to concentrate on the 'simple' Wordsworth, make a distinction between his kind of nature poetry, and that of less glorious writers.

A rough scale of 'nature-poetry' can be constructed. The first level is that of 'nature-notes', the counting of the streaks of the tulip.[57]

Wordsworth, says Danby, does not fall into this category; 'His characteristic poetry is not predominantly visual'.

The second level is that at which the observer sees not only single details but is interested in the whole scene. The words *draw* and *scene* are significant here . . . The eighteenth century abounds in nature-poetry of this sort. It is . . . the century of the picturesque.[58]

Whilst the 'third level' of nature-poetry locates the feelings of the subject with respect to the natural world, it is the 'fourth' level on which Danby places Wordsworth:

The basic Wordsworthian concern is with the transactions that take place between the living person and his environment . . . What Wordsworth was trying to describe was something almost organic. It had to do with the traffic between the inner and the outer.[59]

This naive–sentimental hierarchy could equally be used to organize critical perspectives and it firmly separates what are considered to be objective, visual accounts from subjective, psychological or philosophical accounts.

The idealist model of Wordsworth's poetry as an internalization of the natural world, a reconciliation of subjective and
objective, either consciously articulated or silently at work in the
texts, has become a critical commonplace and the accompanying
distinction between and opposition of the visual and sensuous
and the mental and verbalized has accordingly and unquestion-
ingly become an entrenched part of many critical approaches to
the poet.

Geoffrey Hartman, whose book on Wordsworth's poetry has,
according to the critic David Simpson,

established the scope and direction of Romantic studies for the twenty
years since . . . [and] prepares the way for the deconstructive enterprise
in that Wordsworth is taken out of the historical and put into the
visionary mode[60]

bases his critical vision on this distinction, which is everywhere
reinforced in his writing. As L. J. Swingle says:

Mr Hartman invites us to think dialectically about the intellectual
tensions in Wordsworth's poetry, viewing them as shadowings forth of
a contest in Wordsworth's own consciousness. Wordsworth's struggle,
in Hartman's view, is to avoid the isolation of self that would result from
acknowledging imagination in its purest, apocalyptic form . . . and his
poetry, accordingly, manifests tension between the pressures of apocalyptic imagination and those forces [he] marshalls to bind imagination down to nature.[61]

Nature, in Wordsworth, is an antivisionary or anti-selfconsciousness
principle[62]

says Hartman, and:

One impulse vexes the creative spirit into self-dependence, the other
exhibits nature as the spirit's highest object. The poet is driven at the
same time from and toward the external world.[63]

Wordsworth's later poetry in particular, works by displacing
simple 'description':

There is more descriptive vigor — more observations and pictures from
nature — in an ordinary topographical poem like Wordsworth's own
Evening Walk or *Descriptive Sketches* than in all of *Lyrical Ballads*
together . . . What is truly distinctive . . . is Wordsworth's enlarged
understanding of the setting to be incorporated. This is never landscape
alone.[64]

The collapse of Wordsworth's personal view of the relationship between nature and imagination into an account of the relationship between description and expression in his poetry reveals the origins of this sentimental reading which, like all such, is an enactment of a critical issue, in this case the problem of description/expression in Romantic criticism.

But it is Wordsworth who is understood as being divided:

To follow nature meant, on his part, an extraordinary mimetic effort that reacts against the awakening or reawakening of apocalyptic thoughts.[65]

The dynamic of Hartman's criticism is the opposition between what he calls the 'bodily' and the 'intellectual' eye[66] and this idealist opposition of nature, or the material world, and subjectivity or consciousness underlies, in a different way, the criticism of Harold Bloom.

In *The visionary company*, Bloom says that the mainspring of Wordsworth's *Prelude*, and indeed of all Romantic poetry in England at that time, is the submerged conflict between the creative imagination and the natural world:

The inner problem of *The Prelude*, and of all the poetry of Wordsworth's great decade, is that of the autonomy of the poet's creative imagination . . . the single most crucial problem of all that is vital in English Romantic poetry. Even Wordsworth, the prophet of Nature, is uneasy at the prospect of the spirit's continual dependence on it.[67]

In terms very close to those used by Schiller, Bloom describes the sentimental distancing from nature which brings the birth of self-consciousness and articulacy, as compared with the proximity to nature that is associated with unconsciousness and silence. Of Wordsworth, he says that:

In the presence of too eloquent a natural image, he is speechless. Nor does he attempt, after *Tintern Abbey*, to particularize any local habitations for vision.[68]

The drama that Bloom presents − alienation and internalization − derives directly from idealist philosophy, staged in the psyche of the poet in such a way that there is no distinction between the conscious expression by Wordsworth of an idealist philosophy, his unconscious revelation of the structure of his own psyche and his own relationship to nature, assumed to be the same as that expressed in the texts. Like *The visionary company*, *Poetry and repression* dramatizes what is effectively the relationship between description and expression in aesthetics. Wordsworth 'knows that poetry cannot take on the authority of the natural world, but must assault the supposed priority of the natural object over the trope'.[69]

Both Bloom's psychoanalytic readings – see, for example, 'The internalization of quest-romance'[70] – and Hartman's more phenomenological approach – see, for example, 'Romanticism and anti-self-consciousness'[71] – describe the mechanism of Romantic poetry in terms of an idealist model of the psyche's progress from nature, through alienation, to a higher reconciliation of the two. This model is more explicitly detailed by M. H. Abrams in *Natural supernaturalism*.[72] Abrams describes how Romantic poetry moves from the supremacy of nature and of the 'outward eye' through alienation or separation from nature to a higher union of spirit and nature and to a liberated and creative 'inward eye'. Thus Romantic poetry is not a 'descriptive' poetry but an 'expressive' poetry of the 'inner eye' which transforms 'objective' or 'visual' natural description into the inward landscapes of the mind: a view now well established in Romantic criticism.

While Paul de Man, like Hartman and Bloom, reads Wordsworth's poetry in terms of a similar opposition between nature and the self, he concentrates more specifically on Romantic language and on the relationship between descriptive or mimetic and interpretative or symbolic language, which are, again, assumed to be different:

An abundant imagery coinciding with an equally abundant quantity of natural objects, the theme of imagination linked closely to the theme of nature, such is the fundamental ambiguity that characterizes the poetics of romanticism. The tension between the two polarities never ceases to be problematic.[73]

How, though, can de Man divide the natural objects from the imagery? Or, for that matter, nature and imagination? 'This type of imagery', says de Man of the nineteenth-century poetic image,

is grounded in the intrinsic ontological primacy of the natural object. Poetic language seems to originate in the desire to draw closer and closer to the ontological status of the object.[74]

Whilst there is undoubtedly a case for describing Romantic thought as preoccupied with the relationship between things and words – at least in Coleridge's case – it is de Man's own

Romanticism which identifies that philosophical problem as described and discussed by the Romantics with the structure of Romantic poetry itself – it is his Romanticism which identifies what the words *say* with what they *are* and collapses content into form in sentimental structuralization. As we saw in chapter 2, he says that:

At times, romantic thought and romantic poetry seem to come so close to giving in completely to nostalgia for the object that it becomes difficult to distinguish between object and image, between imagination and perception, between an expressive or constitutive and a mimetic or literal language.[75]

What does de Man mean by the 'object' which is difficult to distinguish? His idiom suggests that the poetry can almost be divided into a substantial, material element and a spiritual and imaginative component which are then mingled by the poet. And whilst it is fair to say that Wordsworth refers to or talks about the idealist issue of the relationship between mind and matter, de Man seems almost to imply that the two *actually* interact in the text. Moreover, his assumption that there are two languages, one 'expressive' and one 'mimetic', needs to be questioned. Whilst one language can both express and refer, it is difficult to make a case for the possibility of separating out the two functions in either semantic or structural–syntactical terms.

De Man similarly identifies form and content in *The rhetoric of Romanticism*, analysing 'Composed by the Side of Grasmere Lake':

Tranquillity, it seems, is the right balance between the literal and the symbolic vision, a balance reflected in a harmonious proportion between mimetic and symbolic language in the diction of the poem.[76]

De Man turns what is really a change of direction in Wordsworth's thought into a change in the structure of his language itself:

Up to the phrase 'Is it a mirror?' in line 9, which marks the turning point of the poem, we have been using the outward eye of direct perception. The relationship between landscape and poet has been that of observer and thing observed, and consequently language has been mimetically descriptive throughout.[77]

This amounts to a claim that poetic language mimics what it is about: descriptive language for talking about description, nature and the outside world, symbolic language for talking about the self. Surely all that de Man is really isolating is a change in the reference of the language, not a change in its structure?

For de Man, Wordsworth creates paradoxical and 'mixed' landscapes and, in common with other Romantic poets, describes 'the passage from a certain type of nature, earthly and material, to another nature . . . mental and celestial'[78] but, de Man reminds us, the ultimate locus of this nature is material and we are not ultimately removed from earth to a transcendental sphere. Like Albert Wlecke (*Wordsworth and the sublime*), who speaks of

Wordsworth's insistence that the 'presence' is universally 'interfused' and his catalog of its dwelling-places . . . suggest that he wishes to keep the location of the ubiquitous 'presence' thoroughly within the natural world, despite the flight of elevated thoughts,[79]

de Man stresses the fact that Wordsworth does not actually pass beyond nature. The symbolic aspect, this critical position states, is incorporated into bodily vision and location by the poetic imagination. And yet, quite at odds with this, there is the claim that the two kinds of vision or language are identifiably different and that this mingling of mimetic and figurative is something especially Romantic.

Whether this literal–figurative relationship is understood as an achieved synthesis on the part of the poet or as a contradictory manifestation of the battle between nature and consciousness, revealed in the fragmentation of the text at sublime moments; it plays the central role in recent Romantic criticism. Cynthia Chase, in 'The accidents of disfiguration' makes the usual Romantic assumption that there is such a thing as 'ordinary' language, where reference is fixed and subjectivity or ambiguity all but excluded. Speaking of

a general predicament of the reader of Romantic texts: an erosion of the distinction between literal and figurative modes on which recovery of meaning depends,

she claims that the text 'both requires to be read literally and thwarts attempts to fix its referential status'.[80] And again, in the same article:

The passage at once requires to be read literally and makes literal reading impossible. It is impossible first of all just because of the conspicuous traces of the effaced figures that provide the key terms of the text.[81]

Setting aside whatever it is Chase identifies as the force in the text that 'requires' to be read a particular way, this statement poses problems. On what grounds does Chase propose an opposition between a normative, literal reading, free of metaphorical interference, and a reading in which metaphorical skeletons press through the flesh?

Thomas Weiskel's study, *The Romantic sublime*, revolves round the binary opposition of metonymy and metaphor. Like Chase, Weiskel is idealist, and articulates – as she does not – his allegiance to the Kantian aesthetic. Like Bloom and Hartman, he reads in Wordsworth the rejection of the material:

> In Wordsworth the imagination confers, abstracts and modifies; it dissolves, separates and consolidates; it recoils from everything but the plastic, the pliant and the indefinite, because too great an attachment to determinate objects makes sublimation impossible.[82]

But Weiskel also acknowledges the difficulty of separating the two modes effectively:

> Wordsworth was not a symbolic poet and not a descriptive poet either, if indeed a poet can be descriptive. His landscapes hover on the edge of revelation without revealing anything.[83]

Like de Man's, and Wlecke's point about the locus of Wordsworth's nature, this is an admission of the fact that the literal is itself already subjective and symbolic, that the poetry which is perpetually described in terms of an opposition is admitted, even by the critics who work in those terms, to confuse the literal and the symbolic, because they are not different.

And yet, critics like J. Hillis Miller talk in terms of 'a non-representational meaning present side by side with the mimetic one'.[84] In 'Composed Upon Westminster Bridge,' he talks of 'the dislocations of literal language', and concludes that:

> Between mimesis and emblem, between imitative form and creative form, the images of the poem hang balanced . . .[85]

> To follow the implications of the negatives and the figurative language . . . leads the interpreter away from an unambiguous mimetic reading toward the recognition that the poem expresses an oscillation between consciousness and nature, life and death, presence and absence, motion and stillness.[86]

Hillis Miller's interpretation is, again, intensely sentimental. In its assumption of the possibility of an 'unambiguous mimetic reading' and its construction around a set of balanced opposites, it conforms to the sentimental model. Similarly, his work on the dream pasage in *The Prelude* analyses the notion of 'primacy of consciousness' in Wordsworth:

> Wordsworth would seem, at first, to be a good example of a poet who asserts the primacy of consciousness, who assumes that speech involves the pure presence of an undivided and originating subjectivity, and that writing, to use his own word, is merely a dangerous 'counterspirit'. But, as Hillis Miller shows, the poetry of 'The Prelude' does not sustain the simplicity of such a reading.[87]

Robert Young's introduction to Miller's article summarizes the direction of its argument. Referring back to itself, the dream is about language, 'turns back on itself by presenting in the shell a symbol of its own process';[88] it is an assertion of the power of language and imagination, and of the necessary alienation from nature and self of the consciousness involved in language. Thus we have the 'double' view that Schiller associated with sentimentalism:

> The original voice is already double, divided against itself. There is no originating unity or simplicity at the source, but an initial equivocity.[89]

Because, according to the sentimental critic, poetry is its own criticism — as a result of the collapse of the two discussed earlier — it cannot simply be mimetic. And yet whilst realizing this such critics as Hillis Miller use the notion of a normative reading to propel their criticism forward.

Frances Ferguson, whose position in *Wordsworth: language as counter-spirit* is similar, gives a comparable account. Seeing Wordsworth's repetition, for example, as evidence of a preoccupation with the substantiality of language itself, of words as things, she contrasts the search for fixity — whether in things or language — with the sense of change and of reworking which Wordsworth senses in language: the 'counter-spirit' 'which seems always to threaten the possibility of the poet's changing his internal story into an external story. . . . This dialectic persists through *The Prelude*, repeatedly blurring the boundaries between Nature and (human) nature, so that the boundaries between externality and internality correspondingly blur'.[90] So here is another drama of opposition — internal and external working in dialectic, language against nature leading to that blurring so often selected as a Romantic characteristic.

Referring back to the 'checklist' of characteristics of the Schillerian aesthetic: the structuralizing of history or theory, the formalizing of content, the separation of aesthetic and non-aesthetic (or figurative and literal) and the manipulation of binary opposites, it seems as though many recent critics of Wordsworth have fallen within the category of sentimental criticism, deriving their methodology ultimately from Schiller. Moreover, their criticism can be described in terms of Schiller's own account of the sentimental mode: binary or divided, it constructs a naive object as the means of articulating itself: in this case, the concept of a lateral language, in which reference is fixed, or of a visual apprehension which is immediate and simple. Neither concept is, in the context of language philosophy after Wittgenstein or perception theory after Gombrich, very viable.

The coincidence of sentimental criticism and the poetry that it describes is not surprising, given that it subscribes to the notion of poetry as criticism, as the interpretative process, which is an important aspect of Romantic theory. A corollary of that concentration on poetry as the structure of the interpreting – or creative – consciousness and methodology is, as we have seen, the neglect of the referential or communicative aspects of the literary text and certain critics of Wordsworth have pointed this out. David Simpson, for example, stands against the idealist approach which dominates Wordsworth criticism. Criticizing the aesthetics that neglects any politicized or historically critical readings of Romantic poetry, he points towards

an alternative approach to that which stresses the emergence of the visionary mode (and its 'decline' in *The Excursion*). This alternative . . . will not focus on 'intellectual confusion' or Coleridgean hangovers but on the historical conditions informing a subjectivity that is unassured and a poetry that is indecisive and prone to scruples and qualifications.

At the moment, we have a divided Romantic criticism . . . with the major historical scholars remaining implicitly or explicitly antitheoretical and the 'theorists' ignoring history.[91]

Simpson confirms that the theorists of Romanticism 'are still for the most part locked into a false dialectic in which the search for purity and propositional closure, on the one hand . . . is answered, on the other, by an equally reified counterstatement declaring for universal contamination' and similarly confirms the presence in the criticism of sentimentality of 'some fantasy of an achievable, universal truth'.[92] Deconstruction, he asserts, 'does not investigate the "inabsolute" middle ground between fullness and absence, a middle ground which is *not* at all a merging or fusion of the two extreme positions but rather . . . a denial of the very opposition which their mutual antagonism presupposes'.[93]

Simpson's own criticism of Wordsworth and of Romantic poetry accordingly deals far more with the strategies and the communicative 'intentions' of the poets concerned within a specific context than with modelling their psyches, considering the 'heuristic', reader-directed aspect of the poetry neglected elsewhere.

The emphasis upon self-finding and self-creation, with the consequent disestablishment of the text as an authority and the stressing of its functions as a heuristic stimulus, occur all over Romantic aesthetics.[94]

Undermining authority, confronting the issue of communication; Simpson credits the Romantic authors with a conscious dismantling of naiveté – and a refusal of determinism. The questioning of simple reality in the poetry – of the status of the past, of objective nature – involves a recognition that 'what is regarded as the real has already been figured and processed by the mind'.[95] Thus, rather than accepting and re-enacting a dramatic opposition between reality and figure, Simpson understands it as a problem in Romantic thought and philosophy articulated and communicated by the poetry which does not, however, mirror that issue in its structure.

L. J. Swingle similarly criticizes the dialectical model offered by Hartman *et al.*:

Wordsworth saw himself not as a private but as an essentially public poet, one whose business was . . . to *use* his mental experience artifactually in the service of moving his reader towards some conceived goal.[96]

We need, he says, 'to think about their [the poems'] manipulative designs . . . what they reveal to us about our own minds'.[97] For Swingle,

Wordsworth is not primarily interested in asserting or establishing the objective validity of the mind's perceptions. His concern is not with the mind's ability to discover which of its numerous and contrary perceptions is 'true' . . . Wordsworth is not writing about Truths discovered, but rather about mental processes,[98] and 'employs contrarieties in his poetry in the service of revealing us to ourselves'.[99] There is of course a strong prejudice against this kind of approach, which makes some estimate of the original intentions or context of the poems as a communicative act. But it is a sentimental ideology that has brought about that prejudice. The separation of 'aesthetic' language from ordinary language, which refers and communicates, is responsible for the current impossibility of talking about poetry in terms of ordinary language.

CONCLUSION

It was plain from the account of Wordsworth's critical writings given in chapter 2, that he did not really endorse the idealist aesthetic that governs the kind of reading of his poetry offered by many critics. Instead, he emphasizes prosaic communication between human beings sharing a community and a language, trying to avoid the separation of poetry from 'life'. However, both Wordsworth criticism and criticism of Clare are and have been intrinsically idealist, employing the sentimental mechanics of opposition, dividing literal and figurative, descriptive and expressive, nature and consciousness. Even where these opposites are believed to interact or are discovered in their partners, it is their difference that is the perpetual dynamic of both kinds of criticism.

In the case of Clare, the opposition works against Clare's 'transcriptive' or 'mimetic' work, contrasting it with Wordsworth's 'expressive' poetry. In the case of Wordsworth, that same opposition is dramatized in his texts which, formally read, reveal a divided consciousness, typical of that which Schiller described:

The sentimental poet therefore is constantly dealing with two opposing concepts and emotions, with reality as boundary and with his idea as the infinite, and the mixed feeling which he excites will always bear witness to this double source.   (*NS*, p. 42)

In either case, acts of meaning, carried out within the context of a shared language system and set of reading or writing conventions, are excluded from consideration. The aesthetic is set adrift, cut loose from the real situations in which it is voiced, a formal, autonomous entity answerable to no one.

The existing distinction between Clare as a naively transcriptive or 'descriptive' writer and Wordsworth as a sentimental, 'expressive' poet is clearly reductive and inadequate. It fails to account for either poet in the context of his history or aesthetic, or to recognize the pressures of popular aesthetics. Moreover this distinction can be even more closely criticized, and it is through such a criticism in my next chapter that I hope to review attitudes to Clare and Wordsworth.

4

UT PICTURA POESIS

I

OVERVIEW

My last chapter showed how *practical* critics from Clare's time onwards have used a pictorial analogy to define Clare (and similar poets) as 'descriptive', and to contrast 'descriptive' poetry with a non-visual or 'expressive' poetry.

This chapter examines the origins of that sight–insight distinction in *theoretical* aesthetics, and shows how deeply and frequently aesthetics, or critical theory, betrayed not only the philosophical understanding of its time, but also its own philosophical origins, in order to support this opposition between the visual and the non-visual.

I start by looking at how eighteenth-century *mimetic* theory popularized the visual analogy for poetry, which was understood as an imitation of nature, just like painting. I then move to nineteenth-century practitioners of *expressive* aesthetics who rejected that definition of poetry, and were writing alongside philosophers of language whose account of poetry rendered the mimetic theory obsolete. I argue that, despite this, nineteenth-century critical theorists clung to the concept of a purely descriptive, visual poetry which they contrasted with the new, expressive poetry to the glorification of the former. In this way, I suggest, these critics were using the old theory of poetry as a 'naive' contrast to their contemporary sentimentalism.

The comparison between painting and poetry which dominates eighteenth-century criticism was based on an enthusiasm for art which manifested such qualities as fidelity to nature, vivacity, and clarity. This chapter shows the way in which the pictorial analogy was transformed by nineteenth-century critics, for whom these qualities were no longer what constituted the true essence of poetry.

The second section of this chapter reviews the pictorial analogy, as used by both eighteenth and nineteenth-century critics, from the perspective of twentieth-century theories of perception and visual art. Starting with a straightforward critique of the concept of visual art as imitative prevalent throughout both the eighteenth and nineteenth century, I move on to other nineteenth-century concepts of visual art as a sensuous embodiment of meaning. Finally, I look at the alternative accounts of visual art offered by twentieth-century critics, and notably by the pragmatic philosopher, Nelson Goodman, in his book *Languages of Art*.

Goodman's account challenges established – and particularly idealist – theories about art. He insists that painting, like poetry, is cognitive. Both arts are *symbol systems*, which we understand in a similar way to a language, but they differ in the organization of their respective systems. To differentiate visual from verbal art, Goodman introduces the idea of the comparative 'density' or 'articulation' of the terms within those systems in each case. Painting is a 'denser' symbol system than poetry.

I explain this account, and suggest that we can use it to reformulate the received relationship between naive and sentimental, usually supported by the versions of the pictorial analogy considered above. That is, we can formulate a different pictorial analogy for poetry, using the notion of density. This new version of an old formula would suggest that certain texts are 'dense' with respect to critical systems within which they are constructed while others are 'articulate'. These terms are relative and do not make any statement about the intrinsic characters of the texts in question, only their relationship to a system. I use this analogy to suggest how we could re-read John Clare, and counteract the descriptive/expressive opposition – a suggestion taken up in my last chapter. Thus this chapter begins with a critique of the pictorial analogy and ends by turning it around to provide an alternative to the opposition it has fostered.

EIGHTEENTH-CENTURY THEORIES OF POETIC LANGUAGE

The term 'descriptive', as it is used in eighteenth-century aesthetic and critical writings, implies a particular, visual or 'imaging' relationship between language and the world. As Ralph Cohen says:

So long as language was considered 'pictured' in the eye of the imagination, the critic quite correctly compared particulars of poetry with those of painting and created discriminations which coincided with this view.[1]

The comparison between poetry and painting which dominated eighteenth-century criticism and which gave rise to the vogue for 'picturesque' and 'descriptive' poetry implies a particular understanding of the way words work and how they compare with pictures. As Stephen Land explains in his study, *From signs to propositions*,

The eighteenth century inherited the tendency . . . to think of signs in terms of reference, a tendency which yields what can be called a 'picture' theory of words . . . Words . . . 'represent' things either by convention or by virtue of actual resemblance. The meaning of language is a function not of any formal qualities of the language itself but of this quasi-pictorial representation of the referents. Many 'aesthetic' treatises of the first half of the eighteenth century openly adopted this view of language.[2]

This view, whereby words work by causing visual images to rise up through association and according to which language is a *sensible* process, closely associated with perception, is very evident in the writings of eighteenth-century critics. For poetic language in particular was thought to conjure up vivid pictures to the mind's eye and the imagination was believed to work by way of the sight. Thus Addison, whose aesthetics were so influential, claims that:

Our sight is the most perfect and most delightful of all our senses . . . It is this sense which furnishes the imagination with its ideas; so that by the pleasures of the imagination or fancy . . . I here mean such as arise from visible objects . . . We cannot indeed have a single object in the fancy that did not make its first entrance through the sight.[3]

The imagination 'is but opening the eye, and the scene enters'.[4] Thus his account of poetry as an imaginative art bypasses the workings of language as we might understand it, conceiving of it as representation relayed through the senses and transformed into mental images of sensuous *things*.

Addison is not alone in describing the poetic process as an evocation of visual images. John Dennis, in 1704, describes how Homer and Virgil write frightening poetry:

> to bring an absent terrible Object before our Sight, they drew an Image or Picture of it; but to draw an Image or Picture of a Terrible Object, so as to surprise and astonish the Soul by the Eye, they never failed to draw it in violent Action or Motion.[5]

And Joseph Trapp, in his *Lectures on poetry* (1711–1719) also talks of words as images:

> Thoughts are the Images of Things, as Words are of Thoughts; and we all know that Images and Pictures are only so far true as they are true Representations of Men and Things . . . For Poets as well as Painters, think it their Business to take the Likenes of Things from their Appearance . . . in Description or Painting that is *truly* express'd which is express'd as the Thing *appears* to be.[6]

Here we can see how the 'descriptive' standard was applied: if poetry represented, it was to represent accurately, to give us a clear and vivid picture.

However, whatever the affinities between empiricist epistemology and contemporary aesthetics, the account of how language worked that underlay eighteenth-century critical writings was not in tune with the views of contemporary philosophers, such as Locke or Berkeley. For both these philosophers stress the ambiguous and often distortive relation that obtains between language and *ideas*, insisting that there is no direct word–thing relationship of the kind a copy-theory suggests. Locke emphasizes the fact that words are the signs, conventionally established, whereby we communicate ideas and as such can have an obscure and confusing relationship to the sense-world.[7] Words, especially when used figuratively, when they have abstract or 'mixed' rather than 'simple' referents, are far removed from things as they really are[8] and we use them without having distinct ideas of what they refer to.[9]

Berkeley pursues this line, reminding us that we cannot

visualize or define abstract words, and indeed, do not have access to the meanings of the words we use: 'We are not acquainted with the meanings of our words',[10] he tells us, and 'Even proper names themselves do not seem always spoken with a design to bring into our view the idea of those individuals that are supposed to be marked by them'.[11] Moreover, he stresses that even perception – which for the literary critics provides a standard of clarity and definition – is conventional, not natural, since

it hath been shown, there is no resemblance between the ideas of sight and things tangible . . . We can no more argue a visible and tangible square to be of the same species, from their being called the same name, than we can, that a tangible square and the monosyllable consisting of six letters, whereby it is marked, are of the same species.[12]

Thus, 'visible figures represent tangible figures, much after the same manner that written words do sounds'[13] and the world that we see is as conventionally constructed as that which we write about: Locke concurs in this view that visual apprehension is conventional and learnt.[14]

So, both Locke and Berkeley state not only that language is a conventional system of signs, rather than a natural, sensuous 'imaging', but also that even perception, contrary to the view revealed in Addison's and similar criticism is no natural, direct sensuous access to the world but a convention-governed activity, a kind of knowledge or cognitive activity.

But their contemporaries in the literary critical domain conceive of language and vision in a very different way. Here, poetic language is a kind of vision and vision is a natural apprehension of the real world.

THE SISTER ARTS: PAINTING AND POETRY IN EIGHTEENTH-CENTURY CRITICISM

Il faut donc que nous croyions voir, pour ainsi dire, en écoutant des Vers: Ut Pictura Poesis, dit Horace.[15]

So said the Abbé Dubos in 1719 and this view was echoed by countless of his contemporaries and successors. Poetry should be like painting, in giving the reader a vivid and lucid image in the mind's eye; the history of the comparison between the arts has been traced by Jean Hagstrum in *The sister arts* (see chapter 2,

n. 59 above). As the arts flowered during the eighteenth century, 'the habit of applying terms of painting to the criticism of poetry became more deeply ingrained than ever before'.[16] In the context of the kind of 'visual' account of language in general offered by aesthetics at the time, this is not surprising. Language, although it 'imaged', could not achieve the kind of vividness and naturalness in its 'pictures' that painting could achieve, for words themselves cannot imitate or look like things in the way that pictures can. Poetry must accordingly aspire to the 'natural' imitation of painting, for like painting, language in poetry is believed to 'imitate' the natural world. It is on this basis – the shared principle of *imitation* – that the arts are compared, a principle which, as Todorov puts it, 'reigns uncontested over the theory of art during the first three quarters of the eighteenth century':[17] the classic statement of this aesthetic is Batteux's *Les beaux-arts réduits à un même principe*, (1746).[18]

It is this central conviction that art should imitate that dictates the way in which the relationship between the arts develops, for painting with its 'natural' signs is thought to imitate more accurately and successfully than poetry. It is set up as a model for the latter and accordingly a certain conception of what good poetry should be like develops.

Whilst recognizing that poetry uses conventional signs, critics insist that it 'imitates' and order the arts accordingly. Thus James Harris, in his *Discourse on music, painting and poetry* (1744) states that:

The Mimetic Art of POETRY has been hitherto considered, as fetching its Imitation from mere *Natural* Resemblance. In this, it has been shewn much inferior to *PAINTING*, & nearly equal to *MUSIC*.[19]

And Addison tells us that 'Description runs yet further from the things it represents than painting, for a picture bears a real resemblance to its original, which letters and syllables are wholly void of'.[20] Similarly, Alexander Gerard claims that

that instrument of imitation is doubtless the most perfect, which is capable of producing the most perfect likeness. Among the fine arts, this pre-eminence . . . belongs to sculpture; and more to painting . . . than to poetry.[21]

From here, it is easy to see how, before an alternative aesthetic which could replace the mimetic principle and so put poetry back at an advantage was developed, what was valued in poetry was that which seemed to approximate to painting. Thus for example Richard Hurd, in his *Discourse on poetical imagination*, (1751) tells us that

every object stands forth in bright sunshine to the view of the true poet. Every minute mark & lineament of the completed form leaves a corresponding trace on his Fancy. And having these bright and determinate concepts of things in his own mind, he finds no difficulty to convey the liveliest ideas of them to others. This is what we call *painting* in poetry; by which . . . every single property (is) marked, and the poet's own image set in distinct relief before the view of his reader.[22]

And he notes that: 'The material universe, or what the painters call *still life* is the object of that species of poetical imitation, we call *descriptive*'.[23]

In Addison's criticism, vivacity and clarity — together with a skill in combining images — are general virtues for poetry, around the middle of the century these qualities begin to be associated with a particular kind of poetry — the descriptive. For as aesthetics move away from the mimetic principle, this account of poetry as a lively rendering of the natural world begins to be found inadequate. Language, especially poetic language, is no longer thought of as 'copying' and this means that alternative accounts of poetry and its ideal qualities begin to appear. Description is not rejected, though: it simply becomes one category of poetry. Thus for instance Joseph Warton[24] classified poetry as 'Sublime and Pathetic', didactic, or witty and descriptive: the latter being the least significant kind of poetry, associated with landscape painting. This shift in values can be explained in terms of a more general shift in attitudes to language, as well as in terms of a changing aesthetic.

IMITATION TO EXPRESSION: CHANGES IN PHILOSOPHY OF LANGUAGE AND AESTHETICS, AND THEIR EFFECTS ON CRITICISM

'The concept of the sublime', says Stephen Land, 'provided perhaps the most important single path from representationalism to alternative theories of linguistic signs'.[25] It is this theory which helped to release [a] flood of emotionalism into the aesthetic theory of the period',[26] that we find invading the work of British aestheticians towards the middle of the eighteenth century and which makes its presence felt in the movement away from a neo-classical account of all poetry as imitative, and towards an account of poetry as passionate. What is noticeable, however, is the way in which these critics, rather than abandoning the mimetic principle, experience difficulties as they try to fit the new notion of poetry as primarily 'expressive', derived from the theory of the sublime, into the existing framework of a neo-classical theory. The principles of imitation and expression do not oppose one another as alternative accounts of poetry but are found side by side in the treatises of the time.

Thus John Dennis early on in the century claims at once that poetry 'ought to be an exact Imitation of Nature',[27] and that 'Thoughts are but the Images of Things',[28] or that 'As Poetry is an Art, it must be an Imitation of Nature', whilst he simultaneously insists that poetry works by exciting the reader's passions through figurative language.

Passion, then, is the Characteristical Mark of Poetry, and consequently, it must be every where: For wherever a Discourse is not Pathetick, there it is Prosaick.[29]

Dennis' influence is plain in writers like Lowth, whose Lectures on the sacred poetry of the Hebrews (1753) similarly divides its allegiance between the traditional emphasis on clarity and exact visual representation and an emphasis on poetry's passionate character. Thus, whilst he stresses visual images, saying that, 'poetry abounds most in those images which are furnished by the senses, and chiefly those of the sight',[30] he also says that the most 'amazing power of Lyric Poetry is directing the passions'[31]: two claims that might seem at odds with one another.

And even Burke, whose aesthetic has been said to be the most central of all in providing the new rationale for poetry as expression, rather than imitation, remains firmly within the empirical tradition.[32] Like Locke and Berkeley, Burke points out that we can use words without having access to what they mean or stand for in a definite way. For, he says, we can use words without knowledge of the things they represent, 'and yet afterwards be capable of returning them to others, combined in a new way'.[33] And , like them, he points out that words cannot work by sensuous representation:

In short, it is not only of those ideas which are commonly called abstract, and of which no image at all can be formed, but even of particular real beings, that we converse without having any idea of them excited in the imagination . . . Indeed, so little does poetry depend for its effect on the power of raising sensible images, that I am convinced it would lose a considerable part of its energy if this were the necessary result of all description.[34]

So here we have an account of poetic language which strongly resists the notion that it copies sense-objects or that it is an imitation and which provides the ground for a movement away from the comparison of poetry with painting. But even Burke continues to fall into the old idiom. At one point he notes that:

The images raised by poetry are always of this obscure kind, though in general the effects of poetry are by no means to be attributed to the images it raises . . . But painting . . . can only affect simply by the images it present.[35]

Swiftly retracting his phrase 'the images raised', Burke often uses the idiom of representation: although he insists that

poetry and rhetoric do not succeed in exact description so well as painting does; their business is to affect rather by sympathy than imitation;

he goes on to talk of poetry as 'displaying' this effectiveness –

to display rather the effect of things on the mind . . . than to present a clear idea of the things themselves.[36]

And elsewhere he still speaks of poetry as, in certain cases, being imitative art.[37]

The fact that Burke's challenge to established accounts of poetry was formulated within a basically empirical framework is significant. When we look at British criticism around this time, we find that the movement at a theoretical level from an imitative to an expressive account of language was accommodated within criticism as a 'synchronic' contrast between two kinds of poetry: the 'descriptive' (from the mimetic principle) and the 'expressive' (from the 'sublime' theory). Rather than moving from one general account of poetry to another – as studies like M. H. Abrams' *The mirror and the lamp* tend to suggest – most critics accommodated the changing view of poetic language by conceding that *certain* kinds or aspects of poetry were 'expressive', others 'descriptive'.

Edward Young, whose 1728 essay on lyric poetry and 1759 'Conjectures on Original Composition' draw on the theory of the sublime, exemplifies the way in which the newly acknowledged expressive aspects of poetry are associated with a limited aspect or class of poetry: the Lyric, or Ode.

The Ode, as it is the eldest kind of poetry, so it is more spiritous, and more remote from prose, than any other, in sense, sound, expression and conduct.[38]

Similarly, we saw that Joseph Warton classified poetry downwards from the 'sublime and pathetic' to the descriptive, whilst Trapp says that 'Beauty in writing may be consider'd as twofold: Either the *Elegant*, or *Sublime*'[39] and claiming that 'it is the great art of poetry to work upon the passions',[40] placed the latter over the former in his hierarchy: the lyric was for him 'of all kinds of Poetry the most poetical'.[41] Thus the sublime is contrasted with artificial diction, wit and description.

It is Sir William Jones, K. G. Hamilton tells us, who makes 'the first clear distinction between imitative and expressive poetry'[42] and, again, this distinction evolves from unease with the concept of imitation as a rationale for poetry. Jones argues that a poem may be partly imitative, partly expressive. He starts off in his 1772 essay, 'On the arts, commonly called imitative', by saying that

almost all the philosophers and criticks, who have written upon the subject of *poetry, musick*, and *painting* . . . seem of one mind in considering them as arts merely *imitative*; yet it must be clear to anyone, who examines what passes in his own mind, that he is affected by the finest *poems, pieces of musick*, and pictures, upon a principle, which, whatever it may be, is entirely distinct from imitation. M Le Batteux has attempted to prove that all the fine arts have a relation to this common principle of *imitating*: but, whatever may be said of *painting*, it is probable, that *poetry* and *musick* had a nobler origin.[43]

Jones then associates poetry with original utterance, calling it 'a strong and animated expression of the human passions' – in its original form. Like Dennis, he speaks of 'the language of the violent passions, expressed in exact measure, with strong accents and significant words'.[44]

Having distinguished poetry from the imitative arts on the

grounds that it is thus passionate, Jones goes on to suggest that painting can in many cases be included in this non-imitative category. From here, he arrives at a position in which all the arts are partially imitative, partially expressive.

It is asserted also that *descriptive* poetry, and *descriptive* musick, as they are called, are strict imitations; but, not to insist that mere *description* is the meanest part of both arts, if indeed it belongs to them at all, it is clear, that words and sounds have no kind of resemblance to visible objects: and what is an imitation, but a resemblance to some other thing?[45]

Jones seems torn between an imitation/expression distinction based, like Burke's, on the difference between the individual arts and an internal division of each art into imitative and expressive — whereby description, the imitative aspect, is the least essential to the art. This is his final conclusion, that each artist will achieve his end

not by *imitating* the works of nature, but by assuming their power, and causing the same effect upon the imagination, which her charms produce to the senses: this must be the chief object of a poet, a musician, and a painter, who know that *great effects are not produced by minute details, but by the general spirit of the whole piece.*[46]

Thus, he finishes

the finest parts of poetry, musick, and paintings, are expressive of the passions . . . the inferior parts of them are *descriptive* of natural objects.[47]

Here, the inherited need to categorize means that opposing ways of understanding poetry or art are transformed into different aspects of one art. Yet 'imitation' and 'expression' and thus 'description' and 'lyric' are incompatible accounts of poetic procedure.

Hugh Blair's *Lectures on rhetoric and belles lettres* (1783) show the influence of Harris as well as of Burke and the sublime tradition. Reflecting the growing discrimination of poetry from painting as an art *more* capable of imitating, by virtue of the flexibility and resourcefulness of language in evoking images, Blair continues to consider poetry as an imitation and to place emphasis on the word's ability to call up a visual image. Poetry and eloquence, he says, have

a greater capacity of Imitation and Description than is possessed by any other art. Of all the means which human ingenuity has contrived for recalling the images of real objects, and awakening by representation, similar emotions to those which are raised by the original, none is so full and extensive as that which is executed by words and writing . . . Hence it is usual among critical writers, to speak of Discourse as the chief of all the imitative or mimetic arts.[48]

Here, the concept of imitation as poetic principle has not been seriously disturbed by the recognition that words work in a different way from pictures. Blair goes on to admit that poetry and discourse are not altogether imitative, but rather, descriptive.

Imitation is performed by means of somewhat that has a natural likeness and resemblance to the thing imitated . . . such are statues and pictures. Description, again, is the raising in the mind the conception of an object by means of some arbitrary or instituted symbols . . . such are words and writing. Words have no natural resemblance to the ideas or objects which they are employed to signify, but a statue or a picture has a natural likeness to the original.[49]

Even where Blair acknowledges the conventionality of words, he conceives of the effect of poetry as much the same as that of painting — to represent things or ideas. Poetic description achieves this without resemblance, whereas painting relies on natural symbols: hence the limitations of pictorial art. Blair's lectures also involve the notion of poetry as passionate or heightened figurative language which derives from the Longinian tradition, together with a sense of early language as poetic. Poetry is 'the language of passion, or of enlivened imagination, formed, most commonly, into regular numbers':[50] an account similar to that given by John Dennis. And accordingly Blair gives the Ode as poetry in 'its first and most antient form' and its most passionate.[51] But along with this definition of poetry as essentially passionate, calling on the emotions, is an accent on the descriptive capacity whereby a poet enables the reader to visualize what he describes:

a true Poet makes us imagine that we see it before our eyes; he catches the distinguishing features; he gives it the colours of life and reality; he places it in such a light, that a Painter could copy after him. This happy talent is chiefly owing to a strong imagination, which first receives a lively impression of the object; and then, by employing a proper selection of circumstances in describing it, transmits that impression in its full force to the imagination of others. In this selection of circumstances, lies the great art of Description.[52]

Description, when good, is such that 'a Statuary or a Painter could lay hold of, and work after' it[53] and in this it is still closely related to the plastic and visual arts; although the particular qualities of the verbal medium have been recognized, they still work within the same framework and to the same end.

Thomas Twining, whose 1789 dissertation 'On poetry considered as an imitative art' also differentiates poetry from painting and sculpture, similarly employs the concept of description as a particularly poetic form of imitation. Whilst Twining begins by pointing out that when 'We are told that Poetry is an imitative art . . . In order to conceive how it is so, we naturally compare it with painting, sculpture, and such arts as are strictly and clearly imitative. But in this comparison the *difference* is so much more obvious and striking than the *resemblance*',[54] he goes on to list those ways in which poetry does imitate.

The most general and extensive of these senses is that in which it is applied to DESCRIPTION, comprehending, not only that poetic landscape-painting which is *peculiarly* called descriptive Poetry, but all such circumstantial and distinct representation as conveys to the mind a strong and clear idea of its object, whether *sensible* or *mental* . . . The more distinct and vivid the ideas are of which this picture is composed, and the more closely they correspond to the actual *impressions* received from nature, the stronger will be the resemblance, and the more perfect the imitation.

This descriptive imitation is distinguished from other kinds of imitation – of actions or passions, for instance – rather as Platonic imitation from Aristotelian mimesis. Here again, the changing definition of imitation is accommodated within the text and one concept is set against another. It is description which is the most obvious kind of poetic imitation: it is

of all the extended or analogical applications of the words . . . perhaps, the most obvious and natural. There needs no other proof of this than the very language in which we are naturally led to express our admiration of this kind of poetry, and which we perpetually borrow from the arts of strict imitation. We say the poet has *painted* his object; we talk of his *imagery*, of the lively *colors* of his description, and the masterly touches of his *pencil*.[55]

Imitations of visible objects of this kind are distinguished from imitations of sounds or music and then from imitations of the passions and other mental objects or internal effects. All these kinds of imitation are classed together as 'descriptive' and further distinguished from 'fictive' imitation, which does not resemble impressions received from things, but other ideas. Here, Twining's classification is stretched almost beyond belief and even he admits that these are extended uses of the imitative concept. His final category of imitation is personation where, in drama, the poet speaks as another character. 'It is scarce necessary to observe', Twining admits, 'that these different species of imitation often run into, and are mixed with, each other . . . Descriptive imitation is, manifestly, that which is most independent on all the others'.[56] This notion of description Twining takes up and considers more fully, giving as an example 'that which answers to *landscape* in painting, and of which the subject is, prospects, views, rural scenery, etc. considered merely as *pictures* – beautiful objects to the eye'.[57] Poetic description for Twining is largely identified with the contemporary notion of 'picturesque' writing, which looks like landscape painting. Thus we can see how 'description' begins to be isolated as a separate category or aspect of poetry.

As an understanding of poetic language as primarily emotional and 'expressive' emerges, the favoured account of poetry as 'descriptive' becomes just one category among others. Thus the 'mimetic' account of poetic language, whilst it is slowly being ousted at a theoretical level, can be said to be preserved as a class of poetry, though inferior to the 'expressive' or 'lyric' class.

In this way, the notion of a 'descriptive' poetry is inconsistent with the 'expressive' aesthetic developed by Romantic writers. It would require a different account of poetic language. And this notion of 'descriptive' poetry also depends on a particular account of how painting works. It is on these two notions: of language in poetry as an imitation and of the pictorial or visual mode as naturally imitative and 'objective' that our concepts of what it is to be 'descriptive' rely. As late as 1805, Richard Payne Knight and other critics continued to battle with the principle of imitation, saying that 'sculpture, music, and poetry are all in their principles, as Addison has observed, imitative arts', but admitting at the same time that poetry's strength lies in its associative power, which enables it to generalize and select.[58]

What happens to these notions during the nineteenth century?

We might expect that a changing understanding of poetic language and of the way the arts relate might make it impossible to sustain this idea of a 'descriptive' poetry as a naive pictorialism. However, we have seen that such a concept does survive up to the present day. I now want to look at the kinds of belief about poetic language and about visual art which have encouraged us to continue to distinguish an 'expressive' poetic language, that nineteenth-century aesthetics establishes. I thus extend the critique of the 'descriptive/expressive' opposition, and show how a version of the pictorial analogy continues to support this opposition in nineteenth-century criticism.

NINETEENTH-CENTURY THEORIES OF POETIC LANGUAGE

In considering the background to Romantic theories of poetic language, we have to turn to the philosophy emerging on the Continent and particularly in Germany at the end of the eighteenth and at the beginning of the nineteenth century. Here, language had begun to be considered less as the vehicle for thought – a stable system of signs referring to things or ideas – than as a process, or *form*, with its own origins, history and character. So Culler tells us that:

Rejecting the link between language and mind, the nineteenth century lost interest in the word as a sign or representation. The word became a form which was to be compared with other forms so as to establish the relations between languages, or else a form whose historical evolution was to be traced.[59]

This trend is manifested in the popularity of studies of the origins of language, which emphasize the birth of speech as the expression of emotion and of sensuous experience.[60] Discussing Friedrich Schlegel's work of 1808, *On the language and wisdom of the Indians*, Culler defines the important transformation in attitudes to language that typifies Schlegel's approach – and that of Romantic thinkers like Rousseau, Herder and later, von Humboldt. He says that

language was now conceived as an object of knowledge, something which could be dissected or anatomized like a plant or an animal. No longer was it being studied as the form of thought itself, as a representation of the mind's relations to the world.[61]

Whereas empiricists such as Locke had seen language primarily as a means of communicating thought and thus considered the ways in which it could best carry out this task, the emphasis of a writer such as Rousseau will be on language's natural emergence. And whereas for Locke, figurative language is a distortion of rational language and the orderly relations between words and ideas, for expressivists: 'As man's first motives for speaking were his passions, his first expressions were tropes. Figurative language was the first to be born'.[62]

In this tradition stands Wilhelm von Humboldt, friend and correspondent of Schiller, the Schlegels and their circle, who 'applies the Kantian critique to the philosophy of language . . . Like cognition, language does not merely "copy" a given object; it rather embodies a spiritual attitude which is always a crucial factor in our perception of the objective',[63] and 'aims at nothing less than an analytic correlation of language and human experience'.[64] Given this background, it is hard to see how the Romantic critics and aestheticians could preserve or encourage distinctions between poetic language and 'ordinary' language, given that all language is understood as essentially *creative* and expressive.

However, Schiller's aesthetic involves an important differentiation between poetic language and the language of, for example, science. Discussing this view as Schiller expresses it in certain essays, Wilkinson and Willoughby explain how he insists that

the poet must . . . make 'the dead letter' of his abstract, generalizing, medium take on the breadth of individual life; . . . he first laments the barriers to full communion which are erected by speech, and then exhorts the poet to overcome them by engaging in a love-affair with language: exploiting its outward forms as a lover explores the body of his beloved.   (*AE*, Introduction, p. cvii)[65]

We have already seen how Schiller understands the role of art as that of restoring the sensuous to the rational, the concrete to the abstract and in this, poetic language must overcome the arbitrariness of words to make the poem 'natural' and organic. It must be substantial, bodily and present, overcoming the breach between the sensuous world and conventional signs by resembling a natural object. Clearly, this bodily or organic quality can only really be imagined if we think of language as a *whole*, not as a set of signs or a system. For non-arbitrary, 'natural' signs would be difficult to accept. Indeed, Todorov asks how we can accept this post-Kantian, Romantic view of language with a recognition that language is essentially a set of conventional signs, asking the question:

how are we to reconcile, in Lessing's thought or in that of his successors, from A. W. Schlegel to Jakobson, the observation that linguistic signs are arbitrary and the affirmation that poetry uses motivated signs?[66]

It is here that the idea of the poem as 'organic' whole comes in and helps to establish the idea of poetic language as different from ordinary language. The poem *as a whole* is what matters. From Kant's identification of the symbolic as a *presentational* kind of cognition, where we are given an illustration or example to clarify a concept — a kind of cognition distinct from discursive cognition (*CJ*, 59, pp. 197–198) — through Goethe and Schiller to the Schlegels and Coleridge, the notion of the 'symbol' as a unit of meaning which is in some way pictorial or plastic develops. Goethe writes to Schiller of his experience of perceiving objects as symbolical: 'eminent cases which, in characteristic variety, stand as the representatives of many others'[67] and, as the examples Todorov gives in his account of Goethe's theory of the symbol show, conceives of the latter as something sensuous, a unit of a representation, a picture, a significance: 'the symbol speaks to perception (along with intellection); the allegory in effect speaks to intellection alone'.[68] We see this kind of distinction in Coleridge, for whom, Swiatecka states in a discussion of his theory of the symbol, 'a symbol has the same genesis as an Idea, but is its outward, sensible complement.'[69] Thus, in *The statesman's manual*, Coleridge tells us that

by a symbol I mean, not a metaphor or allegory or any other figure of speech or form of fancy, but an actual and essential part of that, the whole of which it represents

and makes the same distinction as Schiller between a discursive and an intuitive or presentational understanding — which ultimately derives from Kant.[70] Whilst poetic language is ideally a union of subjective and objective, rational and sensuous, it is usually described as aspiring towards a natural or organic state. Coleridge says that he 'would endeavour to destroy the old antithesis of *Words & Things*, elevating, as it were, words into

Things, & Living Things too'.[71] This idea of the symbol — or the word — as an embodiment of meaning, which is itself living and organic, extends to the poem as a whole. Goethe tells us that the art-work must be like nature:

something that resembles her phenomena . . . the rival of nature, something spiritually organic . . . both natural and beyond nature.[72]

And A. W. Schlegel claims that: 'In the fine arts, as well as in the domain of nature — the supreme artist, all genuine forms are organical'.[73] We are led to think of poetry not as discourse, but as organic form: poetic language as something substantial: 'Poetry makes everything sensuously present', said Schiller.[74]

If, in Romantic critical theory, poetry imitates the *form* of nature rather than shadowing its appearances, what happens to the comparison of poetry with painting and the notion of a 'descriptive' poetry?

THE SISTER ARTS: PAINTING AND POETRY IN NINETEENTH-CENTURY CRITICISM

In principle, Romantic aesthetic is concerned with the underlying form of *all* the arts and not with the specifics of any. As Schiller says, of painting, poetry and music:

the greater the degree of excellence attained by a work in any of these three arts, the more . . . particular affinities will disappear; and it is an inevitable and natural consequence of their approach to perfection that the various arts . . . tend to become ever more like each other in their effect upon the psyche.   (*AE*, 22nd Letter, p. 155)

Because Schiller and his Romantic successors were primarily concerned with the structure of aesthetic experience and not with art-works as 'objects', the emphasis of their aesthetics is on the *form* or structure of each art as analogous. However, it is a necessary consequence of this view that whatever is formal, abstract and general about art should be emphasized at the expense of whatever is material, concrete and particular. And indeed, this form which underlies all art is identified as a 'poetic' principle which is really just imagination. All the arts are collapsed into a general account of this poetic or imaginative principle, so that for Friedrich Schlegel:

Every art and every discipline that functions through language . . .
appears as poetry. And every art or discipline which does not manifest
its nature through language possesses an invisible spirit: and that is
poetry.[75]

Schelling also insists that this spirit infuse the plastic arts:

Plastic art should . . . be a dumb poetry . . . should, like poetry, express
intellectual thoughts – conceptions whose origin is the soul only; not
by speech, but like silent nature, by shape, by form, by sensuous and
independent works . . . As plastic art has, indeed, its relation to the
soul, in common with poetry and all other arts, that relation in which it
stands to nature, and by which it should be a like creative power,
remains its peculiar character.[76]

Even whilst plastic art retains its 'presence' it is governed by the
imaginative, poetic principle: by subjectivity. Schiller complains
in a letter to Goethe of the extent to which this approximation of
all art to poetry has been adopted, asking

whether the tendency of so many talented *artists* of modern times *to
poetise in Art* is not to be explained by the fact that in a time like the
present, there is no passage to the aesthetic except through what is
poetic, and that consequently all artists, making any pretension to
genius, show poetic imagination even in plastic representations.[77]

The tendency to exalt poetry for its universal quality, its freedom
from the spatial and material hindrances to free form of plastic art
or painting can be said to climax in Hegel's hierarchy of the arts in
which

Poetry is the universal art of the spirit which has become free in itself
and which is not tied down for its realization to external sensuous
material.[78]

Poetry's

characteristic peculiarity lies in the power with which it subjects to
spirit and its ideas the sensuous element from which music and painting
began to make art free.[79]

Here, we have come a long way from Schiller's idea of art as giving
sensuous realization to the rational. Poetry liberates art from its
realization in an alien medium, so that signifier and signified,
form and matter, can be wrought from the same spiritual stuff.
  So the belief that painting is more sensuous, more material,

than poetry persists in the nineteenth century. Schiller's own point, in the essay *On the naive and sentimental in literature*, that

the strength of the ancient artist . . . consists in limitation, explains the high esteem which the visual art of ancient times enjoys over that of modern times and the entire unequal relationship with regard to value in which modern poetry and the modern visual arts stand to both artistic genres in ancient times. A work for the eye finds its perfection only in limitation. A work for the imagination can attain it also by means of the infinite   (*NS*, p. 41)

is typical of his Romantic successors, who tend to arrogate to *poetry* whatever is spiritual and unlimited about visual art.

But this view runs contrary to the belief, also expressed by Schiller, that poetry must *reconcile* the limited and the unlimited, the sensuous and the rational, and that its language must accordingly aspire to plasticity. Painting, whose comparative 'concreteness' in Romantic theory might have provided a model for poetry as it did at the beginning of the eighteenth century, is instead characterized as 'naive' to the poetic 'sentimental' as when, in later eighteenth-century criticism, pictorial or descriptive poetry was set against expressive poetry.

The crossroads at which these two different aesthetics meet is, it can be argued, Coleridge's aesthetic, for Coleridge inherits both the British and the German critical theory. And to a large extent both he and Hazlitt, who is particularly concerned with painting, continue to conceive of that art as less spiritual, less universal, than poetry. In the well-known *Notebook* entry, he exclaims:

The generic how superior to the particular illustrated in Music, how infinitely more perfect in passion & its transitions than even Poetry – Poetry than Painting[80]

placing painting at the bottom of the hierarchy of the arts, as they aspire to the immaterial. Hazlitt endorses this view, using 'poetical' in the Romantic sense of 'imaginative':

We may assume . . . that poetry is more poetical than painting . . . Painting gives the object itself; poetry what it implies. Painting embodies what a thing contains in itself: poetry suggests what exists out of it . . . But this last is the proper province of the imagination.[81]

We can see in the painting/poetry opposition, in which the last term includes and overwhelms the other as a general principle for

art, the naive/sentimental relation, in which the reconciliation of
naive and sentimental, objective and subjective, is at the expense
of the objectivity of the former. The imagination as Hazlitt sees it
is essentially poetic. And, like Burke, Coleridge also insists that
poetry, in being imaginative, is immaterial; the power of words is
their evocative, associative, elusive quality, not any sensuous
presentational or representational capacity:

what are deemed fine descriptions, produce their effects almost purely
by a charm of words, with which . . . we associate *feelings* indeed, but no
distinct *Images*.[82]

As Roy Park says of Coleridge, he 'deplored the influence of
painting on poetry' and

did not demand the object in all its vivid visual detail, but the object as
symbol − created not by observation alone, but by the union of
meditation and observation. It is in this sense that the early nineteenth
century would subscribe to Wordsworth's view that 'sight is . . . a sad
enemy to imagination'.[83]

Insisting that images taken from nature and accurately described
(see ch. 2, n. 29 above) are not adequate for poetry, Coleridge
suggests that there is a kind of poetry that simply does transcribe
nature and which does not achieve symbolic truth. This poetry is
more like painting:

The presence of genius is not shown in elaborating a picture: we have
had many specimens of this sort of work in modern poems, where all is
so dutchified, if I may use the word, by the most minute touches that
the reader naturally asks why words, and not painting, are used? . . .
The power of poetry is, by a single word perhaps, to instil energy into
the mind, which compels the imagination to produce the picture.[84]

Although he says that the imagination 'produces a picture',
Coleridge rejects pictorialism, criticizing the attention to detail of
Erasmus Darwin much as Clare was criticized by his
contemporaries:

Dr Darwin's Poetry . . . a succession of Landscapes or Paintings − it
arrests the attention too often, and so prevents the rapidity necessary to
pathos − it . . . makes the great little.[85]

Painting deals in particulars and so distracts from underlying
forms and from the formal harmony of art.

What Coleridge really isolates is a difference in subject-matter: he finds Darwin insufficiently general or philosophical. There is no intrinsic difference in Darwin's language: and we can see how problematic the idea of the 'symbol' as a distinguishing feature would be. For whilst poetry must be immaterial, the symbol has decidedly material overtones, even pictorial ones.

In a similar vein, Hazlitt condemns Crabbe for his specificity, his attention to detail, as though this were a stylistic trait. In fact it is a question of Hazlitt's sentimental dislike for Crabbe's choice of non-philosophical, insufficiently general or universal topics, a sense that poetry should be about grander things.

Painting is still considered by Hazlitt and Coleridge to be a more concrete, specific, material art and thus the pictorial analogy still works to illustrate what it is for poetry to be descriptive. But now, of course, this is considered a fault. However, we have seen that this descriptive category relies on the kinds of views about language and about visual art that go against the articulated aims of the Romantic aesthetic. In retaining this category, sentimental criticism retains a rejected aesthetic as the 'naive' against which it can determine its 'sentimental': the true Romantic poetry, the true Romantic aesthetic.

But what of the ideal of poetic language, not as abstract and universal, but as sensuously present? the belief that

it is art alone which can succeed in objectifying with universal validity what the philosopher is able to present in a merely subjective fashion.[86]

If we have inherited the descriptive/expressive categories, we have also inherited this view of poetic language which sees it as more corporeal and sensuous than non-poetic language. Nineteenth-century Symbolism, as Lee McKay Johnson explains, asks poetry to aspire to the corporeality, the full presence, of the painting, which *embodies* its meaning rather than referring to it:

The silent communication of painting, which radiates a complex of meaning which is perceived all at once, represents for Baudelaire the highest level of the imagination in operation . . . painting communicates a metaphysical sense directly and concretely, viscerally in fact.[87]

And in this century, too, Northrop Frye argues that:

In painting, sculpture, or music, it is easy enough to see that the art shows forth, but cannot *say* anything. And, whatever it sounds like to call the poet inarticulate or speechless, there is a most important sense in which poems are silent as statues. Poetry is a *disinterested* use of words: it does not address a reader directly.[88]

Here, the Romantic connection between the art-work as autonomous and the distinctive nature of aesthetic experience is made explicit. Unlike cognition, art is experiential, sensuous and immediate – not mental, rational and mediated. The poem – as urn or icon – is untranslatable in the way that we cannot translate words into things or vice versa.

This view of art, adopted by post-Romantic critics is tacitly present in Romantic aesthetics when it understands poetic language as sensuous, the organic poem as autonomous object. And, as Roy Park points out, as well as using an analogy with painting to criticize detail or specificity in poetry, both Hazlitt and Coleridge use it to suggest the *positive* quality of the symbol as the sensuous embodiment of spirit, as the involution of the general in the particular. Roy Park tells us that:

The growing emphasis on the individual and the minute discrimination of the particular were no longer seen as comprising the imaginative nature of art . . . In the transition from a theory of art as ideal to a theory of art as essentially individual, painting was literature's most potent ally.[89]

But nevertheless this understanding of painting as a positive model for poetry still aligns itself against 'descriptive' poetry. For it is 'symbolic', expressive poetry that unites the particular and the universal and embodies the ideal, whilst it is non-Romantic poetry that is comparatively prosaic and straightforwardly referential.

It seems, then, as though non-Romantic poetry can be characterized by a sentimental theory as either material (like painting) and so insufficiently spiritual and universal, or as not material enough (unlike painting) and so prosaic and unpoetic. Either way, it loses out.

CONCLUSION: PART I

So far, I have provided a critique of the way in which poetry has been constructed as 'naive' by sentimental critical theory and shown how the classification of poetry as 'descriptive' or in some way non-Romantic depends on the fostering, within a sentimental account of poetic language, of a *contradictory* account, so that those two accounts can be set against one another as the 'naive' and 'sentimental' categories for poetry. This is the sentimental model which we have already encountered.

It has become clear that the notion of this 'naive' poetry is very dependent on the analogy drawn by criticism between poetry and painting. First of all, 'naive' poetry was thought to work like painting and this accounts for its unpopularity when the mimetic principle associated above all with painting was rejected. For painting continued to be thought of as 'imitative', even after poetry was recognized as 'expressive'. Then, 'naive' poetry was shown to be inadequate when a revised version of the pictorial analogy enhanced the Romantic account of true, 'sentimental' poetic language as sensuous and presentational, an analogy that was to become more explicit in later criticism.

I now go on to criticize and re-evaluate the relationship between the arts as it has been conceived by literary criticism and in aesthetics in the past. By looking at formulations of this relationship in contemporary aesthetics, I scrutinize the analogy as it has rested (1) on a view of painting as 'natural' imitation or representation compared with poetry's conventional expression and (2) on a view of painting as sensuous, presentational form. In either case, painting is conceived as less mediated and more sensuous, than poetry. By dismantling these views of painting, it is possible to dismantle the basis on which the descriptive/expressive opposition rests.

II

PAINTING AS IMITATION OR NATURAL REPRESENTATION: THE EIGHTEENTH-CENTURY ANALOGY CRITICIZED

'There was a time', says E. H. Gombrich in his influential *Art and illusion*

when the methods of representation were the proper concern of the art critic. Accustomed as he was to judging contemporary works first of all by standards of representational accuracy, he had no doubt that this skill had progressed from rude beginnings to the perfection of illusion . . . It is one of the permanent gains we owe to the great artistic revolution which has swept across Europe in the first half of the twentieth century that we are rid of this type of aesthetics . . . Aesthetics has surrendered its claim to be concerned with the problem of convincing representation, the problem of illusion in art.[90]

Changed understanding of visual perception and an increased recognition of the role of interpretation and conceptual thought in the construction of the perceived world has, Gombrich tells us, made the old belief in an objective reality which can be copied, unacceptable. Listing some of the many new theories of perception which have emerged this century, Gombrich shows how these new perspectives render traditional accounts of representation inadequate:

The basic terms which critics, artists, and historians have hitherto used with confidence have lost much of their validity in this assessment. The whole idea of the 'imitation of nature', or 'idealization', or of 'abstraction' rests on the assumption that what comes first are 'sense impressions' that are subsequently elaborated, distorted, or generalized.
(*AI*, pp. 27–8)

Gombrich's study counteracts this inadequacy with an account of representation as a learning process. Towards the end of the book, he says:

In our study of the language of art we have come increasingly to stress one fact – the power of interpretation. We saw it at work in . . . the beholder's share in the readings of images, his capacity, that is, to collaborate with the artist and to transform a piece of coloured canvas into a likeness of the visible world . . . in . . . the artist who interpreted the world in terms of the schemata he made and knew. (*AI*, p. 291)

It is by a 'making and matching' learning process that representation develops and is put into practice, suggests Gombrich, and by testing and retesting, new methods are evolved:

More is needed than a rejection of tradition, more also than an innocent eye. Art itself becomes the innovator's instrument for probing reality. He cannot simply battle down that mental set which makes him see the motif in terms of known pictures; he must actively try that interpretation, but try it critically, varying here and there to see whether a better match could not be achieved. (*AI*, p. 324)

Seeing and knowing are not, Gombrich insists, opposed, as they have often been thought to be, but part of the same process of discovery and learning. Art, Gombrich concludes, is like a kind of language which must be stretched and manipulated but which also has rules which confine the user. In his final chapter, he makes a comparison between visual art and language, suggesting that 'there is more in common between the language of words and visual representation than we are sometimes prone to allow' (*AI*, pp. 361–2). Firstly, visual representation is no more 'natural' in its relation to the world than words – a painting of a sunlit landscape has little in common, in size, shape, dimensions, texture or colour with the real thing. From here, Gombrich goes on to argue that just as a writer or speaker can have a personal 'style', so an artist expresses his or her own subjectivity through the conventions of visual representation. At this point, Gombrich says, we can query that distinction itself:

With the question of personal style we have reached the frontier of what is usually called 'representation'. For in these ultimate constituents the artist is said to express himself. But is there really such a sharp division between representation and expression? The results of our last chapter have made us doubt it, and a comparison with language will confirm these doubts. For language, like the visual image, functions not only in the service of actual description and subjective emotion but also in that wide area between these extremes where everyday language conveys both the facts and the emotive tone of an experience.   (*AI*, p. 366)

Like language, then, art is both 'objective' and 'subjective', representative and expressive at once, but, Gombrich suggests, it is a more limited and restrictive language than that of words and sentences. However, he suggests, it is in these limitations that the strength of visual art lies, because it resists innovation and requires tenacious manipulation:

Where everything is possible and nothing unexpected, communication must break down. It is because art operates with a structured style governed by technique and the schemata of tradition that representation could become the instrument not only of information but also of expression.   (*AI*, p. 376)

We shall return to this concept of productive limitation with respect to poetry at a later stage. Here, Gombrich's conclusion that the artist works *through* familiar images to transparence:

In teaching us to see the visible world afresh, he gives us the illusion of looking into the invisible realms of the mind − if only we know, as Philostratus says, how to use our eyes   (*AI*, p. 389)

is sufficient in its reminder that representation is perhaps even more conventional than language, that it works even more fiercely against the grain of established practice and is even more limited than language. Gombrich's argument effectively overturns the traditional belief that visual representation, like perception, is 'natural'.

Gombrich's perspective is endorsed and expanded by later critics. The belief that visual representation involves conformity to social practices and conventions has been widely adopted. Barry Barnes, for instance, comments in *Interests and the growth of knowledge* (1977) that

In Gombrich, Ivins and similar work, we find an account of the construction of pictorial representations which serves admirably as an informal working model for the construction of knowledge. Pictorial representations are actively constructed from conventions available as the resources of some culture or sub-culture. The successful realisation of paintings, for example, depends on familiarity with existing paintings and illustrations and the conventions implicit in them. Such conventions are meaningful as words are meaningful, and are actively manipulated and organised in the light of particular aims or interests.[91]

Barnes goes on to say that

when a representation conveys knowledge . . . or information about, say, an object, it is by classifying it, by making it an instance of one or more kinds of entity recognised by the culture whose resources are drawn upon . . . Knowledge and object are connected by the representation.[92]

On this view, representations are

actively constructed assemblages of conventions or meaningful cultural resources, to be understood and assessed in terms of their role in activity. Essentially this amounts to making representations analogous to techniques, artistic conventions or other typical forms of culture, rather than considering them in terms of the contemplative conception.[93]

Under this view, we will no longer be concerned with the 'truth' or 'accuracy' of the art-work, but with art as a signifying process, a way of doing and saying something.

Richard Wollheim also says that art is an activity:

art is something we do . . . works of art things that human beings make . . . From the fact that art is something that we do, it follows that in the making of art a concept enters into, and plays a crucial role in, the determination of what is made . . . when we make a work of art, we make it under a certain description – though, of course . . . we may not be in a position to give the description.[94]

Certain concepts determine artistic practice – concepts of what art is – and it is in the relationship between these concepts and the art-works produced in accordance with them that Wollheim is partly interested: for example in the way in which the concept of modern art as *material* might explain such characteristics of modern art as its emphasis on texture and surface. Wollheim looks at art as a process of making in a particular medium and under certain cultural constraints. We can understand the art-work not in relation to what it represents, but in relation to the prevailing concept of what art ought to be.

In *Art and its objects* (1968), Wollheim discusses various hypotheses about the nature of art: that art-objects are physical objects, that they resemble things by virtue of representational properties, or that they express feelings by virtue of expressive properties, that they are mental entities, that they are formal entities of perceptible properties, and so on. Much of the argument revolves round the question of the extent to which art-works have been identified with or distinguished from physical objects with properties and structures.

The first section of the argument deals with these different hypotheses about art-objects, and presents the case against each. For instance, where representational properties such as resemblance are concerned, Willheim points out that

the concept of resemblance is notoriously elliptical, or . . . context-dependent: and it is hard to see how the resemblance that holds between a painting or drawing and that which it is of would be apparent, or could even be pointed out, to someone who was totally ignorant of the institution or practice of representation.[95]

A representation is not a resemblance but 'a visual sign, or reminder' of what it represents, and 'what counts as a representation of what . . . is a culturally determined matter' (Wollheim, pp. 20–1).

Considering the possibility of an art-work having 'expressive' properties, Wollheim similarly relates the notion of an expressive property to a pre-existing concept of what it is to be expressive. That is, just as the concept of what it is to represent and those objects or properties considered representative are mutually determining beliefs about art, so the concept of what it is to express both conditions and is conditioned by what we think are expressive works of art.

> For it is not at all clear that, in the cases where we attribute emotions to objects . . . we have any other way of talking about the objects themselves. There is not necessarily a prior description in non-emotive terms, on which we superimpose the emotive description . . . it is not always the case that things that we see as expressive, we can or could see in any other way. In such cases what we need is not a justification, but an explanation, of our language. (Wollheim, pp. 33–4)

What Wollheim seems to say is that asking *why* a picture represents or expresses something is as irrelevant as asking *why* the word 'sad' represents or expresses sadness. Taking a nominalist rather than an essentialist view, he points out that the picture is sad just because we call pictures of that kind sad, or because it is an example of sadness. This approach runs through the text, so that, for example, with reference to the 'Presentational' theory:

> we do wrong to pick on either the representation itself or the thing represented as providing us with the sure criterion of what properties we directly perceive. But this has not led us to postulate as that criterion some mental image of picture, which is then called the direct object of perception: as traditional theory generally does. If there is such a thing as a criterion of what we directly perceive, it rather looks as though it is to be found in what we would naturally say in response to an outer picture. But if this is so, then there seems little hope that we can, without circularity, define or identify the properties of a picture by reference to what we directly perceive. (Wollheim, p. 51)

His general position, then, is that art is determined in practice and in a context.

> In the first place, in the case of a work of art what the facts are is not something that can legitimately be demarcated . . . whole ranges of fact, previously unnoticed or dismissed as irrelevant, can suddenly be seen to pertain to the work of art. These transformations can occur in a variety of ways as a result of changes in criticism, or as the result of changes in the practice of art, or as a result of changes in the general intellectual environment. (Wollheim, p. 88)

If we consider the aesthetic attitude rather than the art-work, Wollheim goes on to say, we reach the same sort of conclusion — that it is not necessarily possible to define that attitude in terms of anything else, any more than a language could be explained away.

The point is not that there is nothing distinctive of the aesthetic attitude, but rather that there need not be any comprehensive way of referring to what is distinctive of it other than as the aesthetic attitude. In other words, we should regard Wittgenstein's argument as against what he takes to be a pervasive error in our thinking: that of identifying one phenomenon with another phenomenon more specific than it, or that of seeing everything as a diminished version of itself. (Wollheim, p. 96)

This Wittgensteinian approach is sustained through the argument. Wollheim goes on to consider Wittgenstein's phrase 'form of life', and to suggest that 'Art is, in Wittgenstein's sense, a form of life'. He goes on:

The phrase appears as descriptive or invocatory of the total context within which alone language can exist: the complex of habits, experiences, skills, with which language interlocks in that it could not be operated without them and, equally, they cannot be identified without reference to it. In particular Wittgenstein set himself against two false views of language. According to the first view, language consists essentially in names: names are connected unambiguously with objects, which they denote: and it is in virtue of this denoting relation that the words that we utter, whether to ourselves or out loud, are about things, that our speech and thought are 'of' the world. According to the second view, language in itself is a set of inert marks; in order to acquire a reference to things, what is needed are certain characteristic experiences on the part of the potential language-users, notably the experiences of meaning and . . . understanding: it is in virtue of these experiences that what we utter . . . is about the world. There are obviously considerable differences between these two views . . . [but they] also have something in common. For both presuppose that these experiences exist, and can be identified, quite separately from language . . . The characterization of language . . . as 'a form of life' is intended to dispute the separation on either level.

(Wollheim, pp. 104–5)

An account of painting, for example, as 'copying' things or 'expressing' experiences might derive from one of these discarded views of language as a separate vehicle for things or experiences. If we adopt Wittgenstein's account, whereby language itself is experience, a 'form of life', then we can give a different account of how painting works.

Wollheim goes on to point out that under this analogy with language it is mistaken either to try to separate art from the medium in which it occurs, or 'to postulate, of each work of art, a particular aesthetic intention or impulse which both accounts for that work and can be identified independently of it' (Wollheim, p. 110). We cannot say that there is something separate from the art-work which it expresses, nor that the medium in which that thing is expressed is arbitrary. Understanding art, moreover, is like understanding a language. Having made this comparison between art and language, Wollheim qualifies it, and points out its limitations. He is very definite about not making a simple equation between art and language (Wollheim, pp. 132–43).

He begins by dismissing the distinction between cognitive and aesthetic often brought up by critics who argue that art, unlike language, is non-cognitive, experiential or emotional. The distinction between language as simply communicative and art as simply expressive, like the division of language into two kinds, cognitive and aesthetic, rational and poetic, is rejected:

the theory that language is essentially concerned with the communication of ideas is a dogmatic notion, which does not even take account of the variety of ways in which ideas are communicated. However, the theory of the two uses of language (as in the critical theory of I. A. Richards) constitutes no real improvement on it, incorporating as it does the original error: for it would never have been necessary to postulate the poetic use if the account of the scientific use had not been taken over unexamined from the theory of the single use. (Wollheim, p. 137)

This again is significant in the critique of the previous uses of the pictorial analogy, and particularly the second, which relies on a distinction between two kinds of language. Wollheim goes on to qualify the comparison of art and language. Firstly, he says, literary arts are already in language: can they then be compared with it? This will not concern me here, since I am not attempting to define art in general, but to relate visual to verbal art. Secondly, he points out, language is more rule-bound than art and art is more ambiguous: both spectator and artist demand this.

It would therefore be quite alien to his purpose if there were rules in art which allowed him to construct works which could be unambiguously correlated with a 'meaning'. (Wollheim, p. 139)

However, it seems that it is possible to get round this objection by arguing, firstly that language can be used with different degrees of ambiguity in ordinary and poetic language and secondly that the difference between this language and that of visual art might just be ambiguity – that is what in some sense Nelson Goodman, whose work I shall turn to in a minute, suggests. There is no need to posit a difference of kind between ordinary and poetic language in order to claim that language is used differently, in the context of poetry.

Wollheim concludes by suggesting that there is 'some kind of scheme of reference, or framework, within which a work of art can be identified' (p. 146) and that art 'is essentially historical' (p. 151). That is, it is not simply socially determined, but determined with respect to its own history, the existence of concepts of what art might be.

The arguments put forward, for example, by Gombrich, and by Wollheim, seem sufficient refutation of the belief that art is imitative or natural representation. Both critics suggest that visual art might be more like language than we expect, in its social, historical, and conventional aspects, and both critics also suggest that it differs from language in specific ways. For Gombrich, the 'language' of visual art is more restricted, more tied to representation, than verbal language, and its strength is in pushing that limitation as far as possible in order to express individuality. For Wollheim, visual art – and, he suggests, poetry – differ from ordinary language in being more ambiguous, less rule-bound. Having thus put forward the case against 'ut pictura poesis' as a way of filling out the notion of 'description' as accurate representation, we can consider the second, more Romantic conception of the art – literature relationship.

PAINTING AS FORMAL UNITY AND SENSUOUS PRESENTATION OF MEANING: THE NINETEENTH-CENTURY ANALOGY CRITICIZED

Nineteenth-century critical thought tends to distinguish the aesthetic from the cognitive, following Kant, and to conceive of art as the sensuous presentation or embodiment of ideas, the filling-out of the rational skeleton with an instantaneously apprehended realization in sensuous form. The only way in which the difference between the aesthetic and the cognitive put forward by this critical trend is really conceivable, is in visual or plastic terms. The aesthetic is somehow patterned, formal, sensuous language, presentational language, language to be grasped and appreciated for itself, as a substance or an arrangement, a unity, rather than language as a vehicle pointing beyond itself to other things. Poetic language cannot be paraphrased, it is claimed, out of its specific presentation or realization in the particular poem. Thus Coleridge distinguishes the symbol from other tropes, which are extrinsic to what is being expressed, decorative, superfluous:

> by a symbol I mean, not a metaphor or allegory or any other figure of speech or form of fancy, but an actual and essential part of that, the whole of which it represents. Thus our Lord speaks symbolically when he says that 'the eye is the light of the body'.   (see n. 70 above)

The obvious answer to this is that 'the eye is the light of the body' *is* a metaphor, and language can never be paraphrased, is never anything but part of what it represents, in a general sense: this much has been said by the German theorists themselves. And the whole idea that there might be a language in which words were simply signs for an absent and separable reality has already been dismissed within philosophy of language. When Coleridge makes distinctions between Allegory as 'a translation of abstract notions into a picture-language which is itself nothing but an abstraction from the senses' and Symbol which 'always partakes of the reality which it renders intelligible'[96] he is guilty both of the typical sentimental transformation of contradictory accounts of language into alternative poetic categories, and also of drawing on the analogy of language with visual art in two different ways. For both the symbol and the allegory are effectively explained in visual terms, the allegory as a 'picture-language' in the eighteenth century sense, and the symbol as a visual unit embodying meaning, something that has spatial extension, that can be 'translucent'. It is in this latter sense that formalist accounts of poetry as object draw on the pictorial analogy. But what of accounts of painting that conceive of pictures as the sensuous realization of meaning? Could such an account of the way in which painting is apprehended, be defended?

Such views of art depend primarily on a distinction between

the cognitive and the aesthetic mode derived, ultimately, from Kant. As Roger Scruton says in *Art and imagination* (1974):

This is the theory which seeks to define the aesthetic attitude by contrasting it with scientific (cognitive) attitudes on the one hand, and with moral (practical) attitudes on the other . . . When I appreciate an aesthetic object, it is said, I am not interested in comparing it with objects of a similar kind: I have no concern to derive universal laws. Kant went further, insisting that in aesthetic judgment the object is not brought under concepts at all. Hence the faculty of appreciation is quite distinct from that of the pure understanding, and involves a sort of mental leap in which the individuality of an object is seized and made present to thought. This part of the theory survives, in an altered form . . . in the expressionism of Croce and Collingwood, with its celebrated contrast between intuition and conception.[97]

Scruton does not challenge the Kantian distinction between cognitive and aesthetic: indeed, it is on such a distinction that his own argument rests.

In *Art and imagination*, Scruton aims 'to sketch a theory of aesthetic judgment and appreciation in terms of an empiricist philosophy of mind' (Scruton, p. 1). That is, to fill out Kant's account of aesthetic experience as a distinct, autonomous kind of knowledge with an empirical account of the way in which the mental process involved differs from other mental processes. Thus he aims to give an empirical and epistemological, rather than a formal semantic or transcendental idealist, explanation of the aesthetic experience. Different mental states can be analysed 'in terms of their criteria, the observable states of affairs that warrant their application'. (Scruton, p. 9) He suggests that

we should be able to classify *some* mental activity as aesthetic appreciation, and . . . be able to analyse it so as to show its differences from and resemblances to, for example, practical and moral attitudes.
(Scruton, pp. 20–1)

What characterizes this mental activity? Scruton begins by insisting that

whatever aesthetic appraisal is, it must involve just that kind of interest in the *uniqueness* of an object which Kant and Croce, in their several ways, attempted to describe.   (Scruton, p. 22)

As it is this isolation of the aesthetic as a formal, unified experience that can be said to have generated the kind of idealist, formalist and structuralist views of literature that are in question here (for their sense of the poem as object, poetic language as self-referential, and so on), it is worth examining Scruton's argument briefly.

Two basic premises underlie his theory. The first is that there is such a thing as a 'non-descriptive' use of words.

> Our words as a whole can be used in a new way without a change of meaning. This might occur when I describe a dream: here the normal referential function of my words is, as it were, held in abeyance, but if what I say is to be understood then the words must have their normal meanings . . . words may be used with their standard meanings but out of context . . . because the point of using these words is here entirely different. (Scruton, pp. 49–50)

We might ask what the 'normal referential function' of words is. Scruton seems to combine a basic theory of words as having stable references with an additional theory whereby words acquire different meanings in different contexts. But the first theory is neither necessary, nor defensible. If I say 'I dreamt about Roger Scruton' and go on to describe my dream, there is no reason to suggest that the 'normal referential function' of those words is in abeyance, any more than if I said, 'I saw Roger Scruton on television' or 'I saw a documentary about Roger Scruton', or even 'I saw Roger Scruton in Oxford'. It is surely the understanding of the word 'dream', from having come across it before, that leads a listener to interpret the first sentence in a particular way. Scruton goes on to argue that when Wittgenstein, in *Philosophical investigations*, suggests describing Tuesday as lean and Wednesday as fat, he is using the words 'fat' and 'lean' in a special, extended way.

> Now Wittgenstein's example has much in common with certain kinds of aesthetic description – descriptions of the 'warmth' of a colour scheme, of the 'weight' of certain visual effects . . . of the 'heaviness' of a musical style . . . And clearly there is a continuum from this kind of description to the suggestive comparisons of criticism, as exemplified in Baudelaire's description of Chopin's music as 'un brillant oiseau voltigeant sur les horreurs d'un gouffre'. (Scruton, p. 51)[98]

Why should this be a special, aesthetic use of language? Even Locke pointed out that many abstract uses of words derive from what we call 'concrete' uses, as did Kant.[99] Why is the use of 'weight' to describe a concrete block more normal and standard than the use of 'weight' to describe an opinion, or an authority, or a piece of music? And even if we insist that there is a difference, it is surely impossible to draw an exact dividing line between the normal and the extended use. Although Scruton claims that there is a difference between the two ways of using a word, he insists that in both cases the word has the same meaning. So he implies that meaning is different from use — an unWittgensteinian conclusion. It seems that Scruton might be making the kind of mistake that the deconstructionists accuse philosophers of making: as Christopher Norris says in *The deconstructive turn*:

Philosophers like Locke and his latter-day positivist descendants devote a great deal of their thought to establishing a discourse of dependably logical and referential meaning such that philosophy can carry on its work undisturbed by the beguilements of rhetoric . . . Deconstruction . . . shows just how omnipresent and potentially disruptive are the effects of this 'buried' figural dimension.[100]

Scruton argues that he is not talking about a figural use of words. The whole point of saying that music is sad is that we know what *sad* normally means. But then, why make the distinction between the two uses at all? On what grounds is one more normal than the other?

The second premise, analogical to the above, is that there are two kinds of perception: seeing, and 'seeing as'. Again, the second term derives from Wittgenstein.[101] Basically, Scruton describes 'seeing as' as an imaginative, interpretative version of ordinary seeing.

To add imagination to seeing is to change it from seeing to 'seeing'. We have a new activity of the imagination . . . [which] has already been referred to as aspect perception, or 'seeing as'.   (Scruton, p. 108)

Again, Scruton begs questions in assuming that ordinary seeing does not involve the intentionality, the verbal aspect or the immediate knowledge that he ascribes to 'seeing as'. Quite the opposite has been argued, for example by N. R. Hanson in *Patterns of discovery*. Whilst he does not identify the two, Hanson makes it clear that they cannot be separated as straightforwardly as Scruton suggests:

Something of the concept of seeing can be discerned from tracing uses of 'seeing . . . as'. Wittgenstein is reluctant to concede this, but his reasons are not clear to me. On the contrary, the logic of 'seeing as' seems to illuminate the general perceptual case. Consider again the footprint in the sand. Here all the organizational features of *seeing as* stand out clearly, in the absence of an *'object'*. One can even imagine cases where 'He sees it as a footprint' would be a way of referring to another's apprehension of what actually is a footprint.[102]

He goes on to argue that seeing, like 'seeing as', involves both the visual and the verbal.

Seeing is, as I should almost like to say, an amalgam of the two – pictures and language. At the least, the concept of seeing embraces the concepts of visual sensation and knowledge.[103]

A similar case is argued by Rudolf Arnheim, who not only insists that seeing involves thinking, but that thinking involves seeing.

We assert not only that perceptual problems can be solved by perceptual operations but that productive thinking solves any kind of problem in the perceptual realm because there exists no other arena in which true thinking can take place.[104]

He explains how the process of visual structuring has two aspects, an *intuitive* and an *intellectual*, which together make up the picture.

The process of structuring, in which each element receives its character by taking its place in the whole, occurs to some extent below the level of consciousness. What the viewer 'sees' in the picture is already the outcome of that organizational process.[105]

Such theories militate against Scruton's distinction. However, it is on the basis of the two premises mentioned above that he develops his theory of imagination. For he concludes that

the relation between 'seeing as' and perception mirrors the relation between imagination and belief. 'Seeing as' is like an 'unasserted' visual experience: it is the embodiment of a thought which, if 'asserted' would amount to a genuine perception, just as imagination, if 'asserted' amounts to genuine belief. This point is very important, since . . . the 'unasserted' nature of 'seeing as' dictates the structure of aesthetic experience. (Scruton, p. 120)

It is difficult to see how 'seeing as', which after all involves interpretation and which is in fact an interpretative act, is 'unasserted'. Scruton would claim that when we see a picture of a man, we do not assert 'there is a man' because what we see is also a collection of lines and colours. But surely we assert, 'there is a picture of a man' and, when we see a real man, we also see a collection of shapes and colours. His argument really depends on the claim that we know we are looking at a picture, not a person, when we see a collection of lines on a page 'as' a man. But in what way is this different from seeing a collection of shapes as Roger Scruton? It seems that Scruton believes that in the first case, the physical or formal existence of the art-object can be separated from our interpretation of it 'as a man' and in the latter case, the two are one and there is no slippage between the two. But it is surely possible, particularly at a distance, that I might see Roger Scruton as something else?

From his analogy of aspect-perception and aesthetic experience, Scruton suggests that an aesthetic experience, like a perceptual experience, is 'sensuous' and that this sensuous experience is located in the aesthetic object.

in the case of the visual arts at least, the analysis given leads immediately to a connection with perceptual experience, and, therefore, explains in part why the connection of the aesthetic and the sensuous has so often seemed inevitable. The principal manifestation of aesthetic interest is attention to an object, which, since it cannot go beyond the object in the manner of practical or theoretical judgement, must come to rest in the perception of the object itself.   (Scruton, p. 154)

It has become clear that the view of perception on which this point is based can be criticized: the extent to which 'sensuous', 'cognitive' and 'emotional' experiences can be distinct in the way Scruton suggests is doubtful, at least where definitions are concerned. However, Scruton defends his view of art as experience and largely 'sensuous' experience, against the challenge of cognitive theories of art.

He begins by attacking the possibility that art is like a language, and that we understand it as a system of signs. Language, he insists, 'is bound by truth, and by the requirements of truthful expression', whilst 'there is nothing (besides itself) that music means'. (Scruton, p. 169). In other words, language means, or refers, whilst music just is. Without going into what Scruton means by saying that language is bound by truth and logic, we can question this distinction between language as semantic and music as non-semantic by looking at Scruton's account of what music *is*.

Music, he says, is not something that can be conceptually taught or explained and yet understanding it involves being able to detect or follow certain patterns.

> Musical understanding involves, then, the sense of rational development. Phrases and notes are felt to connect with each other in various ways . . . The principal point to grasp . . . is that the capacity to understand music in this sense is an auditory capacity: it is a matter of being able to hear certain things. It is not a matter of being acquainted with a body of principles or rules.   (Scruton, p. 171)

And yet, as Scruton acknowledges, it is only if we are acquainted with the background of music, if we are musically 'educated', that we can appreciate the patterns he identifies with what we understand in music.

> What is most important in music is clearly the way in which an intellectual grasp of structure and meaning can . . . become part of an auditory experience.   (Scruton, p. 180)

He concludes that music is 'hearing as', a process whereby our identification of pattern and structure becomes 'embodied' in the experience of music itself. In other words, it is an 'interpretative experience' such that,

> the thought itself can never be fully specified independently of the 'perception' in which it is embodied. We can now see that there are cases – the hearing of melodies and the seeing of patterns – where the element of thought has been reduced to something entirely formal. There is no way of achieving even a partial description of the *content* of the musical thought: we can only point once more to the experience in which it is 'embodied'.   (Scruton, pp. 180–1)

What he seems to be saying is that we learn to interpret sounds as patterns or to organize them in particular ways, according to certain rules and in the context of a familiarity with music as a practice. These patterns cannot be explained in words or paraphrased out of the medium in which we apprehend them. This is what Scruton calls a 'perceptual thought', reminding us of Kant's and Schiller's 'presentational' thought.

We have, then, taken the idea of a perceptual thought well beyond the point at which it could even be indicated apart from a perception. And what is interesting is that such thought-impregnated perceptions seem to lie at the heart of our understanding of art. It is because we can see patterns and figures that we can see representation in painting, and it is because we can hear melodies and sequences that we can hear expression in music.   (Scruton, p. 181)

Apart from its failure to deal with the role of the creator or crafting process, this account is lacking in that it seems to be tautologous and to say little more than that music is an auditory medium. The fact that it cannot be translated into verbal rules or concepts is not surprising: translating philosophy into music would be equally problematic.

When it comes to literature, Scruton's account of art as experiential becomes more complicated.

The sensuous element in the appreciation of literature is far less easy to locate. It is arguable, nonetheless, that there must be a sensuous element: for my interest in a work of literature is by no means an interest in its paraphrase; it cannot, therefore, be an interest merely in what the poem or novel *says*.   (Scruton, p. 155)

He picks this point up, saying that

to understand a poem is not to understand what it literally means: Blake's poem *The Sick Rose* expresses a thought that could be grasped by anyone with a knowledge of the language whether or not he understood it as a poem.   (Scruton, p. 183)

The distinction between understanding what a poem says, and understanding it 'as a poem' is the old distinction between 'standard reference' and a special, contextualized or extended meaning. But what exactly this special meaning is, is still not clear, even to Scruton. He suggests that poetry has a special form, a kind of grouping of words, but has to admit that

although the appreciation of poetry is, like the appreciation of all the arts, essentially perceptual, we see that its relation to sense is at once more subtle and more abstract than that of the other arts.
                                                          (Scruton, p. 186)

We might ask whether the differentiation of the two kinds of meaning is very useful. Certainly, music is sensuous, like taste, but is it useful to say that our understanding of it is sensuous, or experiential? And where literature is concerned, the purpose of the notion of 'perceptual thought' seems even more superfluous.

But Scruton defends his position, attacking 'semantic' explanations of art, like that of Nelson Goodman, which I shall be considering. He concludes that:

In arguing that appreciation is not primarily cognitive I have intended to maintain that the aesthetic attitude is not one of discovery, and its end point not the knowledge of facts, whether about the work of art or about the world to which it 'refers'. No cognitive theory of aesthetic experience can explain why one should desire to listen to a symphony again.   (Scruton, p. 226)

Finally:

What the subject learns from the painting – what the painting ‘brings home to him’ – is something that he learns in the *experience* of the painting, and only in that experience . . . This suggestion corresponds to the Hegelian (and to some extent Kantian) theory that a work of art has expression through being the 'sensuous embodiment' of an idea . . . It is the look of the picture that provides the elaboration of my thought.
                                                                        (Scruton, p. 236)

Scruton acknowledges that understanding or learning *is* part of aesthetic experience, but tends to suggest that the sensuous object is simply the occasion for our interpretations rather than explain how it is constructed or conceived. Moreover, he does not really give an account of the way in which that understanding can be embodied or sensuous, except inasmuch as the medium of the art-work is itself sensuous.

The central problem with the Kantian aesthetic and its adoption by the post-Kantian thinkers is, as Scruton's aesthetic illustrates, the implementation of a distinction between cognitive and aesthetic modes. Scruton is determined to separate out states of mind and to distinguish them in an empirical fashion. He differentiates literal and figurative, seeing and thinking, belief and imagination and so on. But such discriminations have a tendency to collapse, as the 'subjective' can always be revealed in the 'objective' partner.

However, criticism has widely adopted the notion of a distinctive, poetic language and Scruton's aesthetic shows just how the analogy with painting (and music, in his case) helps to reinforce the conception of poetry, allied with the other arts, as a more sensuous or embodied kind of thinking. Even if we were to accept this description of music or painting, it becomes difficult, as Scruton says, to show just how poetry might be sensuous, self-referential and non-cognitive.

PAINTING AS SYMBOL SYSTEM: NELSON GOODMAN

I now want to consider a third, alternative account of the relationship between poetry and painting, which has quite different consequences for criticism.

Part of the problem with Scruton's account of art is his belief about language. At least where criticism is concerned, the view that language has 'standard' and 'extended' uses, in the sense discussed above, is inappropriate in a contemporary context. Nelson Goodman, however, stands in a different tradition from Scruton and offers an aesthetic based on a very different view of the way language works: part of what Richard Rorty calls the 'post-philosophical' trend; pragmatic and anti-metaphysical.[106] Goodman would not claim to define truth, art or the imagination but offers instead an account, much closer to Gombrich's or Wollheim's, of the practices, context and conditions for the production of art-works. I turn now to his *Languages of art* (see Introduction, vi, 1–5).

This book is, Goodman explains, 'an approach to a general theory of symbols' (Goodman, p. xi) and is characterized by its breaking down of the distinction between 'literal' and 'figurative' which is usually central to such theories.

'Symbol' is used here as a very general and colorless term. It covers letters, words, texts, pictures, diagrams, maps, models, and more, but carries no implication of the oblique or the occult. The most literal portrait and the most prosaic passage are as much symbols, and as 'highly symbolic' as the most fanciful and figurative.

(Goodman, p. xi)

As Scruton says, Goodman 'refuses to acknowledge a clear distinction between cognitive and non-cognitive states of mind' (Scruton, p. 189). This is as much the mainstay of Goodman's aesthetic, as the opposite is of Scruton's.

In the first section of *Languages of art*, Goodman considers the problem of 'representation' and its habitual association with concepts of 'copying' or 'imitation'. Demystifying the possibility of a picture or sculpture really looking like what it represents, Goodman examines the conventions whereby we come to think of a representation as 'realistic'. He concludes that

a picture, to represent an object, must be a symbol for it, stand for it, refer to it . . . no degree of resemblance is sufficient to establish the requisite relationship of reference . . . A picture that represents – like a passage that describes – an object refers to and, more particularly, *denotes* it. Denotation is the core of representation and is independent of resemblance. (Goodman, p. 5)

In this way, representation is like description, in that:

Reference to an object is a necessary condition for depiction or description of it, but no degree of resemblance is a necessary or sufficient condition for either. Both depiction and description participate in the formation and characterization of the world; and they interact with each other and with perception and knowledge. They are ways of classifying by means of labels having singular or multiple or null reference. (Goodman, p. 40)

The way in which either a description or a representation relates to what it denotes is variable and flexible: there are many ways of representing something, many kinds of pictures of the same thing. In this first section, then, Goodman concludes:

What we have done so far is to subsume representation with description under denotation. Representation is thus disengaged from perverted ideas of it as an idiosyncratic physical process like mirroring . . . Furthermore, representation is thus contrasted with non-denotative modes of reference. (Goodman, pp. 42–3)

(An example of the latter would be a picture of something that did not exist, a picture with no specific referent.)

In his second section, Goodman considers 'expression' and how it might differ from 'representation'. Expression, he suggests, seems less 'literal' than representation, in that 'the feeling or emotion or property expressed is remote from the medium of expression: a painting may express heat, a musical composition may express color or fragility' (Goodman, p. 46). And, moreover, expression seems more 'direct and immediate' (Goodman, p. 47) than representation. 'Expression, then, can be tentatively and partially characterized as involving figurative possession' (Goodman, p. 51). He then clarifies this suggestion, refining the notion of 'possession' into that of 'exemplification', which is 'possession plus reference' in the sense that a tailor's sample 'exemplifies only those properties that it both has and refers to' (Goodman, p. 53). That is, within the tailor's system it doesn't refer to the weight of the whole bolt of cloth, or when it was manufactured, but to its weave, colour and so forth. Having defined exemplification, Goodman goes on to reach a definition of 'expression'.

What is expressed is metaphorically exemplified. What expresses sadness is metaphorically sad. And what is metaphorically sad is actually but not literally sad, i.e. comes under a transferred application of some label coextensive with 'sad'.   (Goodman, p. 85)

Thus a painting does not express pictorial qualities, such as size or colour, but qualities which within a system are 'constant relative to those properties', such as, for example, sadness relative to being blue. A picture is determined as a picture within a system of properties considered pictorial, which it exemplifies, and as an expressive work in a system of properties metaphorically associable with those pictorial properties.

Thus expression, like representation, is a symbolizing process and one that can apply to the verbal as well as to the visual arts. Goodman's account makes quite certain that we distinguish the 'sensuous' – or what might be thought of as sensuous – properties of the art-work (such as its weight or colour) from those we are interested in *qua* art-work, such as sadness. The relationship between them is one of convention, metaphorical convention.

What, then, of the relationship between the arts? So far, it has seemed as though representation is just like description and that both arts can express in the same way. For example

a passage or picture may exemplify or express . . . without being a description or representation at all – as in the case of some passages from James Joyce and some drawings from Kandinsky.   (Goodman, p. 92)

If both representation and description, visual and verbal art, are symbol systems, then, suggests Goodman, they can be distinguished as such.

In the third section of the text, he points out one obvious difference between the arts. This is the distinction between what he calls an 'autographic' and an 'allographic' art, where the former is an art whose works cannot be reproduced without loss of value and the latter an art where they can. Painting is autographic, because a reproduction is not the same as an original, whereas writing is allographic, because there is no concept of the work (*qua* work) as original: many copies can be produced. Music is also allographic. In the fourth section, he attempts to account for this distinction with a 'theory of notation', and in the fifth he applies this theory to the arts. To summarize: to account for this difference between 'autographic' or original works and 'allographic' or copiable works, Goodman looks at the symbol systems within which they are respectively constructed. If we take a musical work we can extrapolate from the individual performance(s) a *score* or notational system which is a syntactically and semantically *determinate* and *unambiguous* language with highly articulated characters. This means that the score can be used to generate identical – for our purposes – performances. In the case of a poem, the *script* does not generate instances or performances, but is identified with the work itself. However, it exists within a language, which, whilst it is semantically ambiguous, has determinate syntactic rules. By contrast, a painting has neither score, nor script: it does not exist within a notational system, scheme or language. The work is not generated by any identifiable and separable system, of which it is an instance and to whose rules it conforms. Thus, we have seen that

a musical score is in a notation and defines a work; that a sketch or picture is not in a notation but is itself a work; and that a literary script is both in a notation and is itself a work. Thus in the different arts a work is differently localized. In painting, the work is an individual object . . . In music, the work is the class of performances compliant with a character. In literature, the work is the character itself.   (Goodman, p. 210)

The arts can thus be differentiated according to whether the artwork concerned is in a notational system, and if so, whether the 'character' in that notational system is identified with the work itself or not.

In the concluding chapter, Goodman explains the significance of this distinction between the different symbol systems of the arts, and in particular, the way in which it affects traditional understanding of what 'representation' is.

The respective symbol systems within which art works, poems and so on are constructed explain the differences between those works. Whereas the symbol system of music is highly 'articulate': determinate, syntactically and semantically in that each character has a very definite and unambiguous reference and 'grammatical' function, language is semantically more ambiguous and less articulate in that one word can mean different things. But it is syntactically articulate; it has a clear grammar. Where painting is concerned, the symbol system is very inarticulate or 'dense' in that its characters are not determinate or defined either syntactically or semantically. We cannot distinguish individual 'characters' or a 'grammar' for painting in the way that we can for music and for language. Characters in an articulate symbol system are clearly differentiated, refer in a determinate or predictable way and are governed by definite rules. It is not the intrinsic nature of a character but the degree or articulacy of the symbol system to which it belongs that decides whether it is representational or not.

Nonlinguistic systems differ from languages, depiction from description, the representational from the verbal, paintings from poems, primarily through lack of differentiation – indeed through density (and consequent total absence of articulation) of the symbol system. Nothing is intrinsically a representation; status as representation is relative to the symbol system. A picture in one system may be a description in another; and whether a denoting symbol is representational or not depends not upon whether it resembles what it denotes but upon its own relationships to other symbols in a given system. A system is representational only insofar as it is dense; and a symbol is a representation only if it belongs to a system dense throughout or to a dense part of a partially dense system. Such a symbol may be a representation even if it denotes nothing at all.   (Goodman, p. 226)

The consequences of this account are dramatic and their effect on art criticism far-reaching. Paintings are not different from writing because they resemble what they represent, or because they are more sensuous or experiential or immediate, but because they occur as instances within a *dense* rather than an *articulate* symbol system.

Descriptions are distinguished from depictions not through being more arbitrary but through belonging to articulate rather than to dense schemes; and words are more conventional than pictures only if conventionality is construed in terms of differentiation rather than of artificiality. Nothing here depends upon the internal structure of a symbol; for what describes in some systems may depict in others.
                                        (Goodman, p. 230)

For example: a Chinese character that 'looks like' a house: it can be either a character in a language or a picture in its own right. Its internal characteristics are then irrelevant.

   Consequently, 'we have to read the painting as well as the poem' (p. 24) and, presumably, revise the common belief that aesthetic experience is passive recipience, sense-experience. One of the reasons for the persistence of this kind of belief about art, Goodman suggests, is the domineering dichotomy between the cognitive and the emotive. On the one side, we put sensation, perception, inference, conjecture, all nerveless inspection and investigation, fact and truth; on the other, pleasure, pain, interest, satisfaction, disappointment, all brainless affective response . . . This pretty effectively keeps us from seeing that in aesthetic experience the *emotions function cognitively* . . . Cognitive use involves discriminating and relating them in order to gauge and grasp the work and integrate it with the rest of our experience and the world.

(Goodman, pp. 247–8)

Aesthetic experience, Goodman concludes, 'is cognitive experience distinguished by the dominance of certain symbolic characteristics and judged by standards of cognitive efficacy' (Goodman, p. 262): this does not exclude, but exploits and involves the emotions.

'Density', the characteristic which distinguishes the different symbol systems of the arts may, Goodman proposes, also be taken as a characteristic of the aesthetic: semantic density, syntactic density and what he calls 'syntactic repleteness'. For:

As we have seen, syntactic density is characteristic of nonlinguistic systems, and is one feature distinguishing sketches and scripts from scores; and relative syntactic repleteness distinguishes the more representational among semantically dense systems from the more diagrammatic, the less from the more 'schematic.' All three features call for maximum sensitivity of discrimination.   (Goodman, p. 252)

This will mean that, in general, the plastic and visual arts are more 'aesthetic' than the verbal arts: for example, a painting is more 'aesthetic' than a diagram, and so on. But the classification is to be flexible:

Classification of a totality as aesthetic or nonaesthetic counts for less than identification of its aesthetic and nonaesthetic aspects.

(Goodman, p. 255)

The other characteristic of the aesthetic is 'exemplification' which, Goodman points out, demystifies 'immediacy' just as 'density' demystifies 'ineffability' in talk about the arts, explaining our ideas about art 'showing' rather than 'saying' as a relationship between a label and a sample, no closer, but different in direction, from that between a label and what it denotes.

Languages of art deftly cuts through the kinds of problems which have been encountered in literary criticism, relating to the 'representational' or 'expressive' character of art-works. Expression is not more intimately sensuous than representation; it is just a different kind of relationship between symbol, thing and label:

Representation and description relate a symbol to things it applies to. Exemplification relates the symbol to a label that denotes it, and hence indirectly to the things . . . in the range of that label. Expression relates the symbol to a label that metaphorically denotes it, and hence indirectly not only to the given metaphorical but also to the literal range of that label.   (Goodman, p. 92)

Representation, moreover, is nothing to do with likeness, but is, like description, a kind of denotation. This clarification of the process involved in the making and interpretation of art, together with the conclusion that each art works through cognitively apprehended symbols, goes a long way towards demolishing accepted beliefs about the difference between the arts and about the sensuous, non-cognitive nature of art in general.

This revised view of the relationship between painting and literature clearly militates against the possibility of there being in literary criticism a category of poetry called 'descriptive', where 'descriptive' equals 'representational' in the old sense of naturalistic, imitative or realistic, and where 'descriptive' is opposed to 'expressive'. For Goodman turns the comparison between 'description' and 'representation' around to tell us that the latter is like the former in that both are based, not on copying, but on denotation. Nor does a painting or a poem *either* denote *or* express. A sad painting of Roger Scruton would denote him, but express sadness; similarly a sad poem about Nelson Goodman. So Goodman's argument does not rely on the usual oppositions: natural–conventional, cognitive–aesthetic, literal–figurative and in many ways it breaks down beliefs about the way in which the two arts differ. This in turn is an attack on many beliefs about the way in which kinds of poetry can differ since these have been shown to depend on similar beliefs about the nature of language and the difference between visual and verbal modes.

However, Goodman does provide an explanation for the way in which the arts differ and in so doing, creates the possibility of a new version of the 'ut pictura poesis', a new concept of what it might be for poetry to be 'pictorial'. Or, to put it another way, a new way of explaining those characteristics of, for instance,

Clare's poetry which have in the past been called 'pictorial'. For although such a comparison may seem difficult, Goodman has made it clear that there is no definite boundary between the arts: what is a representation in one symbol system can be a description in another. Density is a relative, not an absolute characteristic and as such does not clearly limit the different arts.

DENSITY AND NAIVETÉ: A POSSIBLE ANALOGY

Accepting Goodman's account of the relationship between the arts means rejecting accounts of naive poetry that rely in one way or another on the pictorial analogy. We cannot compare painting with poetry on the grounds that it is imitative, objective or sensuously presentational. However, although both arts are cognitive symbol systems, they can be compared and they are different.

For according to Goodman painting is more 'dense' than poetry. Density is a relative quality with respect to the symbol system within which an art-work occurs or is constructed: it does not tell us anything intrinsic about the art-work itself. It only tells us that we cannot extract from the particular art-work a notational system which would explain that particular work. The dense work is thus resistant to abstract systematizing. An articulate work, one which is 'allographic' rather than 'autographic', is one which occurs in an articulate symbol system, such as language, where each character is distinct and determinate enough for us to be able to extrapolate the system from the work.

Now, it seems that Goodman's understanding of the relationship between the arts might be helpful in reformulating the existing relationship between the 'naive' and the 'sentimental'. For his 'dense/articulate' distinction is one of *degree*, not *kind*: it tells us nothing about the work itself, only about its relationship to a system – and thus to other works and systems. This means that we might adopt his position and ask the question: how, in the context of aesthetics or literary theory, might a particular text be 'dense' or 'articulate'? That is, how might some texts seem dense to a critical reader and others seem articulate? What we would effectively be asking would be: to what extent can we provide a system such that the poem is an instance of that system and to what extent is the poem intractable with respect to systematizing?

Clearly, the critical conventions and habits that surround such questions are similar to those surrounding art or literature in general – whether a poem is tractable or not will be to a certain extent a function of what that system demands and expects.

In other words, this is partly a question about a poem's approximation to a critical system, and as such can be construed in many ways. 'Is the poem "articulate" with respect to the system?' might mean: is it standard English? or, again, can it be read to be about the kinds of things we are interested in, without difficulty? An 'autographic' or dense poem will resist critical elaboration not because it is simple or difficult, but because it resists that particular system. For example, a poem entitled 'Badger' which refers to the habits of the badger and which is written in dialect could be described as 'dense' with respect to a practical critical system, but not to a badger-expert from the region of the dialect. A poem would thus be dense because it occurred within a particular system. We can now see that a 'naive' poem can be described as a poem which is 'dense' with respect to sentimental critical systems. This is partly historical, partly to do with changing interests. Sentimental critical systems are essentially idealist and will find articulate or systematizable those poems which can be construed as idealist or which produce idealist readings.

Now, this is only a question of degree: nothing militates against reading the badger-poem as a poem about the subject–object relationship, but it is less amenable to that reading than, for example, *The Prelude*. This may be nothing more than habit, but given that words refer, we can argue that the two poems are about different things and that different critical theories have different things at stake.

This may seem to say little that is new, but the advantage of introducing this concept of 'density' – albeit a cautiously relative one – is that it will help to avoid the polarization, which is so value-laden, of such poets as Clare and Wordsworth. At the same time it offers some explanation of why they are different. And it is worth noting that Goodman provides an antidote to our sentimental values when he suggests that 'density' is one of the distinctive features of the aesthetic: a demystified version of the 'ineffability' of art.

It is with this in mind that I offer a reading of Clare in my last chapter. For with this in mind, it can be argued that Clare's poetry, usually diminished by critical accounts which construct his work as moving teleologically towards a Wordsworthian sentimentalism and away from naiveté is, in its naiveté – or what we can now call *density* – no less to be valued than Wordsworth's and perhaps more so, if we value resistance.

This reading of Clare as *dense* can be seen to coincide with what John Barrell said in praise – and others in criticism – about Clare's resistance to convention and about his insistence on writing about specifics rather than about universal topics. It is easy to see how this would make him 'dense' for a sentimental system, as would his literal inarticulacy.

Seeing Clare's poetry as 'dense' allows us to review his work which, because we are so accustomed to sentimental standards and methods, we have found it hard to approach. It allows us to stop characterizing him as 'naive' in relation to the sentimental aesthetic.

CONCLUSION

This chapter shows how the pictorial analogy in literary criticism was used by both eighteenth-century and nineteenth-century critics to bolster the belief that there could be a kind of poetry which simply and directly represented the external world. Whilst pre-Kantian aesthetics tended to use this analogy positively for *all* poetry to show that poetry, like painting, can represent the world, post-Kantian aesthetics rejects the notion of simply mimetic poetry and sets it against an expressive true poetry, which is illustrated again by the pictorial analogy. This time painting suggests a special, sensuous, presentational language which characterizes true poetry. Idealist aesthetics still takes this view of poetic language and opposes it to the straightforward, prosaic language which relates directly and one-to-one with the world.

After criticizing the grounds on which criticism has compared poetry to painting to the disadvantage of certain kinds of poetry and notably to that of poets such as Clare, an alternative analogy was sought. Borrowing Nelson Goodman's theory of the arts as symbol systems which are more or less *dense* than each other and more or less susceptible to articulate notation which can account for individual art-works, I suggested that Clare's poetry could, on the pictorial analogy, be described as more 'dense' than that of Wordsworth. 'Density' does not imply a different use of language in general or a different poetic consciousness, but non-susceptibility to a particular kind of systematizing. It may be possible to pin it down to details: of vocabulary, register and so on, but it is strictly a question of specificity of reference: of reference limited by context so as to make the poem intractable for a critical system in search of general, structural readings of the kind demanded by sentimental aesthetics.

In my next chapter I shall expand this point, looking at the way in which sentimental aesthetics from Schiller onwards demands a particular kind of reading or is interested in particular aspects of poetry to the exclusion of others. This sentimentalism, I suggest, characterizes post-structural as well as post-Kantian aesthetics, and explains the difficulty criticism has in accepting a poet such as Clare, whilst accommodating an 'articulate' poet such as Wordsworth. Is it possible, I ask, for an aesthetic to avoid not only the traps of pre-Kantian thought, but also those of post-Kantian sentimentalism? That is, can an aesthetic and a criticism be provided, that will supply readings of texts as naive in the sense outlined above? Can the 'descriptive', or referential aspect of poetry be accounted for without criticism slipping into banality or into constructions of poems as unselfconscious and straightforward transcriptions of reality? On the other hand, can this 'naive' aspect of texts be explained or accounted for at all without the slippage into sentimentalism whereby all specific reference is undermined and revealed as covertly other than it seemed? and whereby all descriptions of badgers are really only descriptions of aesthetics?

5

POST-KANTIANS AND POST-STRUCTURALISTS

OVERVIEW

In this chapter, I argue that post-structuralist critical theory conforms to the model of a 'sentimental' aesthetic described in my first chapter. Post-structuralism can be described as an exaggerated and contemporary version of post-Kantian sentimentalism: a point put by Richard Rorty in a different way.[1] This explains why contemporary criticism emphasizes the relative, self-referential, unstable, processual aspect of texts at the expense of the determinate, referential, stable, productive aspect, and why it gives no account of what is specific about a text, what it is about and what differentiates it from another.

Post-structuralist theory can be said to set up these aspects of a text as a 'naive' which is at once preserved as a means of articulating a radical sentimentalism and collapsed into that sentimentalism. In a sentimental theory, the naive is always only a pseudo-object: an apparently stable, autonomous entity which is then revealed to be subjective process and flux. In this way, a 'text' works like the Romantic 'organic' system: an objectification of a creative process which is then revealed as boundless process.

In this chapter, I consider Derrida's post-structuralist reading of the *Critique of judgment*,[2] and argue that Kant's insight into the subjectivity of aesthetic judgments, whilst it is controlled within his own aesthetic, gives way to an uncontained relativism in that of his successors. Whereas Kant had contained his aesthetic within a wider Critique and ensured that judgment played not only a 'reflective' role in the third, but a 'determinant' role in the first Critique, it is the 'reflective' or aesthetic aspect of judgment

163

alone that is taken up by his successors. From the Romantics onwards, increasing emphasis is placed on the relativism of aesthetic judgments, and the art object is increasingly collapsed into the subjective process of apprehending or constructing it. Eventually, the only account of art that we have is of a highly subjective aesthetic process, which has no way of discriminating between art works, or describing them.

But, I argue, we need to be able not only to show our post-Kantian awareness of the way in which texts are *relative* to contexts, but our naive awareness that contexts *determine* texts. And, I suggest, Kant employs just such a 'double' methodology in his Critique. Although essentially 'subjective' because it excludes the absolute and only discusses knowledge *as we know it*, his system successfully sustains countless internal discriminations between objective and subjective, absolute and relative. Judgment, for instance, can be either *determinant* – that is, constitutive of what we see as external reality – or *reflective* – that is, constitutive of internal reality. Reflective judgment in turn can be either *teleological* (externally or objectively purposive) or *aesthetic* (internally or subjectively purposive). In both these (and many other) cases, the same faculty can be applied *externally* or *internally, constitutively* or *regulatively*. This brings us back to my earlier argument about 'dense' or 'articulate' readings. These terms describe the way texts are read with respect to a critical system. A text read as relative to a system is 'articulate'; a text read as determined by a system is 'dense'. This gives us a new rationale for the distinction between, for instance, Clare and Wordsworth. In accordance with this rationale, I go on in my next chapter to give a reading of Clare as 'dense' which draws on his positioning with respect to a critical system as well as on the way in which his work is biographically, contextually and referentially determined.

PROBLEMS OF SENTIMENTAL AESTHETICS: SCHILLER AND AFTER

In the *Essay on the naive and sentimental in literature*, Schiller describes the dangers of abstraction to which the sentimental tendency is prey:

The sentimental genius . . . is exposed to the danger of removing all barriers, of suspending human nature completely, and of *idealising* or elevating himself, not merely, which is right and proper, above every particular, and limited reality to the absolute possibility, but of going on outside possibility itself or of *indulging in visionary ravings*.

(NS, p. 72)

It is for this kind of abstraction and imaginative self-indulgence that the idealist philosophers have been taken to task. Mary Warnock, for example, says that:

It is all too easy to lapse with Schelling into a gasping sentiment of the profound which for many people is still what they believe philosophy ought to bring them.[3]

The generality or vagueness of these writers is, David Simpson reminds us, not without significance. Where Kant is concerned, the avoidance of specific example is deliberate:

Given Kant's aims, any excessive concentration on examples, consisting as they must in empirically embodied *things* such as statues or paintings, must tend to induce us to believe that he is establishing some sort of canon of beautiful *objects* . . . Thus the almost total absence of examples from the *Critique of Judgment* is meant to alert us continually to its concentration upon acts of mind rather than upon already created objects.[4]

Schelling is similarly abstract and void of example. Associated with this lack of particulars is a tendency to use terms in conflicting ways. Claud Sutton, in *The German tradition in philosophy*, accuses the post-Kantian idealists of a sloppy attitude to words: 'by the misuse of the words "ego" and "self consciousness" they frequently leave it obscure whether they are speaking about the individual person in his society or whether they are talking about some timeless absolute'.[5] René Wellek echoes this accusation:

They use words loosely, shift their meanings quickly and without warning, indulge in many equivocations and private games of naming. We must be on constant guard against the tricks of their language, though we should also recognize that they would have defended their practice by a contextual theory of language and by the argument that philosophical creation is also linguistic.[6]

These failures – or dangers – can be seen as deliberate ruses and Wilkinson and Willoughby, in their introduction to Schiller's

Aesthetic education, see Schiller's cavalier treatment of Kant's concepts, his self-contradictions and the chameleon fluidity of the treatise as a whole as deliberate policy.

> Such contraries are so frequent, so flagrant, and often so symmetrically placed, that it would seem far more plausible to assume that they are of the order of deliberate paradox rather than of inadvertent self-contradiction.   (*AE*, Introduction, p. xlix)

Schiller's strategy, they say, 'is not linear but circular'.

> This is not to say that within the several parts he does not sometimes pursue the more familiar course of a line of argument leading straight to a conclusion. But he often pursues a kind of delaying tactics too.
>   (*AE*, Introduction, p. li)

His purpose is 'not to fix the mind, but to keep it moving' (*AE*, Introduction, p. lvi) and through chiasmus and other such devices, he tries to 'exhibit the dynamics of the psyche, rather than analyse or describe them' (*AE*, p. lxx). This account is perhaps rather idealist – the distinction between a text 'exhibiting' and 'describing' is one devised by the post-Kantian idealists, for whom presentational thought was a possibility. But it is fair to say that Schiller uses philosophical words, normally fixed by conventions or by the strict terms of the discourse itself, in a changeable fashion; it is not clear in what context we should apply his terms.

The looseness of reference which characterizes idealist or 'sentimental' thought can be linked with an awareness of linguistic relativism or the role of language in constructing a philosophical system: how something is said affects what is said. As Schiller himself suggests, such sentimental systems are better at conveying a general spirit than they are at saying anything specific. Comparing the sentimental with the naive, he says that:

> The sentimental genius . . . abandons reality in order to ascend to ideas and to dominate his material with free spontaneity; since, however, the intellect always strives for the unconditional according to its own laws so the sentimental genius will not always remain *sober* enough to keep itself uninterruptedly and uniformly within the restrictions which the concept of human nature brings with it and to which the intellect, even in its freest operation, must here remain always bound. This could only come to pass through a relative degree of responsiveness which, however, in the sentimental poetic spirit is predominated over by the

spontaneity just as much as it predominates over the spontaneity in the naive genius. If, therefore, in the creations of the naive genius one at times misses the *spirit*, so in the fruits of the sentimental genius one often looks in vain for the *subject-matter*. Thus both will fall into the fault of *emptiness*, although in a quite contrary way; for a subject without spirit and a play of the spirit without a subject are both a nothingness when judged aesthetically. (*NS*, p. 73)

If this account of the pitfalls of naive and especially of sentimental literature is considered in a critical context, it gives a useful insight into the problems of sentimental criticism, some of which have already been encountered. Schiller sets spontaneity against responsiveness, saying that the former dominates the sentimental mode, as the latter dominates the naive. The tendency of the sentimental mode towards self-expressive, exploratory, spontaneous extension means that it tends also to surpass or overflow the limits of the actual – the constraints encountered by practical demands – by reality, by data, and by particular cases. This means that it seems disembodied and general, without any specific subject-matter or content: a free-floating spirit. This description seems to coincide neatly with what critics have subsequently had to say about Schiller, Schelling and the post-Kantian idealists in general – or about the Romantics. Although these writers capture a general feeling, it is thought, they are hard to pin down to specific example or to apply to any particular case. Clearly, this is a disadvantage where literary criticism is concerned, at least if we want to say things about particular authors. As Schiller says:

Reason in its creations takes far too little notice of the boundaries of the sensual world and the idea is always carried further than experience can follow it. (*NS*, p. 73)

That is, it becomes problematic relating what insights the theory in general offers to the particulars of any one text or another.

We have already seen what difficulties Schiller himself encountered when trying to pin down authors as 'naive' and how that description tends to collapse into sentimentalism, as apparently 'objective' descriptions can be revealed as secretly subjective and expressive. Similarly, the post-Romantic accounts of Clare which are not just nature-notes tend to collapse Clare into the canonical Romantics: to argue, as Harold Bloom does, that Clare's work is a postscript to Wordsworth's (see chapter 3 above). To account for specificity, for locality and for definite reference – those 'naive' characteristics which have begun to be associated with Clare – is beyond the scope of a sentimental theory. So far, this problem has only been illustrated with respect to nineteenth-century theory. But it can be shown to be equally present in contemporary critical thought.

POST-KANTIANS AND POST-STRUCTURALISTS: VARIETIES OF SENTIMENTALISM

It may have already become clear that the kinds of characteristics associated with the 'sentimental' aesthetic are similar to those associated with post-structuralist theory. The connection between post-Kantian idealism and post-structuralism has been convincingly argued for by Richard Rorty, in his essay, 'Nineteenth-century idealism and twentieth-century textualism'. In this essay, Rorty argues that the 'textualists' (the Yale school, Bloom, Hartman and others; post-structuralists, Derrida and Foucault and others who 'write as if there were nothing but texts' – Rorty, p. 139) make the same points that the idealists were making in the last century.

The two movements are similar in that both are aware of the way in which ideas or words *construct* the world and thus both are suspicious of claims by scientific discourse to have authority. They

> both insist that we can never compare human thought or language with bare, unmediated reality. The idealists started off from Berkeley's claim that nothing can be like an idea except another idea. The textualists start off from the claim that all problems, topics, and distinctions are language-relative – the results of our having chosen to use a certain vocabulary, to play a certain language-game. Both use this point to put natural science in its place.   (Rorty, p. 140)

Thus, Rorty proposes, 'textualism' is 'the contemporary counterpart of idealism – the textualists as spiritual descendants of the idealists, the species having adapted to a changed environment' (Rorty, p. 140). The change in environment is a function of the fact that we are now a 'post-philosophical' culture, one in which metaphysical theses about the nature of things are no longer thought authoritative or defensible. But although textualism is 'literary' where idealism was 'philosophical' and although textualism is located in the field of fictional texts whereas idealism was located in the field of philosophical theses, they are united in their belief that 'what is most important for human life is not what propositions we believe but what vocabulary we use' (Rorty, p. 142). This thesis Rorty calls 'romanticism'.

He goes on to attack the textualists, primarily for being unoriginal:

> As usual with pithy little formulae, the Derridean claim that 'There is nothing outside the text' is right about what it implicitly denies and wrong about what it explicitly asserts.[7] The *only* force of saying that texts do not refer to nontexts is just the old pragmatist chestnut that any specification of a referent is going to be in some vocabulary . . . There are, alas, people nowadays who owlishly inform us 'philosophy has *proved*' that language does not refer to anything nonlinguistic, and thus that everything does not refer to anything nonlinguistic, and thus that everything one can talk about is a text. This claim is on a par with the claim that Kant proved that we cannot know about things-in-themselves. Both claims rest on a phony contrast between some sort of nondiscursive unmediated vision of the real and the way we actually talk and think. Both falsely infer from 'We can't think without concepts, or talk without words' to 'We can't think or talk except about what has been created by our thought or talk'. (Rorty, pp. 154–5)

Rorty draws our attention to the way in which textualism argues against reference by setting up the shibboleth of a final and determinate and unmediated word–thing relationship, and then belabouring it. Whereas, in fact, there is no reason to believe that referring depends on this finality. That we can use words to refer without having a definite concept of what it is we refer to is a point with which we are familiar from Wittgenstein's philosophy of language.[8]

If textualist theories frame reference in this way, then what they are doing is constructing a 'naive', just as Schiller does, as a foil for a sentimental theory and for the purposes of self-articulation. This is the view that Rorty takes elsewhere, noting that

> in England and America philosophy has already been displaced by literary criticism in its principal cultural function – as a source for youth's self-description of its own difference from the past.[9]

It is this need to sever the modern, sentimental consciousness from the classical naive that was the dynamic of Schiller's aesthetic. The essay discussed is a defence of the new poetry against classical norms and it was in this cause that the naive was enlisted, as the 'unconscious' of the new consciousness.

With this in mind, we can look briefly at the question of reference in 'textualist' critical theory.

THE REFERENT AS NAIVE

'Someone stole the referent, and we are overrun with sliding signifieds and floating signifiers'. Thus exclaims Vincent Leitch, in his discussion 'The borders of reference overrun', in *Deconstructive criticism*.[10] The *referent* has become a lost object, something substantial and material, a piece of property which we can contrast with 'sliding' and 'floating' signifiers and signifieds. Referring, as an activity in language, is replaced by a contrast between language as an autonomous web of words and the referent as the elusive fish that has slipped through the net. Leitch is perhaps rather high-handed with Derrida, whose own formulations are less risky:

the signified always already functions as a signifier. The secondarity that it seemed possible to ascribe to writing alone affects all signifieds in general, affects them always already, the moment they *enter the game*. There is not a single signified that escapes, even if recaptured, the play of signifying references that constitute language.[11]

Both Derrida and de Man quote C. S. Peirce in making this point: that every signified is also a signifier. De Man says that:

The interpretation of the sign is not, for Peirce, a meaning but another sign; it is a reading, not a decodage, and this reading has, in its turn, to be interpreted into another sign, and so on *ad infinitum*.[12]

One might want to ask how we could decode language into anything but language. De Man implies that there could be an alternative to understanding words in words and implies that words might be translated into something simpler, into things, for instance. But, as Rorty indicated, the fact that we cannot turn words into things does not mean that we cannot refer; language would not be much use as language if it were not the medium in which we talked about the world. But the step taken by de Man is one that Jonathan Culler, in *On deconstruction*, also seems to take:

Reading is an attempt to understand writing by determining the referential and rhetorical modes of a text, translating the figurative into the literal, for example, and removing obstacles in the quest for a coherent result, but the construction of texts – especially of literary works, where pragmatic contexts do not so readily justify a confident distinction between the literal and the figurative or the referential and the nonreferential – may block this process of understanding.[13]

Like de Man, Culler tricksily sets up an opposition in order to dismantle it. His argument seems to be that reading is translating figurative into literal. However, this is difficult because literal and figurative are not easily distinguished. Given this position, we might ask: why make the distinction in the first place? The answer may be that it generates a literary theory. But we must surely reject the idea that reading is a question of finding a 'coherent result', of achieving a literal closure or finality. Why should we not just be able literally to understand language in all its ambiguity and figurativeness, just as we understand the familiar figures that saturate ordinary speech? De Man says that difficulties arise when

we have, on the one hand, a literal meaning and on the other hand a figural meaning, but . . . it is impossible to decide . . . which of the two meanings . . . prevails. Rhetoric radically suspends logic and opens up vertiginous possibilities of referential aberration.[14]

Now, this seems to go against our experience of reading or, for that matter, of having a conversation. Firstly, there are surprisingly few situations, verbal or oral, in which these vertiginous possibilities make interpretation impossible, though it may be a question of choosing what fits the context. Secondly, the suggestion that there is a choice between a 'literal' and a 'figurative' meaning seems mistaken: these are words that can only really apply to contexts, not to something intrinsic about a particular expression. Otherwise there would not be the possibility of 'taking something literally'. And if they are only contextual, then all de Man is saying is that we can choose how we interpret language, according to context. And this is, above all, a question of reference, of extra-textual situations. We can argue against de Man and Culler that understanding ordinary language in speech or in writing is a skill that we learn with language which involves what can be called 'figurative' as well as 'literal' expressions, since language does not make that distinction.

Understanding 'Roger Scruton is a block of ice' need not be any more problematic than understanding 'Roger Scruton is a philosopher', since we will have learned how 'block of ice' can be applied to individuals. Both Culler and de Man imply that we understand language from the *outside*, as a puzzle, when we are in fact already inside and think and speak in the kinds of puzzles they suggest we might have to decode into something else. This problem is a pseudo-problem and might remind us of what Schiller says about the sentimental failure to acknowledge or respond to actuality or experience when constructing theories.

Derrida's account of reference also concentrates on the possibility of 'closure', of establishing determinate meaning with a given system. Concepts such as 'centring' or the 'transcendental signified' involve the notion of an ultimate point of reference, which would close off and put a full stop to the interplay of numerous signs.

> Peirce goes very far in the direction that I have called the deconstruction of the transcendental signified, which, at one time or another, would place a reassuring end to the reference from sign to sign. I have identified logocentrism and the metaphysics of presence as the exigent, powerful, systematic, and irrepressible desire for such a signified. Now Peirce considers the indefiniteness of reference as the criterion that allows us to recognize that we are indeed dealing with a system of signs. *What broaches the movement of signification is what makes its interruption impossible. The thing itself is a sign.*
>
> (*Grammatology*, p. 49)

There seem to be two issues to consider here. The first is that meaning is always constructed within a linguistic system and is accordingly not absolute. There is no non-linguistic meaning; we only have access to things through words. Or, more simply, words are not things. The second is that any one language or way of saying something can always be replaced by another alternative. But as Rorty says, this is nothing new. What is more interesting is the critical model which is constructed in spatial or structural terms, even whilst it attacks them. We are told that

> structure – or rather the structurality of structure – although it has always been at work, has always been neutralized or reduced, and this by a process of giving it a center or of referring it to a point of presence, a fixed origin. The function of this center was not only to orient, balance, and organize the structure . . . but above all to make sure that the

organizing principle of the structure would limit what we might call the play of the structure. By orienting and organizing the coherence of the system, the center of a structure permits the play of its elements inside the total form. And even today the notion of a structure lacking any center presents the unthinkable itself.[15]

It must be pointed out that this model is Derrida's own. Even while deconstructing the notion of a text or system as a structure with a centre, he is establishing that as a norm. A text or a system has always been thought of as a structure with a centre which stabilizes the many possible meanings that might be generated. But this is not strictly the case. There are many other ways in which we can think of writing or reading other than as a structure: this is very much a Romantic, and subsequently a new critical or a structuralist way of thinking. But it is quite otherwise, for example, that we talk about books, when interested in what they are about or their historical positioning. What Derrida describes is the sentimental model for literature or criticism which, as we have said, is highly structural. But why set up this notion of a text as a closed structure just in order to knock it down? We could never think of conversation in this way.

The instability of reference to which the textualists always refer is a concept closely bound up with the concept of the text as a structure or system, a concept which is set up as the condition for the possibility of reference. When there is no centre, no system, no limit to the text, then there is no more reference. I now want to consider this question of the 'limits' or borders of the text.

THE NAIVE AS LIMIT IN A SENTIMENTAL SYSTEM

There are two texts: the old and the new. The old 'text' possesses a title, margins, signature (author), a beginning, an end, overall unity, and limited content. Outside its frame lies a 'referential realm'. This piece of writing is distinguishable from reality, the world, history, life, and speech; and it is distinctive from the realms of the body, mind, consciousness, the Unconscious, politics, and economics. All these boundaries, frames, divisions, limits — borders — mark out and enclose the old 'text', making it a very special and highly differentiated entity and object. Since the late 1960s, however, a new text has come to our attention. It touches and tampers with — it changes and spoils — all the old boundaries, frames, divisions, and limits. The identity of 'text' alters. The overrun of all the old borders forces us to rethink the 'text'.[16]

What Leitch is doing here is creating a 'naive'. All criticism before the 1960s considered a text to be an autonomous, defined entity, which related to a separate reality 'out there'. Post-1960s criticism has realized that there is nothing outside the text and that the world is not separable from language. We have already seen that this is not a new insight, but one which was at the heart of Romantic theory — as was the interest in language as autonomous, living form which has resurfaced, now cut adrift even from a community or a history. The idea that the physical limits of the book, or the closure of meaning, were particularly important before this reversal is just another way of saying that aesthetics was less relativistic, that one system or reading could have priority over another.

The idea of the old text as something bounded and limited which has since been overrun or surpassed must surely remind us of Schiller's account of the sentimental spirit. In this account, the naive counterpart is confined, limited, and contained, while the sentimental spills over any existing limits into the absolute:

> For all poetry must have an infinite value, this alone is what makes it poetry; but it can fulfil this demand in two different ways. It can be infinite in form if it represents its subject *with all its limitations*, it individualises it; it can be infinite in substance, if it *removes all limitations* from its subject, if it idealises it, therefore, either by means of an absolute representation or by means of the representation of an absolute. The naive poet takes the first path, the sentimental the second.
>
> (*NS*, p. 64)

The sentimental spirit, Schiller tells us, 'abandons reality in order to ascend to ideas' (p. 72) and 'takes far too little notice of the boundaries of the sensual world' (p. 73). The sentimental is that which goes beyond or through established limits. This is how Leitch characterizes the post-structural age, in which 'the world becomes an infinite, borderless text'.[17]

What is significant is that both for Schiller and for Leitch the naive or limited is necessary for the articulation of the sentimental; it is not possible to go beyond a limit unless a limit exists. This is a principle central to sentimental aesthetics. If we look, for example, at Schelling's *System of transcendental idealism*, we find him explaining that '*The self is unlimited as a self only in that it is limited* . . . the condition of all becoming is limitation or restraint' and that 'Boundedness . . . is thus the condition under which alone the self as self can be infinite'.[18] The limited and the unlimited must be united in transcendental idealism, since each depends upon the other. And although for the purposes of systematic thought they are distinct, they are essentially and fundamentally one.

The real, originally striving into infinity, but to be limited for the sake of self-consciousness, is nothing without the idea, for which, in its limitation, it is infinite . . . Conversely, the ideal activity is nothing without the to-be-intuited, the limitable, and on that very account, the real . . . Just as idealism and realism mutually presuppose each other, so also do theoretical and practical philosophy; and in the self as such there is initial union and combination of what we must hereafter separate, for the sake of the system now to be established.[19]

Schelling places more emphasis than Schiller on the necessary complicity and underlying unity of the two modes, realism and idealism, naive and sentimental. And yet, like Schiller, he must work through them and what he ends up with is definitely theoretical idealism rather than practical realism. The acknowledgement of the importance of the real, the naive, as a way of articulating the ideal, or sentimental, is something that we also come across in 'textualism'. For example, in *Of grammatology*, the opposition between 'natural' speech and 'conventional' writing, whilst it is being demolished, is the dynamic of the whole critique: we tend to forget that this opposition is something that is in the first place set up as the given. And this opposition, as it is found in Rousseau, for instance, is exactly that of the 'naive' and 'sentimental':

Nature, as self-proximity, comes to be forbidden or interrupted, when speech fails to protect presence, writing becomes necessary. It must *be added* to the word urgently. I have identified in advance one of the forms of this *addition*; speech being natural or at least the natural expression of thought, the most natural form of institution or convention for signifying thought, writing is added to it, is adjoined, as an image or representation. In that sense, it is not natural. (*Grammatology*, p. 144)

The nature–culture relationship, where nature is inscribed in culture, or the speech–writing relationship, where speech is inscribed in writing, is analogous to the naive–sentimental relationship: setting up the natural–conventional opposition of speech and writing according to which the voice, producer of *the first symbols*, has a relationship of essential and immediate proximity with the mind . . . Between being and mind, things and feelings, there would be a relationship of translation or natural signification; between mind and logos, a relationship of conventional symbolisation.   (*Grammatology*, p. 11)

Derrida then uses it against itself. Writing, we are told, threatens or violates speech whilst preceding it:

I would wish . . . to suggest that the alleged derivativeness of writing, however real and massive, was possible only on one condition: that the 'original', 'natural' etc. language had never existed, never been intact and untouched by writing, that it had itself always been a writing . . . writing was, by its situation, destined to signify the most formidable difference. It threatened the desire for the living speech from the closest proximity, it *breached* living speech from within and from the very beginning.   (*Grammatology*, pp. 56–7)

The 'presence' of speech as the undifferentiated, primordial and 'natural' language is, like Schiller's naive, a construction of and dependent upon, writing, as that which differentiates and thus makes articulation and meaning possible. So, as Derrida says of Rousseau:

The displacing of the relationship with the mother, with nature, with being as the fundamental signified, such indeed is the origin of society and of languages. But can one speak of origins after that? Is the concept of origin, or of the fundamental signified, anything but a function, indispensable but situated, inscribed, within the system of signification inaugurated by the interdict?   (*Grammatology*, p. 266)

Because the 'fundamental signified', the naive, primordial presence 'will never be given to us in person, outside the sign or outside play', because we always construct the naive within language, there is, Derrida argues, no original naive, only the point at which displacement or difference occurs.

For the point of nonreplacement is also the point of orientation for the entire system of signification, the point where the fundamental signified is promised as the terminal-point of all references and conceals itself as that which would destroy at one blow the entire system of signs.
                              (*Grammatology*, p. 266)

The moment of articulation (or of the birth of culture), when it is no longer possible to be naive, is also the point at which the naive can be constructed as an ideal or goal. We saw this in Schiller. And Derrida's own system, like Schiller's, depends – if in a more complex way – on and is the articulation of the sentimental against the naive or difference against presence. To go back to what Schiller says about the organization of the sentimental:

The sentimental poet . . . is constantly dealing with two opposing concepts and emotions, with reality as boundary and with his ideas as the infinite, and the mixed feeling which he excites will always bear witness to this double source. (NS, p. 42)

The sentimental critic deals with reality as boundary and the idea as infinite, using the opposition of naive and sentimental to generate a sentimental system. As Schelling says, 'The necessary factor in production therefore lies in the opposition as such'.[20] This means, in the end, that the sentimental system knows no limits, for it will always collapse any limits that it sets up into sentimentalism. I now want to look at the way in which the internal divisions of such a system are undermined.

THE PARERGON

Culler describes deconstruction as 'the twin principles of the contextual determination of meaning and the infinite extendability of context.'[21] Which is to say that, where a text is rendered determinate or closed by its context, it is never in fact limited, for any context will itself be limited by a context and so on without end. And Leitch concurs: 'The context limits the text . . . Once borders are overrun and difference is set loose, context multiplies itself to infinity'.[22] What is text, what context, is no longer clear. Again, the text–context model is one set up by deconstruction: we can argue that we can quite easily recognize that language is not sectioned off into determinate texts, and still insist that it refers determinately.

For the deconstructive argument seems to be: a text is indeterminate because it is interpreted within a particular system, which can itself be re-interpreted. This seems rather like saying that a word is relative to a sentence is relative to a paragraph, to a page, to a text and so on. It is certainly true, if we look at it that way round. But we could equally well say that a language determines a book, which determines a chapter, which determines a page and so on. And in fact this seems more sensible, given that the whole point of a system (like language) is that with respect to the terms it contains, it should be determinant, even though the system may be relative with respect to other systems. For instance, if we draw a frame round a picture, our idea of what is art can certainly be questioned. But nevertheless, given that idea, the frame does determine the picture: what is in the frame is a picture, given the conventions of framing.

The difference here is between arguing outwards from specifics to generals and arguing inwards from generals to specifics. Which way we argue is a question of what we are interested in. Derrida, for example, argues outwards, in 'The parergon'. Aesthetics, he tells us, insists upon a distinction 'between the internal or proper meaning and the circumstances of the object in question', and this demand

> organizes every philosophical discourse on art, the meaning of art and meaning itself, from Plato to Hegel, Husserl, and Heidegger. It presupposes a discourse on the limit between the inside and the outside of the art object, in this case *a discourse on the frame*.
>
> (*Parergon*, p. 12)

The *Critique of judgment*, for instance, tries to distinguish the beautiful from the conceptual and the aesthetic from the cognitive. But, Derrida argues, such discriminations between intrinsic and extrinsic are not possible, for the frame or 'parergon', is itself relative to what it defines.

> The parergon is distinguished from both the *ergon* (the work) and the milieu; it is distinguished as a figure against a ground. But it is not distinguished in the same way as the work, which is also distinguished from a ground. The parergonal frame is distinguished from two grounds, but in relation to each of these, it disappears into the other. In relation to the work, which may function as its ground, it disappears into the wall and then, by degrees, into the general context. In relation to the general context, it disappears into the work.   (*Parergon*, p. 24)

The frame is thus a borderline between two areas, disappearing into one or the other. What we are doing when framing is defining something not in a determinate, but a relative or reflective way. Rather than drawing a border around a pre-existing art-work, we are making something into an art-work by drawing a border around it.

In Kant's case, Derrida says, judgment works like a parergon. For whilst it is supposed to be a separate faculty, it is really only articulated with respect to the others.

> The *Mittelglied*, intermediary member, must be treated as a detachable part, a separate part . . . But also as a non-detachable part, a nonseparate part, since it constitutes the articulation between two others . . . Kant thus seems to contradict himself: it is necessary to disengage the middle member as a detachable part, but it is also necessary to remember the whole by reconstituting the nexus, the connection, the reannexation of the part to the two major columns of the corpus.　　　　(*Parergon,* p. 6)

The whole problem of the Critique, according to Derrida, is whether judgment is constitutive or merely regulative: whether it exists on its own terms, or only as a way of relating the other faculties. He concludes that although the aesthetic is supposed to be autonomous, it is only determined with respect to the other faculties. And correlatively, we cannot describe an art-work with respect to its intrinsic qualities, but only by framing it in a system: the aesthetic is just this framing process.

Here, Derrida is treating the Critique very formally, much in the idealist manner of Kant himself rather than considering what 'judgment' might involve in a more referential sense: so he assesses judgment in the Critique with respect to its 'context' rather than with respect to its 'content'; that is, what 'judgment' intensively covers as a working term is less relevant than how it extensively relates to other terms, which relationship is thought to undermine its autonomy. This is analogous to a conception of the art-work as something to be structurally defined within a system rather than something to be cognitively understood on the terms of that system. We might want to argue that whilst it is of course important to recognize that the internal discriminations of a system are relative to that system, they can also work to determine and refer, just as words, whilst relative to a language, also refer even if reference is never determinate or absolutely stable and complete.

Derrida notes that

> the distinction . . . between reflective and determinant judgment controls all of the book's internal divisions . . . The faculty of judgment *in general* allows us to think of the particular as contained under the general (rule, principle, law). When the general is given first, the

operation of the judgment subsumes and *determines* the particular. It is determinant (bestimmend), it defines, narrows, comprehends, compresses. In the opposite assumption, *reflective* (reflektirend) judgment begins with the particular and must return, retrace, the way to the general: the example (what matters to us here) is given prior to the law, and may thus be revealed in its exemplary unity. Current scientific or logical discourse proceeds according to determinant judgments . . . But in art and in life, any place where we must, according to Kant, proceed by means of reflective judgments and assume . . . an end whose concept is not given, *the example precedes.*   (*Parergon*, p. 16)

Kant's distinction between determinant and reflective judgment – analogous to that between constitutive and regulative principles – rests on the belief that we can either judge an object under a concept or law (for example, as a member of a genus), or 'formally' for itself and its own inner purposiveness. In the latter or 'reflective' judgment, we derive the law from the object itself, apprehending it as a formal whole: this is what happens in aesthetic judgments of taste:

If pleasure is bound up with the mere apprehension . . . of the form of an object of intuition, without reference to a concept for a definite cognition, then the representation is thereby not referred to the object, but simply to the subject, and the pleasure can express nothing else than its harmony with the cognitive faculties which come into play in the reflective judgment, and so far as they are in play, and hence can only express a subjective formal purposiveness of the object.
                 (*CJ*, Introduction, VII, p. 26)

This is how the aesthetic judgment is differentiated from other kinds of judgment. It is important to remember that this aesthetic judgment describes not an object, but a way of apprehending an object, an experience in which our faculties, rather than resolving themselves into a concept, simply interrelate in formal harmony.

The distinction between the reflective and determinant or regulative and constitutive – or of course, aesthetic and cognitive – can be said to be the central principle of Kant's aesthetic and that which gives rise to the post-Kantian tradition. If we consider Derrida's method in this essay in this light, it can be argued that what he does conforms very nearly to what he describes as 'reflective' in Kant. Kant, he argues, works outwards from a centre. He:

confines the theory of aesthetics within a theory of the beautiful, the theory of the beautiful within a theory of taste, and the theory of taste within a theory of judgment. (*Parergon*, p. 30)

This framing is artificial, a device for distinguishing what is not really distinct. But we can argue that this is just reading Kant one way – the 'reflective' way, or outwards from the particular to find a universal. We could equally well read the 'determinant' way, downwards from the containing principle. This gives us limited determinacy at each stage. Thus the theory of aesthetics is meaningful and determinate within a theory of the beautiful. And the theory of the beautiful is meaningful and determinate within a theory of taste, and taste within judgment, and judgment within the Critique, and the Critique within Kant's metaphysics. This is why we can make sense of Kant's distinctions, even whilst being aware that of course the aesthetic is contained inside the cognitive and so all cognitive judgments involve a subjective or aesthetic aspect. Even if we know that any 'objective' statement can be deconstructed and revealed as 'subjective' – for example, any scientific theory that does not negate the 'determinant' reading, according to which that theory holds with respect to what it determines, the experiments, principles and so forth that it governs. Within the scope of a particular theory or system, a particular distinction, there can be this determinacy.

Derrida, it seems, reads 'reflectively' or outwards, from text to context, to context-of-context – and this will always reveal the instability of meaning. But it is also possible to read 'determinately' or inwards, from context-of-context, to context, to text, and this is perhaps more like the way in which we usually – as readers, not critics – read. In this sense, such 'determinant' reading could be called 'naive' and would provide what we think of as specific, stable meanings. This model of two possible directions of reading can, it seems, be a way of combining or at least holding together the naive and the sentimental awareness. It is reminiscent of Goodman's account of the difference between representation and expression as a difference in direction:

expression, like representation, is a mode of symbolization; and a picture must stand for, symbolize, refer to, what it expresses. The symbolization or reference here runs . . . in the opposite direction from denotation – runs up from rather than down to what is denoted.

(Goodman, p. 52)

This is to say, that if a picture 'expresses' sadness, the label 'sad' denotes the picture. But if a picture 'represents' a house, the picture is a label for the house: expression runs from label to picture, representation from picture-as-label to referent. That is, in the case of expression, we have the particular, the picture, and move upwards to what it is an instance of, to what it expresses and in the case of representation, the representation is the 'universal' which determines what it refers to, which classifies it in a particular way. Thus expression is the 'reflective' and representation is the 'determinant' judgment.

If we consider critical accounts in this way, we can argue that sentimental criticism prefers to move in the 'expressive' or 'reflective' direction, whilst naive criticism prefers to move in the 'representational' or 'determinant' direction. This would include post-structuralist critical theory in the sentimental category.

The frame, then, need not be considered, as Culler says in a résumé of Derrida's view in the essay, 'as a frame-up, an interpretive imposition that restricts an object by establishing boundaries'[23] but as a useful and necessary way of making critical distinctions and thinking systematically at all. It has become plain that sentimental theory must depend on the boundary for its self-definition. Vincent Leitch puts the sentimental viewpoint across:

Although the idea of context depends on a concept of intertextuality, it reduces it in the name of law. Context serves as border patrol.[24]

Criticism, that is, compromises itself, abandons risk and integrity, when it sets limits. We can compare this with what Schiller says about naive poets:

They are hated by the critics, the actual border guards of taste, as *boundary breakers* who should rather be suppressed.   (*NS*, p. 38)

Naiveté, that is, *is* defiance, risk, integrity and the resistance of critical systems; the 'dry truthful' voice of naive common sense makes the critical laws seem artificial and the critics uneasy.

KANT TO DERRIDA: AN INCREASINGLY SENTIMENTAL JOURNEY

I have characterized sentimental criticism as highly 'formal' in its concerns. It reveals general patterns and processes, rather than dealing with specifics or what writing communicates or refers to.

And yet, when Schiller reworked Kant's aesthetic, he was motivated by the belief that Kant was too 'formal', that he had secluded the aesthetic from the rest of life in order to distinguish it as a separate faculty. Kant did not account sufficiently for the content of art, what it had to say and consequently for its significance for humanity. For Schiller, an account of the aesthetic experience as purely formal is inadequate, since for him the aesthetic is characterized by the struggle between the form and the matter (or between freedom and necessity, reason and sense) which is to some degree resolved in aesthetic unity. As he wrote to Goethe:

It seems that a portion of the poetic interest lies in the antagonism between the subject and the representation.[25]

Eva Schaper makes this point about Schiller when she explains that:

As a Kantian, he accepted that sense and intellect, morality and reason, were distinct domains; but their separation was . . . something to be overcome. He recognised that this conflict was one of the mainsprings of his creative ability.[26]

Art, for Schiller, is the opposition and, ideally, the resolution of a resistant, recalcitrant matter and a shaping spirit or form, of the content, the ideas, the material – and the subduing of that content to aesthetic form. He finds Kant inadequate, in that his aesthetic appears to give an account of art as the aesthetic experience, as a purely subjective, formal interplay of the imagination and the understanding in the subject of the experience. He thus searches for an aesthetic which would preserve the autonomy of art, whilst taking into consideration those aspects of art which are not formal. Wilkinson and Willoughby argue that:

Schiller was not of course suggesting that art gives us 'knowledge', empirical or ultimate, or can ever be a surrogate for science, philosophy or religion; not trying to go back behind distinctions so painstakingly established by Kant. But were these as they stood really adequate to account for the nature and effect of an art such as literature, whose very medium is already weighty with meanings? . . . Kant's demand that in aesthetic experience the psyche should delight in the free play of all its faculties was all very right and proper. But was such free play only to be achieved in the *absence* of vital, or even disturbing, interests?

(*AE*, Introduction, p. xxiv)

Schiller's motive, then, is to counteract what he perceives as an excessively formal aesthetic, which does not give a proper account of what art is like as a creative process or as significant for culture. However, it can be argued that what he achieves is quite the opposite of what he set out to achieve. His reading of Kant can be shown to be particularly narrow and negative and the solution that he devises can be revealed as opening the way for increasingly formalist and subjectivist or 'sentimental' aesthetics.

It is not difficult to see why Schiller should have construed the third Critique as he did: this construction can be put down to a particularly problematic tendency in the Critique towards an ambivalence between the formal play of faculties in the subject in the aesthetic experience and the same formal play as in some way 'in' the aesthetic object. This is an ambiguity 'which derives from the core of Kant's thought', discussed by Michael Podro in *The manifold in perception*.[27] For although Kant insists that judgments of taste do not tell us anything about the object itself, only about our own representation of the object: 'it is only aesthetical and involves merely a reference of the representation of the object to the subject' (*CJ*, 6, p. 46), nevertheless he often seems to be talking about aesthetic objects themselves and to be stipulating that the only kinds of objects that are aesthetic are those which are in themselves purely formal. For example, in the discussion of taste as independent of 'charm and emotion' (*CJ*, 13–14) he says that:

In painting, sculpture, and in all the formative arts – in architecture and horticulture . . . the *delineation* is the essential thing; and here it is not what gratifies in sensation but what pleases by means of its form that is fundamental for taste.   (*CJ*, 14, p. 61)

Kant goes on in the problematic section on free and dependent beauty to say that

delineations *a la grecque*, foliage for borders or wall papers, mean nothing in themselves; they represent nothing – no object under a definite concept – and are free beauties . . . In the judging of a free beauty (according to the mere form) the judgment of taste is pure. There is presupposed no concept of any purpose which the manifold of the given object is to serve, and which therefore is to be represented in it. By such a concept the freedom of the imagination which disports itself in the contemplation of the figure would be only limited. (*CJ*, 16, p. 66)

This kind of statement, which seems to imply that only non-representational art is real art, accounts for the tendency to read Kant as formalist. David Miall, for instance, in an essay on the Critique, says that

Kant . . . constructs an aesthetics of extreme formalism. A beautiful object is being judged only in relation to the purposiveness it shows (merely its adaption to the cognitive faculties), apart from any considerations of its use, purpose, perfection, or agreeableness, and in the absence of any concept. Its purpose can in fact only be to display a certain form, and the only form of judgement possible in such a case is that of contemplation.[28]

However, while such arguments seem to take Kant to task for failing to accommodate the non-formal aspects of art, it can be argued that the Critique does not imply that art-works do not have cognitive, or material, or representational aspects, nor that recognition of these aspects is not part of aesthetic experience, but only that the kind of judgment we make in aesthetic experience is itself formal: formality is a characteristic of the judgment or the kind of attention involved, not of the object about which we are saying nothing. It is the final reference of the aesthetic judgment to the subject rather than the object which distinguishes it, rather than any character of the object itself. Thus Schaper says that:

Aesthetic judgements of taste do apply concepts but not in the way that judgements of experience do. The concept of beauty and its associates are not descriptive . . . Aesthetic judgements refer feelings to a subject as their 'determining ground'; descriptive empirical judgements take the objective turn by referring sense representations to an object as 'determining ground'.[29]

Although Kant confuses us by talking about wallpaper patterns, one way of accepting his claim that this kind of pattern is exemplary 'free beauty' is to remember that it is always a kind of judgment, rather than an object, that he is talking about and that this can be taken as an illustration of the interest-free nature of aesthetic judgments of pure beauty, rather than a statement about the objects of those judgments. That is, whatever other interests may be involved in the object, the final judgment must resolve those interests into formal neutrality; it must be a judgment of the object as fitted to the subject and thus only of the subject's experience. There seems to be no reason why the Critique cannot be read not as excluding non-formal elements, but simply as resolving them, in aesthetic judgment, into a formal experience. This resolution is essential to the basic premise of Kant's metaphysics, which is that it is concerned not with the object, but with the object-for-the-subject.

In trying to include into a basically Kantian account of aesthetic experience an account of the beautiful object itself, Schiller necessarily splits the Kantian unity of subject and object in experience. In the *Aesthetic education*, he talks ambiguously about the two drives, the sense-drive and the form-drive (which correspond to necessity and freedom, sense and reason, and so forth) as unified in the subject, in beauty and in the subject, in an aesthetic state, in which we are both free and constrained. As Michael Podro says:

> For Schiller, that there is this harmony between an external form and an autonomous play of the imagination which is prompted by the form, is the very focus of his theory.[30]

But in positioning the harmony of sense and reason *in* the object as well as in the subject, Schiller makes it difficult for us to understand how the two relate: he reopens the question that Kant's aesthetic solved. He takes the relationship of the imagination and understanding which constitutes the aesthetic state in Kant and objectifies it as play of form and content *in* the art-object.

This unification of two opposing drives *in* the object is Schiller's way of resolving the dichotomy of sense and reason in Kant. Just as the aesthetic object in Schiller is an object which seems both free and necessary in that it determines its own form and subdues its own content; so the aesthetic state of mind is one in which the sensuous state and the rational state are unified. Because

> in the enjoyment of beauty, or aesthetic unity, an actual union and interchange between matter and form, passivity and activity, momentarily takes place, the compatibility of our two natures . . . hence the possibility of sublimest humanity, is thereby actually proven.
>
> (*AE*, 25th letter, p. 189)

Objectification, or the understanding of the aesthetic state as a unity of, rather than a mediation between, sense and reason, provides the possibility of resolving the dichotomy. There are obvious disadvantages to this solution. Schiller's dislike of the dualism that separates aesthetics from cognition will have the same consequences as the general dislike among the post-Kantian philosophers for Kant's dualism separating the phenomenal from the noumenal. That is, it can only be resolved by recourse to an intensified subjectivity. We can clarify this by looking at the general movement towards subjective idealism after Kant. David Simpson describes the way in which Kant's successors

saw as their task the closing of the gaps he had created: between nature and freedom, phenomena and noumena (things as they appear and as they must be thought to be in themselves), the empirical and the moral . . . In closing these gaps, they often claimed the authority cf an absolute, the knowledge of an essential or 'noumenal' identity about which Kant himself had been objectively hypothetical. And, in arguing away the various dualisms at the heart of Kant's thought, his successors were also obliged to reopen the very questions he had meant to avoid by relegating them to the non-critical writings. If there is once again a unified subjectivity and a wholeness continuum in the philosophical explanation of experience, what single principle of force then becomes the mainspring? Despite all the saving gestures . . . their philosophies more and more admit . . . a philosophy of will – by which I mean one more and more explicitly founded upon the modifications enacted upon subjectivity.[31]

In abolishing the Kantian dualism, Schelling and Fichte rely on the subjective principle to maintain unity between the self and the world. Whereas Kant had argued that the self is bound up with the world-for-the-self – that is, the relative world as we see it – the post-Kantians insist that this *is* the real world beyond which there is nothing. They take the transcendental into subjectivity, into what we construct for ourselves and into the act of construction. As Robert Brown says in *The later philosophy of Schelling*:

Schelling rejects the Kantian phenomenal–noumenal distinction, and affirms that the external objects of our experience are the real objects themselves. The mind does not simply project onto the natural world the structures of its organization. The order of nature is objectively real because unconscious spirit is operative in nature, paralleling the conscious spirit that is the knowing subject.[32]

Underlying the dualism of nature and self in Schelling's philosophy is a single subjective principle. For although Schelling claims to be more 'objective' than Fichte and although his system includes a philosophy of nature as well as of the subject, the two halves – unconscious nature and conscious subjectivity – must in the end be united in subjectivity: in the self thinking itself as object. Art, in which the *System* culminates, is the locus of that unity of subject and object, which consists in the spirit or idea being objectified, so that in the art-object principle and realization are one. Copleston gives an account of this in his *History of philosophy*, saying that

beauty exists where the particular (the real) is so in accord with its idea that the idea itself, as infinite, enters into the finite, and is intuited *in concreto*. Aesthetic intuition is thus the intuition of the infinite in a finite product of intelligence. Further, the conformity of a thing with its eternal idea is its truth. Hence beauty and truth are ultimately one. [33]

It is to this aesthetic unity of spirit and form that philosophy also aspires: all philosophy, Schelling says, is like art, only it is productive in a different way:

For whereas in art the production is directed outwards, so as to reflect the unknown by means of products, philosophical production is directed immediately inwards, so as to reflect it in intellectual intuition. [34]

Philosophy, like art, will be a unity of form and content:

The principle of philosophy must thus be one in which content is conditioned by form, and form in turn by content – not the one presupposing the other, but each in reciprocity. [35]

The philosophical system is an organic unity: 'every system must contain the ground of its subsistence' and it is thus that, as Paul Hayner says in his study of Schelling, philosophy

becomes genetic, i.e., it lets the entire necessary series of our representations, as it were, arise and end before our eyes. [36]

So, it can be said, aesthetics has absorbed philosophy; the philosophical system itself is an aesthetic unity or at least that is the new way of talking about philosophy. Post-Kantian aesthetics can be characterized by a dual tendency. It posits an organic unity, a system which is itself an art-work where an art-work is an organic unity. Then it puts forward a subjective principle as the mainspring of that unity. This means that the apparently objective art-work, the organically structured system, can always be collapsed into subjectivity. This 'constant objectifying-to-itself of the subjective', as Schelling put it,[37] is summarized by Charles Taylor in *Hegel*: Schelling has

taken up Schiller's vision, and beyond Schiller Kant's third critique, whose two main topics, beauty and teleology, are now put at the apex of the system. But Schiller's notion of the aesthetic as the locus of recovered unity between freedom and necessity is now given an ontological foundation. Art is the point where the conscious and unconscious meet . . . And this meeting-point is . . . foreordained in the ontological fact that nature and consciousness have ultimately the same source, subjectivity.[38]

This quotation reminds us that in taking up Kant's third Critique, Schiller and subsequent theorists lose the Kantian distinction and ambivalence between the 'determinant' and 'reflective' aspects of judgment. The dual aspect of judgment in Kant's Critique means that, as Copleston says in his volume on Kant:

In . . . the *Critique of Pure Reason* . . . judgment simply subsumes particulars under . . . 'universals' as under something given a priori. This is an example of *determinant* judgment. But there are obviously many general laws which are not given but have to be discovered . . . We have to discover the general empirical laws under which we subsume particulars. This is the work of *reflective* judgment, the function of which, therefore, is not merely subsumptive; for it has to find the universal, as Kant puts it, under which the particulars can be subsumed. And it is with this reflective judgment that we are concerned here [in the third Critique].[39]

Judgment, that is, works in two ways. In the first Critique, it is considered as the mediating faculty in cognition, bridging the gap between understanding, which provides us with particulars, and reason, which provides us with universals. It is the means of bringing particulars under a universal, the principle whereby we can think of particulars as being *in principle* conformable to law. Here, in cognition, judgment works determinantly, subsuming particulars under already given universals. In the third Critique, it similarly allows us to think of particulars as in principle 'purposive', orderly and conformable to law. But in aesthetic judgment we do not actually subsume the particulars under a pre-given law. Instead, judgment works reflectively, considering particulars as conforming or purposive with respect to the subject of the aesthetic experience's cognitive faculties. In this way, *reflective* judgment can be described as a way of attending to an object 'formally' and 'subjectively', as a purposive unity which conforms to the subject's faculties. In this kind of judgment, we learn nothing about the object itself, only relate a representation to ourselves as subject and thus only judge the object-for-the-subject. As Kant says:

> That which in the representation of an object is merely subjective, i.e. which decides its reference to the subject, not to the object, is its aesthetical character; but that which serves or can be used for the determination of the object (for cognition) is its logical validity. In the cognition of an object of sense, both references present themselves.
>
> (*CJ*, Introduction, VII, p. 25)

In Kant's system, then, although cognition and judgment are distinct, determinant judgment is also part of cognition. Aesthetic or reflective judgment, taken on its own, can be described as a suspended or abbreviated version of cognition, whereby we never get as far as subsuming the representation we construct under a definite concept. Kant separates aesthetic judgment from cognition, as purely *reflective* judgment, but sustains the connection through the *determinant* judgment, which both belongs to the realm of judgment, *and* plays a part in cognition. This is achieved by way of his carefully structured tripartite system, whereby judgment is treated at once as an autonomous faculty, and as the third member of the cognitive trio: reason, judgment and understanding.

However, when Schiller and subsequently Schelling adapt the Kantian aesthetic, they take it out of its context in the system as a whole and abandon the subtle relationship between judgment considered as part of cognition and judgment considered autonomously: between the determinant judgment and the reflective judgment. That is, they lose Kant's careful dual perspective whereby we can always consider any object either 'objectively' or 'subjectively', either 'autonomously' or 'relatively'. For when Schiller puts forward the idea of the aesthetic unity as the locus of the reconciliation of necessity and freedom, he takes Kant's separate and irreconcilable faculties of understanding and reason and locates them in a formal harmony of the kind described in the third Critique as produced by the reflective judgment. The formal unity that ensues is thus itself 'subjective' in the way that the unity of cognitive faculties in interplay is subjective in the third Critique's account of aesthetic judgment. And indeed, Schiller's account of beauty reveals a very spatial conception of this unity: he talks of the 'oscillation' of the 'equilibrium' (*AE*, 16th Letter, p. 112) within the bounds of the unity.

In order to describe a figure in space we have to set limits to infinite space; in order to imagine a change in time, we have to divide up the totality of time. Thus it is only through limits that we attain to reality, only through negation or exclusion that we arrive at position or real affirmation, only through the surrender of our unconditional determinability that we achieve determination.   (*AE*, 19th Letter, p. 129)

The above can be said to be a statement of the central insight of post-Kantian aesthetics – in theory. We have seen that Schelling similarly stressed the 'limit' whereby the subjective objectifies itself to itself and Fichte equally emphasizes the boundary between self and other on which self depends for its articulation.[40] However, despite this insight, the trend of aesthetics after Kant can be seen to be towards undifferentiated unity, the removal of the internal discriminations of philosophy and the 'sentimentalizing' of aesthetics. It can be argued that Kant in excluding 'noumena' – the 'transcendental signified' as Derrida would have it – did exactly what Schiller suggested: surrendered unconditional determinability in order to achieve determination. For whilst his system as a whole deals only with a world conditional on our knowledge, within the terms of that system it is perfectly possible to distinguish different ways of knowing things. Now, when Schiller does away with the transcendental proviso and makes the *aesthetic* system absolute rather than relative, relativism can be seen to be *taken into* and involved in the system, whereas before it was safely outside: the dichotomy is relocated within the aesthetic and the subjective. So, apparently moving towards greater autonomy and objectivity, Schiller and his followers achieve the opposite. We could say that Schiller removes the outer 'frame' of the Kantian system and consequently the internal divisions of that system.

If we look now at post-structuralism, we can suggest that a similar 'unframing' has been made analogous to the text of philosophy: both are organic unities subjectively produced and truth is their reconciliation in art. But the post-structuralist enterprise is to de-centre or unframe system itself, to open up the text and the world so that there is no longer anything beyond the text. This can be seen to be the next step in sentimentalization, in relativism. As we saw earlier:

> The function of this center was not only to orient, balance, and organize the structure . . . but above all to make sure that the organizing principle of the structure would limit what we might call the *play* of the structure. By orienting and organizing the coherence of the system, the center of a structure permits the play of its elements inside the total form.[41]

This 'play' we have already encountered in Schiller, whose 'play-drive' is that at work in the aesthetic unity as the opposing 'sense' and 'form' drives interact. But whereas in Schiller play is contained within a system, in Derrida play will be made unlimited as the system is unframed. So deconstruction 'refuses the traditional violation of the text that links it to an outside'.[42] The effect of unframing is to bring relativism into the 'text' or 'system', and yet, in contradictory fashion, to assert more forcefully the absolute nature of that system. Whereas Kant's metaphysic by excluding the transcendental insists on the limits of its own domain: 'the bounds of sense', Schiller's or Schelling's system assert their access to the absolute, whilst Derrida's has no bounds at all and includes everything. Thus as the sentimental tradition progresses, it becomes at once more relativistic and more absolutist.

CONCLUSION

What I have tried to suggest in this chapter is that the prevailing sentimental tradition in aesthetics is only one way or direction of looking at literature. Its particular mixture of relativism ('texts' have no limits, are not determinate) and absolutism (there is nothing but texts, texts include everything) can be set against what we might call the 'naive' view whereby texts are determinate but do not include everything. And this comparison should not always imply that the sentimental view is the more sophisticated or critical. For in fact Kant, the original 'critical' philosopher, could be read as taking a 'double' perspective, at once naive and sentimental. Indeed, he himself says that:

This twofold sense or twofold point of view is necessary to our transcendental judgment, but also the illusion which arises from the confusion of the one with the other is natural and unavoidable.

(*CJ*, 57, p. 184 'Solution of the antinomy of taste')

That is, he all the time balances objective and subjective as *different perspectives on the same domain.*

The sentimental urge is the urge to make those perspectives one: to insist that it is necessary that we decide on one theory, one approach. And the necessary consequence of this drive towards monism is, as we have seen, extreme subjectivism: the collapse of distinctions into amorphous matter or 'text'. This brings with it an aggressive assertion of the priority of the system or theory itself as the only possible one. Internally indeterminate, sentimental theory articulates itself as dominant and determinate against other theory. This is the opposite to the Kantian approach as I have constructed it, whereby theory is always relative to other theories – since we have no access to absolute truths – but can be internally determinate with respect to its own propositions and on its own terms.

It is this kind of critical system, I would like to suggest, that will be particularly useful in combating sentimental tendencies, and in carrying out the task set by this book: the redescription of the 'naive'.

Following Kant (as I read him) I propose, as an alternative to the sentimental aesthetic, a literary theory that employs just such a 'double' perspective as Kant describes. This theory will combine a critique of the text as context-*relative*, with an acceptance of the text as context-*determined*. Such a reading will at once consider the text as a post-structuralist might – a web to be unwoven and revealed as process, as the activity of reading, writing, interpreting – and as a more unsentimental critic might – as the finished product of those activities: the patterned cloth. Literary texts are at once relative to the system that produces them, revealing in their apparent design the textual processes that give them meaning, create them and the results of that system, limited and determined by it. It is just because the system does have limited, meaningful results or products and rules that give those products meaning that it is a system at all. The detection of the process in the product does not make it any less a stable product. Post-structuralist readings often suggest that this unpicking defies determinacy; that the text is not determinate because it can be shown to be language in activity.

This dual perspective which I propose can be related to the Goodmanesque terms formulated in the last chapter, whereby texts were described as being more or less *articulate* or *dense*. These terms, which position texts relative to a critical system with respect to their intelligibility or tractability, can now be aligned with the Kantian alternatives, whereby a text is described by a critical system in a more or less *reflective* or *determinate* way. An *articulate* text, it will be remembered, is one which can be unpicked or unravelled into a theoretical or critical model. We could say that Wordsworth's *Prelude* is articulate with respect to a sentimental system: it is possible to extrapolate a philosophical or theoretical model from the poem which corresponds to the sentimental aesthetic whereby culture, or more specifically poetry, brings about the union of nature and culture, hitherto opposed. We saw that critical readings of Wordsworth such as Hartman's see this sentimental model in the Wordsworthian consciousness his poems display.

Such an *articulate* text is favoured by sentimental or *reflective* critical practice, which emphasizes the theoretical or processual underpinnings and mechanisms of the apparently closed text, revealing the hidden structures of consciousness in statements about nature and self in the 'subject-matter' of texts.

On the other hand, Clare's poetry is not favoured by senti-mental criticism, as we saw in chapter 3, where a selection of critics dismissed Clare's poetry as nothing but 'subject-matter' in the narrow sense of descriptive or observed fact. This poetry is *dense* with respect to a critical system in that it doesn't offer an opportunity for extrapolating a critical model of the kind preferred by sentimental aesthetics. As a result, readings of this poetry will tend to be *determinate*, to consider what the poetry is apparently 'about' or *what it refers to*, not *how that reference is constructed*.

Having redescribed the naive–sentimental opposition in these terms, which remove critical emphasis from fixed stylistic qualities of texts and place it on the way critical systems create readings of texts, organizing differences of reference and interest as formal oppositions between styles, it is possible to go back to the sentimental account of Clare that was described in chapter 3.

In my next chapter, I summarize the ways in which the sentimental tradition has constructed Clare as a naive and, through a rereading of his poetry, show how the accepted sentimental perspective on that poetry can be criticized and radically revised.

6

THE PEASANT POET

OVERVIEW

I have argued that the critical tradition to which Schiller's influential essay *On the naive and sentimental in literature* gives rise fosters the belief in a 'naive' or artless art, against which the truly artful can be defined.

This naive poetry is naturally and literally descriptive where sentimental poetry is artfully figurative and expressive, mastering and transforming the natural through the genius of the creative subject. Whilst the sentimental tradition sets up as ideal the union between natural and cultural, object and subject, naive and sentimental, it perpetually lapses into an opposition between the two, encouraging the categorization of poetry into two classes which diametrically oppose one another.

Clare has been characterized as naive by this sentimental tradition, and I used the critical reception of Clare as an example of the way in which the contrast between naiveté and sentimentalism is drawn in stylistic terms. Clare was credited with an accurate, descriptive style; Wordsworth with an inspired, visionary style.

Whilst there is no doubt that Clare and Wordsworth do differ in their background, their interests and so on, I have argued against this kind of stylistic distinction, showing how naiveté is a construction of sentimentalism, engineered to serve its purposes, and relying on untenable distinctions between the literal and figurative uses of language. However, I suggested, naiveté could be redescribed: as a description of the way in which a text stands in relation to a dominant critical aesthetic, the term 'naive' can be illustrated by borrowing Goodman's term 'dense', which suggests

196

an inarticulacy or recalcitrance with respect to an established system of critical evaluation. This means that naiveté is no longer a question of stylistic immaturity but one of non-conformity to a preferred aesthetic: a non-conformity that can be conceived as semantic or syntactic. We could explain Clare as 'dense' or 'naive' not in terms of his inability to subjectivize the object or translate nature into symbols (a sentimental model) but in terms of his lack of interest in discussing sentimental models. His non-conformity can be explained in terms of his social and cultural position, his local register and dialect vocabulary, or his lack of concern for sentimental, idealist philosophical issues.

This redescription encourages critical awareness of dominant sentimental values, as they have shaped the literary canon, and alters existing value judgments about which are and which are not 'major' Romantic poets.

In this concluding chapter, I give a reading of Clare's poetry in accordance with the view of naiveté outlined above. That is, I suggest that what has been understood as a stylistic characteristic − 'literal', 'descriptive' − of Clare's poetry, be redescribed in terms of Clare's non-conformity to sentimental interests and conventions. Clare is no more 'literal', 'natural' or 'descriptive' than Wordsworth; he is simply not interested in the same things, nor does he put forward the same account of art or nature − a fact which is hardly surprising, given the different class and background of each writer. I do not attempt a comprehensive account of Clare's work, a task adequately undertaken by Clare scholars past and present. Rather, I use Clare's texts to consider the problems of the reception they have had at the hands of the sentimental establishment.

THE ROLE OF ART: CLARE'S UNSENTIMENTAL AESTHETIC

One of the main problems with sentimentalism we saw was its tendency to talk about a poem as a model of or window onto the poet's consciousness: a poem is a psyche or a model of the dialectical movement of the psyche from nature through culture to union. This tendency explains in part why Clare has been understood as naive. For his poetry often asserts the priority of nature over art and such assertions tally with the naive state of mind as Schiller described it — the state in which 'nature is victorious over art' (*NS*, p. 24). It seems almost superfluous to point out that asserting the priority of nature over art is not the same thing as being in a state of nature rather than of art, and yet this is the kind of leap that sentimental critics seem to have made with Clare.

Clare's poems often refer to the eternal values of nature and insist upon the importance of those values for art, which should aspire to the condition of nature. One need only look at 'The Eternity of Nature', where birds' song is described as a 'music that lives on & ever lives / . . . Longer then songs that poets ever made' (*MC*, p. 248) or at 'The Autumn Robin', in which the narrator sees in the imitation of the bird's song the means of achieving posterity. Nature provides eternal archetypes which outlast the vagaries of taste.

That Clare often says that art should imitate nature is no ground for classifying him as naive. He is disqualified simply by being aware of the breach between nature and culture which enables him to appreciate the former against the latter. There would be little difficulty in providing a reading of Clare as 'sentimental' should we adhere to a sentimental framework. Is his idealization of nature necessarily different from Wordsworth's reaction against eighteenth-century poetic diction and his advocacy of the return to rural values and simple language? Clare despises the artificiality of poetic diction as fervently as Wordsworth and is no less aware of its divergence from the real language spoken by ordinary people.

However, there is no reason to remain with established sentimental opposition between nature and culture when there are so many different ways in which Clare could be said to discuss nature and art. For whilst Clare is undoubtedly concerned with the way in which art and artifice constrain and diverge from nature, it can be argued that far from moving in a sentimental dialectic from nature to art and thence towards union, he deliberately resists the pressures put on him to conform to Romantic conventions, and chooses the 'natural' language of his own dialect, articulately insisting that it is to be preferred, for poetry about rural subjects, to a more highbrow, moralizing and philosophizing idiom. This is an issue which almost all Clare's recent critics discuss and which need not be considered in depth.

I simply note that, if Wordsworth pointed the way back to the language of the rustic, Clare's preoccupations were similarly focused on the avoidance of poetic diction. For Clare, however, this was a personal issue, since he came in for so much criticism from the public and from his critics and publishers for failing to modify his dialect vocabulary and idiom. In one of many letters which express his resistance to this pressure, he objects to: 'Putting the Correct Language of the Gentleman into the mouth of a Simple Shepherd or Vulgar Ploughman';[1] elsewhere he complains that he dislikes 'The Peasant Boy' (the long title-poem of *The Village Minstrel*) because 'it does not describe the feeling of a rhyming peasant strongly or locally enough'.[2]

Barrell gives a good account of Clare's preoccupation – stated in his letters – with writing 'locally': it is, he says

this desire to write 'locally' . . . that becomes around 1821 and 1822 Clare's main preoccupation; which informs almost all his poems while he is living in Helpston.   (Barrell, p. 119)

If we can accept that Clare consciously chooses the local and rejects the generalizing language of pastoral convention as Barrell's book suggests, then we can reject the view that Clare was a failed sentimentalist, just as we can reject the view that he was simply naive. Neither aspect of sentimental criticism is particularly apt. It seems that Clare might even have deliberately put forward a view of art and of poetry which opposed the standard sentimental view. What Brownlow and Barrell say about his resistance to grammatical and other conventions seems to bear out this suggestion.

If we develop this notion of Clare as deliberately resisting sentimentalism rather than being unthinkingly and passively naive, we can begin to dismantle beliefs that he 'has no hard core of individuality compelling his perceptions to serve an inner purpose' (see ch. 3 n. 18), or that he was 'a camera, not a mind' (ch. 3 n. 17). We can argue that he puts forward views about nature and art that are unsentimental but not naive and that the poetry in which he puts forward those views is no more 'objective' or 'descriptive' than that of Wordsworth.

Barrell points the way forward in suggesting that Clare's *localness* be understood as a positive resistance or choice and that, moreover, it is the way in which he insists on being local, not only in how he writes, but in what he writes – avoiding philosophical or general speculations – that explains why criticism has found it hard to get a grip on his poetry.

> Clare's descriptions are so complete that his poems are without any of the gaps through which they might have passed beyond themselves . . . Clare's language refuses to let us look beyond the things and actions he names, to anything analogous.   (Barrell, p. 131)

While the idea of a 'complete' description is questionable, what Barrell says here is significant in that the terms in which he describes Clare's avoidance of generalization from the specific situation is so reminiscent of the notion of 'density' put forward in chapter 4. That is, Barrell suggests that Clare's poetry resists interpretation because it has no 'gaps': no occasions for passing beyond the specific to the general. It will be recalled that it was in these terms that Goodman described the 'dense' and inarticulate symbol system; a system in which the terms were so indeterminate, indistinct and undifferentiated or articulated that it could not be extracted from its instantiation in the art-work. In arguing that Clare's poetry is 'dense' with respect to a sentimental aesthetic, we adapt this point of Barrell's to make a point at a theoretical, rather than a stylistic level. Clare is 'dense' or naive because his work does not provide the opportunity to extrapolate metaphysical or systemic truths from the specific incident. This is, in the end, simply a question of the absence of philosophical or generalized terms, or subject-matter.

If we now look at what Clare says about nature and about the way in which it relates to culture, it will be clear that a rationale for this avoidance of sentimentalism is easily derived from his poetry. That is, we can provide a 'naive' or unsentimental aesthetic, which positively resists sentimentalism or the cultural appropriation of nature.

Whereas Wordsworth frequently discusses nature in terms of its influence on humanity, particularly in *The Prelude*, Clare rarely voices an interest in nature's influence or symbolic value. Instead, one of his repeated themes is the importance of nature's autonomy, and unconstrained independence. (This is a point Barrell makes with respect to Clare's opposition to enclosure, pp. 98–120.) Clare certainly contrasts nature and culture, but it is a relationship that is differently constructed from that which

Wordsworth's poetry considers. The two poets have different perspectives onto nature and different interests at stake.

The main burden of Clare's statement about nature is the contrast between the wild and unrestricted countryside and the cultivating activities of man on the land as the landscape is marshalled into conventional conformity. A clear statement of this contrast is given in 'Emmonsales Heath' (*MC*, p. 160), where Clare addresses the moorland:

> In thy wild garb of other times
> I find thee lingering still
> Furze oer each lazy summit climbs
> At natures easy will
>
> Grasses that never knew a scythe
> Waves all the summer long
> & wild weed blossoms waken blythe
> That ploughshares never wrong.

'Stern industry' is set against 'natures easy will' both in this poem and in others. In 'Enclosure' Clare describes how, before people interfered,

> No fence of ownership crept in between
> To hide the prospect from the gazing eye;
> (Tibble, I, p. 419)

whilst in 'The Fens' (Tibble, II, p. 281), change 'cheats the landscape every day'. Whilst many poems praise nature's aimless and random aspect, her 'wild & beautiful neglect' ('Pleasant Spots' *MC*, p. 452), dozens describe human intervention critically, attacking the wood man who 'on spring intrudes / & thins the shadow(s') solitudes'.[3] There is repeated comparison between the unshackled countryside beyond the reach of humanity and the systematization of cultivated fields.

Nature is rarely, if ever, considered as an educative force, something to be assimilated to the human spirit or the mind of man and if anything it is the assimilation of nature to human needs that Clare most fiercely attacks. His concern is with the relationship between human communities and the land they cultivate and live in and whatever lies beyond that – not with the nature that inspires the tourist. Such differences as could be drawn between Wordsworth's and Clare's attitudes to nature would not be difficult to explain in terms of their respective positions.

Clare often describes the relationship between nature and humans as positive, though, most often by dwelling on the pleasure nature affords to those at leisure from work in the fields. Numerous poems describe walks through the country which have no apparent purpose or significance other than enjoyment and it is this that has often led critics to dismiss Clare as 'descriptive'. However, there is no difficulty in turning this round to suggest that Clare positively asserts the values of inconclusiveness and unconstraint. The inconclusive wandering he describes could be read as the human equivalent of nature's undisturbed, private and unrestrained idleness.

'Stray Walks', for instance, is one of many sonnets which describe 'How pleasant it is thus to think & roam / The many paths scarce knowing which to chuse / All full of pleasant scenes – then wander home' (*MC*, p. 454), whilst in 'Pastoral Liberty', he extols 'The unshackled mood as free as air / & pleasure wild as birds upon the wing / The unwronged impulse won from seasons fair / Like birds perennial travels with the Spring' (*MC*, p. 45): the impulse is won from nature, which sets the example of a 'wild' pleasure, such as birds – which do not direct their own migration consciously – experience. It is for this reason that the natural world is, he suggests, satisfied and satisfies us – praise goes to the bramble, the 'spontaneous flourisher in thickets lone' (*MC*, p. 476) and to footpaths like 'crooked shreds' which lead the way for the narrator in their undirected meanderings.

The idyll that Clare's poems repeatedly describe is not one of exalted union with nature but one of natural idleness and lack of constraint. In many poems, the narrator idly stands or sits watching the landscape in front of his eyes and it is the 'leisure hour' which provides the occasion for these reveries. 'The Meadow Grass' (*MC*, p. 269) or 'On Visiting a Favourite Place' (*MC*, p. 275) are examples of poems which describe such contented reveries: in 'Summer Images', another such, the narrator delights in the fact that he can, 'acting as I please / Drop into pleasant dreams or musing lie' (*MC*, p. 60).

It seems, then, that Clare describes quite a different relationship between humanity (or the speaking subject) and the natural world. He does not describe the human mind, or spiritual life, in any detail, nor does he understand the natural world as a way of enriching or developing that life. Daffodils are not to be stored up for the inward eye, but enjoyed as part of the immediately present scene. Should we seek to construct an aesthetic for Clare as an alternative to sentimentalism, it would be possible to argue that this avoidance of any accommodation of the natural to the artificial is deliberate and that he puts forward a deliberate resistance to art's dominance over nature. The confusions of present and past tense that characterize his work, the lack of any summarizing or organizing phrases or sentences and the wanderings of both syntax and semantics (which I go on to consider) could be understood as deliberate as Wordsworth's orchestrations of past and present experience and past experience gathered up into present reflection. For when Clare does describe the human in nature, he often describes him as one among other animals, self-contained in the aimless enjoyment of nature. In 'Summer Images', for instance:

> Cow tending boy to toil unreconsiled
> Absorbed as in some vagrant summer dream . . .
> . . .
> Starts dancing to his shadow on the wall
> Feeling self gratified
> Nor fearing human thrall   (MC, p. 61)

This stanza describes the cow boy − released from labour − as absorbed as the birds and animals described in previous stanzas in his own enjoyment. This could be compared with Wordsworth's account of the alienated self in 'Resolution and Independence'; in both cases nature is self-contained: Clare's thrush 'by self delight embued', Wordsworth's stock-dove cooing over its own voice. However, in Clare's poem the human subject is differently positioned, able to become absorbed in the natural world, rather than moving through it, discontent and self-conscious. Such differences could well be explained in terms of the different positioning of their respective writers with respect to the environment and their different interests in it. But to say that Clare describes naive and Wordsworth sentimental man on this occasion is not to say that that is always the case and certainly not to say that their *own* mentalities correspond to those they describe.

Whilst Clare does sometimes describe humanity at ease with nature ('Sabbath Bells', *MC*, p. 284, is another example) and often insists on that positive inconclusiveness in which leisure enables humanity to fit in with the natural scene, there are poems in which humans interfere with and are a danger to the natural world. Many of the bird and animal poems take this form and stress the way in which the natural world must be protected from intrusion. Clare often describes the way in which humans intrude on nature's secrecy and privacy. In 'The Moorehens Nest' (*MC*, p. 208), for instance, we have the lines

> I hate the plough that comes to dissaray
> Her holiday delights – & labours toil
> Seems vulgar curses on the sunny soil
> & man the only object that distrains
> Earths garden into deserts for his gains;

with the same emphasis on the contrast between the animal and human world. In 'The Nightingales Nest' the speaker seeks out the hidden nest ('Deep adown / The nest is made a hermits mossy cell') – one might compare Wordsworth's 'Nutting' – and then leaves, and insists that

> here we'll leave them still unknown to wrong
> As the old woodlands legacy of song   (*MC*, p. 203)

Whereas the boy in Wordsworth's poem actually does break into nature, for his own advantage, the boy Clare describes himself as having been does not, but places his emphasis not only on the way nature can be used for human growth and advantage, but on the way humanity abuses and manipulates nature.

It can be argued that far from being naively identified with nature, Clare is equally capable of articulating the relationship between human subject and natural object as Wordsworth, but that he articulates it differently. Both in the positive relations between self and nature and those which are criticized, Clare could be seen to be characteristically inconclusive, insisting on a policy of non-interference into nature by art. The closing lines of 'A Morning Walk' (*MC*, pp. 157–8), for example

& oft I sit me on the ground
Musing upon a neighbouring flower
Or watch the church clocks humming sound
To count the passing hour
Or mark the brook its journey take
In gentle curves round many a weed
Or hear the first wind soft awake
Among the rustling reed

are as different from anything in Wordsworth as they could be. Clare ends with alternatives, with the narrative voice inconclusively watching an inconclusive and rambling scene. There is no obvious moral or philosophical statement to resolve this or to gather nature up into human significance. And it is the same with poems like [The Fox] or [The Marten] which do not give any explanation of the animals they describe or accommodate them articulately to the subject's concerns. Instead, they simply end with the animal's retreat into privacy:

He found a badger hole and bolted in
They tryed to dig but safe from dangers way
He lived to chase the hounds another day.[4]

Again, this is a recurrent feature of Clare's poetry which characteristically fails to provide the kinds of explanations that sentimentalism requires, in which nature is appropriated or accommodated to human concerns through philosophical or other reflective means. In Clare, the speaking subject rarely reflects, or draws conclusions.

It is thus not hard to see why Clare should have been understood, or constructed, as naive. But it is equally clear that a failure to draw sentimental conclusions is not the same thing as being naive. It is easy to construct a complex aesthetic to account for Clare's poetry as a viable alternative to the sentimental aesthetic. It can be argued that Clare is concerned to express *not* the approximation of nature to the human subject or its entrance into the human mind, but the importance of refusing to interfere with nature. It could more elaborately be argued that Clare's inconclusiveness in his poetry reflects this desire to resemble nature's disorder: Barrell goes some way towards this view. Such an aesthetic would reflect biographical differences between Clare and Wordsworth without consigning the former to naiveté

Thus when Lindenberger says that Clare 'keeps primarily to visual impressions' whilst Wordsworth draws 'the intellectual from the visual' (see ch. 3, n. 1), or when Lynd suggests that 'the record of his senses is more important than the record of his imagination' (ch. 3, n. 16), one could counter this by arguing that Clare deliberately articulates the non-interference of the imagination or the intellect in the visually apprehended world. This is positive resistance to sentimentalism.

However, and more importantly, it can be argued that Clare is simply not concerned with these sentimental distinctions between self and world and that though he does contrast humanity with nature he – just as much and more than Wordsworth – can be read as cutting across that opposition.

CLARE AND THE ROMANTIC IDIOM

We saw in chapter 2 how sentimentalism isolates the truly poetic, by suggesting that there is a peculiarly poetic idiom found in Romantic poetry which, by way of an interaction of the two 'halves' of a metaphor, brings about a dissolution of the subject–object opposition. The example of this Romantic metaphor which Leppard gives, among others, in his aforementioned thesis is:

> oh, then the calm
> And dead still water lay upon my mind
> Even with a weight of pleasure, and the sky,
> Never before so beautiful, sank down
> Into my heart, and held me like a dream.
> (*The Prelude*, 1805, II, 176–80)[5]

I have already suggested that I do not consider this to be in any way a special case of the use of metaphor. It is simply an example of the way in which Wordsworth, in this poem, talks about the relationship between himself and nature: interaction is the subject-matter, not the structure of the poem. As many critics have mentioned (see chapter 3), Wordsworth can certainly be seen as preoccupied with this interaction between self and nature. What is special about his poetry is the way in which it does constantly dwell on the way this interaction takes place, the way nature enters into the human mind. This is in itself quite in line with sentimental preoccupations: Coleridge is similarly interested in the subjectivization of the external world and this is not surprising given his reading and background.

It is similarly unsurprising that Clare rarely mentions this kind of interactive relationship in articulately philosophical terms: he does not have the background to do so. We would expect, given his expressed aim of writing specifically and locally, to find quite a different sort of relationship expressed – not philosophical or general but personal and particular. However, that is not to say that Clare is unable to talk about the interaction of humanity and nature at all, as critics have implied.

There are many instances in which Clare does talk about the mental and the physical in the kind of way which in Wordsworth might be called 'interactive'. For example, in 'On Seeing Some Moss in Flower Early in Spring' (*MC*, p. 278), we are told that, 'poesys woods & vales & streams/Grow up within the mind/ Like beauty seen in pleasant dreams'. Here, a metaphor naturalizes poetry into a landscape, which is then localized in the mental domain and compared to an abstract, beauty. This kind of quick intermingling of physical and mental terms is not uncommon in Clare. In 'The Moorehens nest' (*MC*, p. 208), he describes how

> I pick out pictures round the fields that lie
> In my minds heart like things that cannot die
> like picking hopes & making friends with all.

Here, pictures are located in the fields and the fields are located in the 'minds heart'. There is then a further mixture of the physical and mental in the phrase 'picking hopes'. The ambiguous 'that' and the sequence of metaphors could be described as constituting some kind of interaction between the mental and the physical but Clare never articulates such an interaction. Indeed, I would argue that the difference between these lines from Clare and those cited from Wordsworth is constituted not by the fact that the latter brings about a union of subject and object, but by the fact that he clearly articulates what a sentimental subject–object relationship is. Both poets can be read as ambiguous, as describing a scene which is at once 'literal' and 'figurative', physically specific and mentally abstract but Clare's, unlike Wordsworth's, never articulates exchange between subject and object. Indeed, it is because Wordsworth describes the subject and object as initially autonomous and independent of one another and then describes their interaction that he is much easier to follow than Clare, who moves from one to the other without distinction. Clare's poetry is 'dense', it seems, not because it fails to blend subject and object but because it is not concerned to articulate their relationship as subject-matter and because it is grammatically highly ambiguous, resistant to construal on that basic level as Wordsworth's is not. What could be clearer in sentimental terms than Wordsworth telling us how:

> the visible scene
> Would enter unawares into his mind
> With all its solemn imagery; its rocks,
> Its woods, and that uncertain heaven, received
> Into the bosom of the steady lake
> (*The Prelude*, V, 408–12)

or less clear than Clare's

> How many pages of sweet natures book
> Hath poesy doubled down as favoured things
>
> Such as the wood leaves in disorder shook
> By startled stockdoves hasty clapping wings
> & such as reach days party coloured skies
> & such the landscapes charms oer field & fen
> That meet the poets never weary eyes,
> (*MC*, 'Nature', p. 390)

where poet as writer and observer, poem as text and real scene, are inexplicably, and inextricably, tangled.

Clare, we can argue, is perceived as naive not because he does not bring visual and intellectual together but because he does not separate them sufficiently and does not make articulate the subject–object relations which sentimentalism finds significant. His idiom could be used, then, as an antidote to the 'Romantic idiom', to illustrate not how subject and object, literal and figurative are interactive, but how they are never distinct in the first place.

Focusing more closely on the way in which Clare's language might be 'dense', I take as example the poem 'The Flitting' (*MC*, pp. 216–21), which describes Clare's move to a new home. Analysis of this poem should show how inadequate accounts of Clare's poetry as naively 'objective' in its description are, how indefensible statements that he failed to pass beyond the 'literal'.

If we compare 'The Flitting' to a poem such as 'Tintern Abbey',

which similarly concerns itself with a comparison between the
past and the present, it is clear that, where Wordsworth uses a
narrative voice which, speaking from the vantage point of the
poetic present looks back on the past and holds the two distinct
through such phrases as 'I cannot paint / What then I was', 'That
time is past', and so forth, Clare constructs no such firmly
established poetic history and no such articulated and reflective
personal. Instead, we are confronted by a mixture of past, and
present, and a rambling and uncertain narrative voice. Not only
this, but the authority of that voice is constantly undermined by
the location of emotions and thoughts not in the speaker, but in
the landscape. For example, in the first verse it is the season that is
a stranger to the narrator, who sits passively, being assaulted by
foreign feelings and presences:

> The summer like a stranger comes
> I pause & hardly know her face

whilst in the third, moving alternately from past to present, he
says:

> I sit me in my corner chair
> That seems to feel itself from home
> & hear bird music here & there
> From awthorn hedge & orchard come
> – I sat on my old bench in June
> The sailing puddocks shrill 'peelew'
> Oer royce wood seemed a sweeter tune

It is not only the transferral of the sense of loss to the chair, but the
use of Clare's favourite 'seems' which gives a sense of uneasy
uncertainty. The bird music 'here & there' seems to be at once in
the present and in the past as the two landscapes, so similar in
Clare's comparison, merge. This is clinched by the past tense of
'seemed' in the last line: here the uncertain assessment is put back
into a past in which it did not yet exist.
   In the next verse:

> The nightingale is singing now
> But like to me she seems at loss
> For royce wood & its shielding bough
> I lean upon the window sill
> The trees & summer happy seem
> Green sunny green they shine – but still
> My heart goes far away to dream

there is the same description of feeling to the bird and this movement away from the feeling subject to the landscape is consolidated by Clare's use of 'my heart' or 'my thoughts' as though they were autonomously acting entities. This leaves a helpless subject, unable to control the situation and this sense of helplessness is exacerbated by the disconnected structure of the verse: from being in the lane, we are suddenly at the window sill and then far away. This quick, interrupted subject-change is very typical; Clare rarely constructs long or sustained sentences or any kind of logical progression. Again, in this verse it is 'the trees and summer' – one of Clare's odd combinations of a specific and a general embracing that specific term – which are happy and are the focus of feeling.

Looking at the sixth to eighth verses, the same characteristics appear:

> I miss the prospect far & wide
> From Langley bush & so I seem
>
> Alone & in a stranger scene
> Far far from spots my heart esteems
> The closen with their ancient green
> Heaths woods & pastures sunny streams
> The awthorns here were hung with may
> But still they seem in deader green
> The sun een seems to loose its way
> Nor knows the quarter it is in
>
> I dwell on trifles like a child
> I feel as ill becomes a man
> & still my thoughts like weedlings wild
> Grow up to blossom where they can

Rather than possessing the feeling of strangeness, the subject says 'I seem / Alone & in a stranger scene' and it is 'my heart' which esteems the lost 'closen'. Again, an unexpected past tense appears: the hawthorns 'here' were hung with may: the past is located in the present scene, rather than the lost one. And the verse concludes with the sun being lost – again, loss is located in the landscape. With this in mind, the next verse, in which the randomness of the speaker's thoughts is described, seems particularly apt. Whilst it talks about loss, the poem also confuses with its distracting syntax, use of tense and description of feelings to objects and abstracts.

This is typical of Clare, who rarely gives a historical or temporal perspective and rarely describes a speaker constructing the past from a secure vantage-point. Almost invariably, past and present tenses blur together.

The localization of thoughts and feelings in the landscape itself, remarkable in this poem, is noticeable elsewhere. In 'Bushy Close' (*MC*, p. 207), Clare describes what at first seems like a real past experience:

> I have crept full many hours away
> To hunt for nests & wood flowers

but goes on to use an ambiguous pair of metaphors,

> for in these
> My boyish heart was living – woods & vales
> Made up my being

One might wonder how a Wordsworthian critic would construe this: the 'boyish heart' commands the verb, separate from the self and actually inhabits the particular scene, just as the 'being' is made up of woods and vales. Clare's poetry is riddled with such ambiguities: in the 'Round Oak and Eastwell', for example, he describes how 'The stray poets memory haunts the spot / Like a friends features time nigh hath forgot' (Tibble, II, 297). There is now no metaphor, but a simile – but similar confusion. Does 'like' compare the memory to the friend's features? Is the place like a forgotten friend, and is it time, or the memory or the poet who does the forgetting? It is as if abstract or mental activities were confused with specific physical locations so that the two cannot be separated.

Whilst we could argue that Clare, like Wordsworth, in the critical views held by many sentimental critics, confused the subject and the object, Clare does not articulate a logic of 'interaction'; he gives no direct, philosophical account of the relationship between self and nature, nor are there any obvious conclusions to be drawn from this ambiguity. The narrative voice which Clare constructs seems deliberately stripped of authority and passively recipient of natural forces and changes. Clare thus makes it difficult, we might argue, to construct a metaphysical system for his work, a master model of subject–object relations:

and if we wanted to press the point, we could argue that this was deliberate resistance to sentimentalism. Persistent ambiguity, despite readings of Clare as 'vivid' or 'accurate', makes it hard to construe a particular scene and the shifting locus of the vague, speaking subject, now present, now past, is far more difficult or *dense*, for sentimental critics, than Wordsworth's 'wholesome separation' of two natures – 'one that feels, the other that observes' (*The Prelude*, Book XIII, 330–1).

One can see how Clare might be 'dense' compared with Wordsworth, without being more 'naive' in the sentimental sense. One reason for this apparent 'density' or resistance to critical interpretations (at least, to sentimental interpretation) is a particular kind of construction in the poetry which, as an antidote to de Man's revealing of sentimental rhetoric in Wordsworth's metaphor, we could see as a 'naive' insistence on the already figurative nature of literal description. This is a typical feature of Clare's poetry, a simile in which the two things compared are already closely related – an apparent trope which in fact is nothing more than a simple statement. For example, in 'The Wild Bull' (*MC*, p. 242):

> The schoolboy runs & whines & pants for breath
> Like fear heart bursting from the chase of death, (*MC*, p. 242)

> While the hoarse bull lord of the pasture reigns
> & lives like terror on the rushy plains. (*MC*, p. 243)

The comparisons introduced by 'like' are pseudo-comparisons where we would expect adjectives describing the relevant nouns – the frightened boy, the terrifying bull. Clare's tendency to introduce unexpected abstracts in this way is marked. In 'The Hailstorm in June 1831' (*MC*, p. 415), for instance,

> Darkness came oer like chaos – & the sun
> As startled with terror seemed to run
> With quickened dread behind the beetling cloud
> The old wood sung like nature in her shroud
> & each old rifted oak trees mossy arm
> Seemed shrinking from the presence of the storm
> . . .
> Like reeds they bent like drunken men they reeled
> Till man from shelter ran & sought the open field

After comparing darkness and chaos – an instance where the

two halves of a simile collapse into one another – chaos and darkness overlap – Clare compares the wood to 'nature in her shroud'. 'Her' is ambiguously applicable to the wood or nature, but in either case, wood-shroud-nature are already sufficiently close and overlapping (nature includes wood, 'shroud' implies the wood in this context) for the simile to retreat into itself. The strong contextual link between trees and nature as part of one and the same scene dominates the sense. Then, the trees bend 'like drunken men': a comparison which holds its shaky ground, but the contingent presence of real, reeling men confuses the men looking like trees with trees like men or like reeds. Personification or animation reinforces the close network of relations between humanity and nature: the sun feels terror, the trees shrink from the storm. Rather than building comparisons between the particular situation and something distinct, Clare uses similes to bring closer the already intimate world of rural life, bringing nature and humanity close, whilst the doubtful presence of 'seems' and 'like' makes the animated scene tremble.

In 'The Thrushes Nest' (MC, p. 399), 'A brood of natures minstrels chirp & flye / Glad as that sunshine & the laughing sky': Clare chooses, rather than having the birds flying through the sky, to compare them to the sky, which is itself animated with laughter. Similarly, in 'On Seeing Two Swallows Late In October' (MC, p. 475), the birds are compared to winds: 'Forsaking all like untamed winds they roam'. Reading this as describing the birds flying on the wind, we should in fact compare the two, animating the one, diffusing the other into the atmosphere.

Such similes do not expand or extend the given particular scene by comparing it beyond itself to something distinct. Instead, they retreat into the particular by only comparing like with what is like, or contingent. For example, in 'The Wild Bull',

> The linnet builds in plumage half as green
> Yet safe she lives as in a pathless wood (MC, p. 242)

Here, 'plumage' – because the bird 'builds *in* plumage' – can apply to the materials of the nest, and the leaves of the wood – through its greenness – as well as to the bird's feathers, whilst the comparison of the habitat with a 'pathless wood' is taken less as a comparison than as a statement of where the bird actually does live. In the same way, in 'Pleasures of Spring' (MC, p. 11), 'The gay

woodpecker with its glossy wing / Green as the plumage of
returning Spring' is less a comparison of the bird with spring than
an intimate association of the two: the bird returns with spring,
and 'plumage' applies as much to the one as the other.

Looking again at 'The Wild Bull', we can see how intricately
Clare can combine a main theme and an illustration in such a way
that the actual scene and what it is compared with become
entangled. Long passages confuse the real incident, where a bull
chases the boys, with similar events in illustrated books and with
the speaker's memory of similar events. In these lines

> Reading made easy such life pictures own
> That still delight from pleasures they have known
> I read such little books at leisures will
> & joy though broken feels the picture still
> I still look oer the cuts of boys at play
> Among old hugh tree trunks or meadow hay
> & read me of bird nesters bursting full
> Of terror running from a roaring bull
> & feel delight as boys with joy can be
> To see him safety-pictured on a tree   (MC, p. 243)

the act of reading is not clearly distinguished from the actions
outside reading, particularly as the descriptions of the book's
illustrations are so similar to those in the rest of the poem of the
real bull chase. Abstract nouns, 'joy though broken' spread the
action from the speaker outwards, seeming to apply to the worn
woodcuts as well as to the fading feeling, whilst the enjambment
'Of terror' loosens terror as an abstract that runs in front of the
bull. Comparisons such as 'as boys with joy can be' or in the final
lines:

> & now I feel by safetys side a joy
> From memorys fears – delightful as a boy (MC, p. 243)

relate the speaker, when young, with the boys he watches, and
with the boy in the book, as the abstracted and diffused emotions
of joy and safety drift loose from their owners. His conclusive
security is thrust back into the thick of the experience, as past and
present, actuality and fiction, mix in the specific experience of the
bull chase.

Abstractions and personified abstracts are clearly important in achieving this animated landscape and Clare's poems are characteristically full of such abstracts. In 'The Summer Shower', for example,

> Amid the yellow furze the rabbits bed
> Labour hath hid his tools & oer the heath
> Hies to the milking shed
> That stands the oak beneath
>
> And there he wiles the pleasant shower away
> Filling his mind with store of happy things
> Rich crops of corn & hay
> & all that plenty brings   (*MC*, p. 185)

'Labour' describes the farm hand, who, in a real milking shed, fills his *mind* with happy things, themselves 'rich crops' that might well be part of the actual surrounding landscape. Clare repeatedly uses 'Beauty' or 'Labour' for individuals and also locates abstractions such as 'health' in the place described: 'Health greets me for I hear her voice' ('On Visiting a Favourite Place', *MC*, p. 275), 'I love green leisure to delay' ('A Seat in The Meadows', *MC*, p. 473) or 'thought so full of talk . . . / Meets pleasure in the walk' ('On Seeing Some Moss in Flower Early in Spring', *MC*, p. 278). These repeated abstractions, wandering through the particular landscape, diffuse it with the subject's feelings and locate those feelings in the place. In certain poems, reading can become difficult because of the concentration of abstract terms. For example, in 'The Meadow Grass':

> Joy half a stranger comes to me
> & gives me thoughts to profit bye
> I think how happy worlds must be
> That dwell above that peaceful sky
>
> . . .
>
> In places where the summer seems
> Entirely out of troubles way
> Where joy oer out door leisure dreams
> As if twas sunday every day
>
> . . .
>
> A calmness quiet loves to find
> In these green summer reveries

A freshness giving youth to age
A health to pain & troubles drear
The world has nought but wars to wage
Peace comes & makes her dwelling here   (*MC*, p. 269)

the action, through the main verbs, is appropriated by abstract nouns which inhabit the landscape: worlds, not humans are happy and dwell above the sky; the summer is out of trouble's way, joy dreams over leisure and so on. But although abstractions crowd the scene, the insistence is still on the specific place and situation: it is *here* that quiet and peace live.

At once particular and uncertain, Clare's poems vibrate with the loosened, free-floating emotions of the human subject, transformed into abstractions that occupy local landscapes. A brief survey of his poetry yields countless examples of the animation of the inanimate and the transposition of human feelings and inanimate characteristics.

Sometimes this is simply a case of a single adjective: the 'crouching corn' in 'The Summer Shower' (p. 153), or the hares who eat 'fearful morsels' in 'A Morning Walk' (p. 154). Sometimes there is a fuller and more complex description of subjectivity to birds and animals: for instance, in 'March' from *The Shepherds Calendar*. Here, the solitary shepherd boy crouches in a den like an animal, observing, passive and uncomprehending, a passing crane which has the loneliness of a human traveller:

the solitary crane
Swings lonly to unfrozen dykes again
Cranking a jarring mellancholy cry
Thro he wild journey of the cheerless sky[6]

Or, similarly, in 'January' from the same poem, the skating children look like birds, whilst the passing moorhen experiences human fear:

The morehen too, wi fear opprest
Starts from her reedy sheltered nest . . .
Skaiting along wi curving springs
. . .
Wi arms spread out like herons wings
They race away[7]

and this description of sensibility to birds or animals is usual with Clare; in 'The Robins Nest' this is combined with the localizing of an abstract:

> & thus these feathered heirs of solitude
> Remain the tennants of this quiet wood
> And live in melody and make their home   (*MC*, p. 252)

Here, the birds are at once 'feathered', ordinary birds and 'tennants' and 'heirs' to the wood: they are heirs to 'solitude' and live in 'melody'. Thus Clare introduces into what remains a description of a bird's nest more complex and wider associations without disrupting that description. By saying that the birds live *in* melody, he widens and diffuses the word, making it more than just birdsong or the song of these birds, but a general atmosphere.

It is possible, then, to point to certain recurrent tendencies in Clare's poetry. First of all, there is his use of comparison or simile. Clare's similes, whilst they allow him to evade assertion and to describe through tentative comparison rather than statement, rarely bring in alien or foreign particulars to the scene described. Instead, they tend to compare the particular in question to an abstract noun or another noun in some way connected to that particular and which might more naturally relate adjectivally to it. For instance, in 'The Woodlarks Nest' (*MC*, p. 470), we are told: 'As safe as secresy her six eggs lie', rather than that her eggs are safe and secret. This allows for the abstract 'secresy' and for a certain tentativeness and vagueness about the description. Similarly, in 'Hares at Play' (*MC*, p. 418), where 'Like toil a resting lies the fallow plough,' and 'Each nimbling hare / Sturts quick as fear': 'toil' and 'fear' are logically connected to the plough (its purpose is toil) and the hares (they feel afraid), so the conscious comparison through a formal simile is noticeable.

In the same way, a comparison may be introduced where what it introduces could any way form part of the description: in 'The Skylark Leaving Her Nest' the

> woods in their dark splendour dreams
> Like heaviness on earth   (*MC*, p. 265)

and in 'The Thrushes Nest', as we saw

> A brood of natures minstrels chirp and fly
> Glad as the sunshine and the laughing sky

where in both cases heaviness on earth and the sunshine and sky, could anyway be part of the scene described. There is, it seems, scarcely enough distinction or distance between what is described and the illustration for these to be proper similes. Why, then, the frequent introduction of 'like' and 'as'? It seems that this could have two functions: firstly, to render more uncertain, more tentatively pointing beyond the specific, the scene described; and secondly, to introduce abstractions, which similarly obscure and enlarge the particular without actually having autonomous status: they are just illustrations. Comparisons of this kind, it can be argued, are one way in which Clare achieves that hesitant and wavering quality which characterizes his very specific localities.

Another important characteristic is his tendency to make abstract or general nouns, sometimes as personifications, the subjects of verbs we might otherwise expect the human subject to command. Thus, in 'The Old Shepherd',

> the shades where my infancy revelled in joy
> The axe has left desolate now   (*MC*, p. 195)

whilst in 'Remembrances',

> silence sitteth now on the wild heath as her own
> Like a ruin of the past all alone   (*MC*, p. 369)

In many poems, the speaking subject is lost among such abstracts, which inhabit and wander the countryside and his feelings are distributed among these and the birds and animals and plants. Animation works together with this abstracting tendency to suggest a countryside not controlled or dominated by the human presence, but living according to its own rules, if such they may be called.

Paul de Man, as we saw earlier, is one critic who has given a rhetorical account of Wordsworth's poetry as possessed of a particular kind of image which 'unites irreconcilable opposites'.[8] Other writers – Isobel Armstrong, for example – have supported this view of Wordsworth's language. I would argue, in view of the analysis of Clare's language given above, that what is notable about Wordsworth is his articulate and structured discussion of the relationship of the human subject and the natural world; a relationship for which he has a philosophical or metaphysical rationale. Throughout *The Prelude* Wordsworth articulates the relationship between man and nature; tells us that nature is significant for man, that it becomes bound to him and so forth. It is in the light of these statements about nature as symbol, as mental power, that de Man and others explain the kinds of metaphors which are no more remarkable in ambiguously describing the mental and the physical than those found in Clare. The difference is that Wordsworth articulates ambiguity. He tells us that the human perceiver

> often is perplexed and cannot part
> The shadow from the substance, rocks and sky,
> Mountains and clouds, from that which is indeed
> The region   (*The Prelude*, Book IV, pp. 254–7)

and thus articulates the difference between what is literal and what figurative. It is this articulation which differentiates him from Clare who, not articulating ambiguity, simply is ambiguous, or *dense*.

Rather than constructing Clare as 'naive' because he is not concerned with giving an account of this idealist union of subject and object, we can recognize that it is just as viable to argue that Clare's idiom manifests a 'dense' aesthetic, as it is to argue that Wordsworth's manifests an 'articulate' aesthetic. But it is simpler to construct the difference between them as a function not of idiom, but of subject-matter. Clare's views are different and in being unsentimental, they are dense with respect to a sentimental aesthetic or criticism. This can be further explained in terms of semantic and syntactic ambiguity.

CONCLUSION

In chapter 4, I suggested that we could redescribe the 'naiveté' that sentimentalism offers as 'other' to sentimental poetry as 'density', understanding the difference between the'sentimental' and the 'naive' poet as one of relative articulacy with respect to a critical system. In this chapter, I have applied this principle to Clare's poetry, showing how the characteristics which differentiate it from that of Wordsworth are not those of 'objectivity' or 'visual' or 'pictorial' accuracy or detail or fidelity to nature, but a different set of expressed beliefs about nature and art and a different degree of articulation of those beliefs.

This provides the conclusion to this book in which I have dismantled the dominant notion of naiveté in poetry, explaining it as an ideological and historical rather than a stylistic category and a category which has been inconsistently used to distinguish and isolate the 'truly' aesthetic from a false or inferior class of poetry.

NOTES

Introduction

1 Herbert Lindenberger, 'Images of interaction in *The Prelude*', *On Wordsworth's Prelude* (Princeton: Princeton University Press, 1963), pp. 69–98, rpt. in Jonathan Wordsworth, M. H. Abrams and Stephen Gill, eds., *The Prelude, 1799, 1805, 1850* by Wordsworth, Norton Critical Editions (London, New York: W. W. Norton and Co., 1979), pp. 642–663, 643.

2 F. W. Schiller, *On the naive and sentimental in literature*, trans. ed. Helen Watanabe-O'Kelly (Manchester: Carcanet New Press, 1981). All references are to this text, and are given parenthetically.

3 Nelson Goodman, *Languages of art: an approach to a theory of symbols* (Indianapolis: Hackett Publishing Company, 1976). All references to this text are given parenthetically as Goodman.

4 John Barrell, *The idea of landscape and the sense of place 1730–1840: an approach to the poetry of John Clare* (Cambridge: Cambridge University Press, 1972). All references to this text are given parenthetically as Barrell.

5 John Clare, *The Midsummer Cushion*, ed. Anne Tibble (Northumberland: Mid-Northumberland Arts Group in ass. with Carcanet New Press, 1978). References to this text are given parenthetically as *MC*. Where possible I have used this text, otherwise the less authoritative text of *The Poems of John Clare*, ed. J. W. Tibble, 2 vols. (London: J. M. Dent, 1935). Where texts not in *The Midsummer Cushion* are available in *John Clare*, The Oxford Authors, ed. Eric Robinson and Geoffrey Summerfield (Oxford: Oxford University Press, 1984) I have used that text, which is less heavily revised than Tibble.

Chapter 1 Schiller and the sentimental tradition

1 Arnold Hauser, *Rococo, Classicism and Romanticism*, Vol. III of *The social history of art* (London: Routledge and Kegan Paul, 1962, rpt. 1984), p. 16.

2 Immanuel Kant, *Critique of judgment*, trans. J. H. Bernard, The Hafner Library of Classics, 14 (New York: Hafner Publishing Company, 1951), 54, pp. 180–181. All references to this text are given parenthetically as *CJ*.

3 Elizabeth Wilkinson and J. A. Willoughby, trans., ed., *On the aesthetic education of man. In a series of letters*, by Friedrich Schiller (Oxford: Clarendon Press, 1967, rpt 1982, 1985). All references to this text are given parenthetically as *AE*.

4 Leonard P. Wessell, 'The antinomic structure of Friedrich Schlegel's "Romanticism"', *Studies in Romanticism*, 12 (Summer 1973), 648–669, 653.

5 Hegel, *Introduction to aesthetics, being the introduction to the Berlin Aesthetics Lectures of the 1820s*, trans. T. M. Knox, with an interpretative essay by Charles Karelis (Oxford: Oxford University Press, 1979), p. 61.

6 Arnold Hauser, *Rococo, Classicism and Romanticism*, p. 108.

7 René Wellek, *The later eighteenth century*, Vol. 1 of *A history of modern criticism 1750–1950*, London: Jonathan Cape, 1955; rpt. 1966).

8 David Simpson, ed., *German aesthetic and literary criticism: Kant, Fichte, Schelling, Schopenhauer, Hegel* (Cambridge: Cambridge University Press, 1984), p. 2.

9 M. H. Abrams, *Natural supernaturalism: tradition and revolution in Romantic literature* (New York: W. W. Norton and Co., 1971), p. 212.

10 'While Schiller, along with Goethe, was the impetus for freeing the romantics from an aesthetic of objectivity and the superiority of classical over modern literature, Kant's *practical* philosophy . . . along with Herder's aesthetic of historical relativism . . . had pointed the way for a revolution in criticism'. Kathleen M. Wheeler, ed., *German aesthetic and literary criticism: the Romantic ironists and Goethe* (Cambridge: Cambridge University Press, 1984). See pp. 6–7 for Schiller's influence on the Schlegels. See also James Engell's comments on 'the drama of the will struggling to fulfil itself', in *The creative imagination: Enlightenment to Romanticism* (Cambridge, Mass.: Harvard University Press, 1981), p. 238.

11 René Wellek, *The later eighteenth century*, pp. 232–233.

12 M. H. Abrams, for example, tells us that, 'This complex of related antitheses – subjective and objective, naive and sentimental, classical and romantic . . . migrated over into the vocabulary of English and American criticism mainly during and after the second decade of the nineteenth century', *The mirror and the lamp* (London: Oxford University Press, 1953), p. 242. See also pp. 216–218 for Coleridge and Carlyle's reading of the German theorists.

13 Frank Lentricchia, *After the new criticism* (London: The Athlone Press; Chicago: University of Chicago Press, 1980), p. 3.

14 Lentricchia, *After the new criticism*, p. 20.

15 Murray Krieger, 'Mediation, language, and vision in the reading of literature' in *Interpretation: theory and practice*, ed. Charles S. Singleton, The Johns Hopkins Humanities Seminars (Baltimore: Johns Hopkins University Press, 1969), pp. 221–242, p. 215.

16 Paul de Man, *Blindness and insight: essays in the rhetoric of contemporary criticism*, 2nd ed. (London: Methuen, 1983), p. 27.

17 Ernest Tuveson, 'Shaftesbury and the age of sensibility', in *Studies in aesthetics and criticism, 1660–1800. Essays in honour of Samuel Holt Monk*, ed. Howard Anderson and John S. Shea (Minneapolis: University of Minnesota Press, 1967), pp. 73–93, p. 80.

18 See Harold Osborne, *Aesthetics and art theory: an historical introduction* (London: Longmans, 1968), p. 96.

19 Walter J. Hipple, *The beautiful, the sublime and the picturesque in eighteenth-century British aesthetic theory* (Carbondale: Southern Illinois University Press, 1957), p. 7.

20 For an account of the 'standard of taste' debate, see Walter Hipple's book (above), or Katherine Gilbert and Helmut Kuhn, eds., *A history of aesthetics* (London: Thames and Hudson, 1956), pp. 233–258.

21 Kant, Preface to the Second Edition, *Critique of pure reason*, trans. Norman Kemp-Smith (London: Macmillan, 1929, rpt 1982), p. 22.

22 Ernst Cassirer, 'Language', Vol. I of *The philosophy of symbolic forms*, trans. Ralph Manheim (New Haven and London: Yale University Press, 1955, rpt. 1977), p. 78.

23 Roger Scruton, *Art and imagination: a study in the philosophy of mind* (London: Routledge and Kegan Paul, 1974, rpt. 1982), p. 3.

24 Osborne, *Aesthetics and art theory*. pp. 115–116.

25 Dieter Henrich, 'Beauty and freedom: Schiller's struggle with Kant's aesthetics', *Zeitschrift für philosophische Forschung*, 11 (1957), 527–547, rpt. in *Essays in Kant's aesthetics*, ed. Ted Cohen and Paul Guyer (Chicago: Chicago University Press, 1982), pp. 237–257, pp. 242, 243, 244.

26 Schiller's letters to Körner, detailing his plans for a treatise on beauty, 'Kallias', are selectively translated and published in *Correspondence of Schiller with Körner, comprising sketches and anecdotes of Goethe, the Schlegels, Wieland and other contemporaries* (London, 1849). See especially 'To Körner', Jena, 21 December 1792, p. 204, and 'To Körner', Weimar, 25 January 1793, pp. 212–213.

27 'It was this very issue between himself and Kant that had provoked him to produce a treatise on aesthetic education' (*AE*, pp. clxxviii–ix). See also Eva Schaper's discussion of Schiller's

revision of Kant's aesthetic, in 'Schiller's Kant: a chapter in the history of creative misunderstanding', in *Studies in Kant's aesthetics* (Edinburgh: Edinburgh University Press, 1979), pp. 99–117, esp. p. 111: 'The dilemma, for Schiller, to whom this kind of formalism was deeply repugnant . . .' etc. Schaper criticizes Schiller's reading of Kant as too formal, showing how he mishandles Kant's terms.

28 'To Körner', Jena, 21 December 1792, *Correspondence of Schiller with Körner*, p. 214.

29 Dieter Henrich, 'Beauty and freedom', pp. 246–247.

30 Rose Frances Egan, 'The Genesis of the theory of "art for art's sake" in Germany', Part I, *Smith College Studies in Modern Languages*, 2 (July 1921), 59–60.

31 Schiller, 'To Körner', Weimar, 25 January 1793, cited by Eva Schaper, 'Schiller's Kant', pp. 104–5. Schaper translates from the German edition of Schiller's letters, *Schillers Briefe*, ed. Fritz Jonas, 7 vols. (Stuttgart: Deutsche Verlags-Ansalt, 1892–1896), III, 237–9. For the English translation, see *Correspondence of Schiller with Körner*, pp. 212–214.

32 Arthur E. Lovejoy, 'Schiller and the genesis of German Romanticism, part I', *Modern Language Notes*, 35 (January 1920), 1–10, 4, rpt. in *Essays in the History of Ideas* (New York: George Braziller, 1955), pp. 207–227. This essay, and the second part published in *Modern Language Notes*, 35 (March 1920), 136–146, give an account of the development of Schiller's and Schlegel's thought, and of the categories 'naive' and 'sentimental' as they are transformed by Schlegel.

33 Schiller, 'To Wilhelm von Humboldt', 26 October 1795, cited Helen Watanabe-O'Kelly (*NS*, Introduction, p. 12), no reference given.

Chapter 2 Myths of Romanticism

1 Jerome McGann, *The Romantic ideology: a critical investigation* (Chicago and London: University of Chicago Press, 1983).

2 Wheeler, *German aesthetic and literary criticism*, p. 7.

3 Leonard P. Wessell, Jr., 'Schiller and the genesis of German Romanticism', *Studies in Romanticism*, 10 (Summer 1971), 176–198.

4 Wessell, 'The Antinomic Structure', p. 656.

5 Ernest Behler, 'The origins of the Romantic literary theory', *Colloquia Germanica*, 1–2 (1968), 109–126, 117.

6 A. W. Schlegel, *A course of lectures on dramatic art and literature*, trans. John Black (London: Henry Bohn, 1846), pp. 26–27.

7 A. W. Schlegel, *A course of lectures*, p. 342.

8 Friedrich Schlegel, *Dialogue on poetry and literary aphorisms*, trans. ed. Ernest Behler and Roman Struc (Pennsylvania State University

Park and London: Pennsylvania University Press, 1968), 'Dialogue on poetry', p. 101; 'Selected aphorisms from the *Athenaeum*', no. 116, p. 141.

9 Peter Firchow, trans. ed., *Lucinde and the fragments*, Friedrich Schlegel (Minneapolis: University of Minnesota Press, 1971), Introd., p. 20.

10 Tzvetan Todorov, *Theories of the symbol*, trans. Catherine Porter (Paris, 1977; Oxford: Basil Blackwell, 1982). Todorov's references are to Ernest Behler's edition, see above, n. 8.

11 Hans-Georg Gadamer points out the problematic nature of Kant's distinction between the 'reflective' and the 'determinant' judgment, when he says that,

> Every judgment about something that is intended to be understood in its concrete individuality . . . is . . . a judgment about a special case. That means simply that the evaluation of the case does not merely apply the measure of the universal principle according to which it is judged but itself co-determines it, supplements and corrects . . . it. From this it follows that all moral judgments require taste.

Gadamer points out the intrinsic particularity and subjectivity of all judgments, and thus the difficulty of distinguishing the 'reflective' and 'determinant', the 'aesthetic' and the 'moral'. *Truth and method*, trans. William Glen-Doepl from the 2nd (1965) edition of *Wahrheit und Methode*, and ed. John Cumming and Garret Burdon (London: Sheed and Ward, 1975, rpt. 1979), p. 37. Other critics have taken up this and similar points: see Karl Ameriks, 'Kant and the objectivity of taste', *British Journal of Aesthetics*, 23 (1983), 3–17, 6, where Ameriks points out that 'only a very special kind of terminology is behind the idea that taste is "non-logical" or "non-conceptual"', and although 'this point may serve in Kant's system to distinguish aesthetic judgments from some moral ones . . . it is a fundamental fact of that system that *no* particular phenomenal features are determinable from concepts alone'.

See also Anthony Savile, 'Objectivity in aesthetic judgment: Eva Schaper on Kant', rev. of *Studies in Kant's aesthetics*, by Eva Schaper, (see chapter 1, n. 27 above), *British Journal of Aesthetics*, 21 (1981), 363–369, 364, where he says that 'there seems to be no reason why Kant's aesthetic judgments . . . will not count as nearly objective as those we are ready to recognize without hesitation as empirical'.

12 Friedrich Schlegel, 'Selected aphorisms from the *Athenaeum*', in *Dialogue on poetry and literary aphorisms*, ed. Behler, no. 116, pp. 140–141.

13 Friedrich Schlegel, 'Literary aphorisms from the *Lyceum*', in Behler, no. 21, p. 122.

14 Ernst Cassirer, *The philosophy of the Enlightenment*, trans. Fritz C. A. Koelln and James D. Pettegrove (1932; rpt Princeton: Princeton University Press, 1951), pp. 276, 278.

15 Wheller, *German aesthetic and literary criticism*, p. 3.

16 Abrams, *The mirror and the lamp*, p. 124.

17 Paul Hamilton, *Coleridge's poetics* (Cambridge: Cambridge University Press, 1983), p. 3.

18 Wellek, *The Romantic age*, Vol. II of *A history of modern criticism*, p. 165.

19 Friedrich Schlegel, 'Literary aphorisms from the *Lyceum*', in Behler, no. 115, p. 132.

20 Friedrich Schlegel, 'Literary aphorisms from the *Lyceum*', in Behler, no. 61, p. 127.

21 Mary Warnock, *Imagination* (London: Faber and Faber, 1976; rpt. 1980), p. 91.

22 Coleridge, *Biographia literaria*, ed. J. Shawcross, (Oxford: Oxford University Press; London: Geoffrey Cumberledge, 1907, rpt. 1949), II, xiv, 10.

23 Coleridge, 'On the principles of genial criticism concerning the fine arts', appended to *Biographia literaria*, ed. Shawcross, II, 220–221.

24 Hamilton, *Coleridge's poetics*, p. 42.

25 See *Coleridge's Shakespearean criticism*, ed. Thomas Middleton Raysor, 2 vols. (London: Constable and Co., 1930). Coleridge says that
> poetry, or rather a poem, is a species of composition, opposed to science, as having intellectual pleasure for its object, and as attaining its end by the use of language natural to us in a state of excitement – but distinguished from other species of composition, not excluded by the former criterion, by permitting a pleasure from the whole consistent with a consciousness of pleasure from the component parts. (Raysor, I, 163)

Distinguishing the poem by way of this concept of a holistic apprehension – a distinction not grounded in the aesthetics of Kant, Schiller, or the German Romantics – he goes on to use an equally vague notion of genius to account for the special nature of poetry:

> this most general and distinctive character of a poem originates in the poetic genius itself . . . which sustains and modifies the emotions, thoughts, and vivid representation of the poem by the energy without effort of the poet's own mind – by the spontaneous activity of his imagination and fancy, and by whatever else with these reveals itself in the balancing and reconciling of opposite and discordant qualities.

Here, the character of the aesthetic in general, as it is described in Kant and Schiller, is ascribed to poetry in particular. See also Raysor,

I, 253–254, II, 66–68, 77–79 and 98, for definitions of poetry; and *Biographia literaria*, II, xxii, p. 97, for Coleridge's claim that language can be divided into the poetic, the prosaic, and the 'neutral' style.

26 Abrams, *The mirror and the lamp*, p. 176.
27 Wellek, *The Romantic age*, p. 180.
28 Wellek, *The Romantic age*, p. 180. Wellek refers to Coleridge's *Miscellaneous criticism*, ed. T. M. Raysor (London, 1936), p. 165, and to *Biographia literaria*, ed. Shawcross, II, p. 209.
29 *Biographia literaria*, II, xv, 16.
30 *Biographia literaria*, II, xxii, 101.
31 *Biographia literaria*, II, xvii, 33.
32 Coleridge, *The collected works of Samuel Taylor Coleridge*, ed. Kathleen Coburn (Princeton and London, 1971), *The friend*, ed. B. J. Rooke, p. 464.
33 *Coleridge's Shakespearean criticism*, ed. T. M. Raysor, I, 197–198.
34 Hamilton, *Coleridge's poetics*, p. 156.
35 *Biographia literaria*, I, iv, 59.
36 Coleridge, 'The statesman's manual', in *The collected works of Samuel Taylor Coleridge*, Vol. VI, *Lay sermons*, ed. R. J. White (Princeton: Princeton University Press; London: Routledge and Kegan Paul, 1972), p. 30.
37 *Biographia literaria*, II, xxii, 102. Coleridge is criticizing Wordsworth.
38 *Coleridge's Shakespearean criticism*, ed. T. M. Raysor, II, 138. See also Raysor, II, 93–4, and I, 212–216, esp. 214, where Coleridge praises Shakespeare for 'so carrying on the eye of the reader as to make him *see* everything – and this without exciting any painful or laborious attention, without any *anatomy* of description (a fault not uncommon in descriptive poetry) but with the sweetness and easy movement of nature'. Coleridge retains the eighteenth-century idea of 'visualizing' poetry, but with this caution.
39 William Hazlitt, 'Mr. Campbell and Mr. Crabbe', *The spirit of the age*, Vol. XI of *The collected works of William Hazlitt*, ed. P. P. Howe (London and Toronto: J. M. Dent and Sons Ltd., 1930), pp. 159–169, 166. See also 'On Thomson and Cowper', Lecture V of *Lectures on the English poets*, Vol. V of *The collected works*, pp. 85–104, 96–97; and *Crabbe: the critical heritage*, ed. Arthur Pollard (London, 1972), p. 301.
40 Mario Praz, *The Romantic agony*, trans. Angus Davidson (London, New York, and Toronto: Geoffrey Cumberlege, Oxford University Press, 1933, 2nd ed. 1951), p. 15.
41 *Biographia literaria*, II, xxii, 102.

42 *Coleridge's Shakespearean criticism*, ed. T. M. Raysor, II, 68.

43 Wellek, *The Romantic age*, pp. 149–150.

44 Abrams, *The mirror and the lamp*, p. 103.

45 Abrams, *The mirror and the lamp*, p. 104.

46 Abrams, *The mirror and the lamp*, p. 111.

47 Hamilton, *Coleridge's poetics*, p. 144.

48 Wordsworth, 'Preface to the Lyrical Ballads' (1850), in *The collected works of William Wordsworth*, ed. W. J. B. Owen and Jane Worthington Smyser, 3 vols. (Oxford: Clarendon Press, 1974), I, 119–159, 123.

49 Wordsworth, 'Preface to the Edition of 1815', *Prose works*, III, 26–39, 26. References to this text are given parenthetically as 'Preface, 1815'.

50 Wordsworth, Appendix to the 'Preface to the Lyrical Ballads', *Prose Works*, I, 160–165, 160.

51 Wordsworth, 'Essay supplementary to the Preface of 1815', *Prose Works*, III, 62–84, 73 and *passim*. References to this text are given parenthetically as 'Essay Supplementary'.

52 Wordsworth, 'Essay upon epitaphs' (III), *Prose Works*, II, 80–96, 84–85.

53 Ralph Cohen, *The art of discrimination: Thomson's 'The Seasons' and the language of criticism* (London: Routledge and Kegan Paul, 1964), p. 139. Cohen refers to J. C. Shairp, *On poetic interpretation of nature* (Edinburgh: David Douglas, 1877), p. 110; and to F. R. Leavis, '"Antony and Cleopatra" and "All for Love": a critical exercise', *Scrutiny* (1931), 158–169. See also F. R. Leavis, 'English poetry in the eighteenth century', *Scrutiny* (1936), 13–31, for a similar viewpoint.

54 Cohen, *The art of discrimination*, p. 139.

55 Cohen, *The art of discrimination*, p. 137.

56 John Locke, *An essay concerning human understanding*, ed. Alexander Campbell-Fraser, 2 vols. (1690, rpt. New York: Dover Publications, London: Constable and Co., 1959), I, 183.

57 Joseph Addison, 'Pleasures of the imagination', *The Spectator*, 411 (21 June 1712), rpt. in *Critical essays from 'The Spectator' by Joseph Addison with four essays by Richard Steele*, ed. Donald F. Bond, Oxford Paperback English Tests (Oxford: Oxford University Press, 1970), pp. 175–176.

58 Cohen, *The art of discrimination*, p. 192.

59 Lee McKay Johnson, *The metaphor of painting: essays on Baudelaire, Ruskin, Proust and Pater*, Studies in the Fine Arts: Criticism 7 (Ann Arbor, MI: UMI Research Press, 1980), p. 2. Johnson cites Jean Hagstrum, *The sister arts: the tradition of literary pictorialism and English poetry from Dryden to Gray* (Chicago: University of Chicago Press, 1958).

60 Roy Park, *Hazlitt and the spirit of the age: abstraction and critical theory* (Oxford: Clarendon Press, 1971), p. 105.

61 Elizabeth Abel, 'Redefining the sister arts: Baudelaire's response to the art of Delacroix', *Critical Inquiry*, 6 (Spring, 1980), 363–384, rpt. in *The language of images*, ed. J. W. T. Mitchell (Chicago and London: University of Chicago Press, 1974, rpt 1980), pp. 37–58, 40–41.

62 Hegel, *Introduction to aesthetics*, pp. 88, 89.

63 Mark Storey, *The poetry of John Clare: a critical introduction* (London: Macmillan, 1974), p. 17.

64 Earl Wasserman, 'The English Romantics: the grounds of knowledge', *Studies in Romanticism*, 4 (Autumn 1964), 17–34, 17.

65 Wasserman, 'The English Romantics', p. 20.

66 Wasserman, 'The English Romantics', pp. 21–22.

67 Abrams, 'Structure and style in the greater Romantic lyric', in *From sensibility to Romanticism: essays presented to Frederick A. Pottle*, ed. Harold Bloom and F. W. Hilles (New York: Oxford University Press, 1965), pp. 527–560. All references to this text are given parenthetically as *GRL*.

68 John Dyer's poem, 'Grongar Hill' was a typical 'loco-descriptive' poem, published in 1726. For an account of this genre, see Christopher Hussey, *The picturesque: studies in a point of view* (London: Frank Cass and Co., 1967).

69 McGann, *The Romantic ideology*, p. 1.

70 Paul de Man, 'The rhetoric of temporality', in *Interpretation: theory and practice*, ed. Charles S. Singleton, pp. 173–209, 178.

71 Paul de Man, 'The rhetoric of temporality', p. 178.

72 Paul de Man, 'Structure intentionnelle de l'image romantique', *Revue internationale de philosophie*, 51 (1960), rpt. and trans. in *Romanticism and consciousness*, ed. Harold Bloom (New York: W. W. Norton and Co., 1970), pp. 65–77, and in *Wordsworth: a collection of critical essays*, ed. M. H. Abrams, Twentieth Century Views (Englewood Cliffs: Prentice-Hall, 1972), pp. 133–144, 133.

73 Paul de Man, 'The intentional structure', pp. 137–138.

74 E. D. Hirsch, *Wordsworth and Schelling: a typological study of Romanticism* (New Haven: Yale University Press, 1960), p. 1.

75 Edward E. Bostetter, *The Romantic ventriloquists: Wordsworth, Coleridge, Keats, Shelley, Byron* (Seattle: University of Washington Press, 1963), p. 4.

76 Isobel Armstrong, *Language as living form in nineteenth-century poetry* (Sussex: Harvester Press; New Jersey: Barnes and Noble, 1982), p. xii.

77 Armstrong, *Language as living form*, pp. xiii, 21.

78 Armstrong, *Language as living form*, p. 20.

79 Armstrong, *Language as living form*, p. 30.

80 Armstrong, *Language as living form*, p. 21.

81 W. K. Wimsatt, 'The structure of Romantic nature imagery', in *The age of Johnson: essays presented to Chauncey Brewster Tinker*, ed. Frederick W. Hilles (New Haven and London: Yale University Press, 1949, rpt. 1964) pp. 291–303, 292. Also rpt. in W. K. Wimsatt, *The verbal icon: studies in the meaning of poetry* (London: Methuen, 1984), pp. 103–116.

82 Wimsatt, 'The structure of Romantic nature imagery', p. 293.

83 I. A. Richards, *The philosophy of rhetoric*, The Mary Flexner Lectures of the Humanities, February and March 1936 (London: Oxford University Press, 1936, rpt. 1979), p. 97. All references to this text are given parenthetically as Richards.

84 Wimsatt, 'The structure of Romantic nature imagery', p. 297.

85 Wimsatt, 'The structure of Romantic nature imagery', p. 297.

86 Wimsatt, 'The structure of Romantic nature imagery', p. 296.

87 He quotes Coleridge, 'The statesman's manual', p. 30 in *Lay sermons*.

88 David Leppard, 'An investigation into the theory and structure of metaphor with special reference to Wordsworth and Yeats', unpub. D. Phil dissertation, University of Oxford, 1983, p. 90.

89 Stanley Fish, 'How ordinary is ordinary language?' *New Literary History*, 5 (Autumn 1973), 41–54, 51.

90 Keith Hinchcliffe, 'Wordsworth and the kinds of metaphor', *Studies in Romanticism*, 23 (Spring 1984), 81–100, 82.

91 Hinchcliffe, 'Wordsworth and the kinds of metaphor', p. 86.

92 Hinchcliffe, 'Wordsworth and the kinds of metaphor', p. 89.

93 Hinchcliffe, 'Wordsworth and the kinds of metaphor', p. 88.

94 Wordsworth, 'Preface to the Edition of 1815', *Prose works*, Vol. 3, 26–39, 32.

95 Herbert Lindenberger, 'Images of interaction in *The Prelude*', *On Wordsworth's Prelude* (Princeton: Princeton University Press, 1963), pp. 69–98, rpt in Jonathan Wordsworth, M. H. Abrams and Stephen Gill, eds., *The Prelude, 1799, 1805, 1850* by Wordsworth, Norton Critical Editions (London, New York: W. W. Norton and Co., 1979), pp. 642–663, 643.

96 Lindenberger, 'Images of interaction', p. 657.

Chapter 3 Critics of Clare and Wordsworth

1 Lindenberger, 'Images of interaction', pp. 661–662.

2 Erich Robinson and David Powell, eds., *John Clare*, The Oxford Authors (Oxford: Oxford University Press, 1984), Introduction, p. xix.

3 John Taylor, Introduction, *Poems descriptive of rural life and scenery*, by John Clare (London: Taylor and Hessey, 1820), p. i.

4 Mark Storey, ed., *Clare: the critical heritage* (London and Boston: Routledge and Kegan Paul, 1973), Introduction, p. 1.

5 Joanna Rapf, rev. of John Barrell, *The idea of landscape and the sense of place*, and of *John Clare: a life*, by J. W. Tibble and Anne Tibble (Totowa, NJ: Rouman and Littlefield, 1972 rpt from 1st ed., London, 1932), in *Studies in Romanticism*, 13 (Winter 1974), 79–84, 82.

6 Unsigned rev. of *The Rural Muse* by John Clare, *Druid's Monthly Magazine*, NS 2 (1835), 131–134. Cited in *Critical heritage*, p. 240.

7 Unsigned rev. of *The Village of Minstrel and other poems by John Clare the Northamptonshire peasant*, *Eclectic Review*, NS 27 (January–June, 1822), 31–45, 31.

8 John Taylor, Letter to John Clare, 14 August 1820, British Museum MS. Egerton 2245 fol., rpt. in Mark Storey, ed., *Clare: the critical heritage*, p. 122.

9 Storey, *The critical heritage*, Introduction, p. 10. Storey refers to John Aikin, *Letters to a young lady on a course of English poetry* (1804), p. 155, p. 291.

10 Cyrus Redding, untitled article, *English Journal*, 22 (29 May 1841), 340–343.

11 Unsigned rev. of *The Village Minstrel*, *Monthly Magazine*, 1 November 1821, pp. 321–325, 322.

12 Arthur Symons, ed., *Poems by John Clare* (London: Henry Frowde, 1908), Introduction, pp. 18–19, 20.

13 Samuel J. Looker, 'The life and genius of John Clare', *Poetry Review*, Sept.–Oct. 1920, pp. 263–4.

14 Harold J. Massingham, rev. of *John Clare: poems, chiefly from manuscript*, by John Clare, ed. Edmund Blunden and Alan Porter (London: Richard Cobden-Sanderson, 1920), *Athenaeum*, 7 (7 January 1921), 9–10.

15 John Middleton Murry, 'The poetry of John Clare', *Times Literary Supplement*, 13 January 1921, pp. 17–18, rpt. *Countries of the mind: essays in literary criticism* (London: William Collins, 1922), pp. 103–119, and in *John Clare and other studies* (London, New York: Peter Nevill Ltd, 1950), pp. 7–17.

16 Robert Lynd, unsigned rev. of *John Clare: poems chiefly from manuscript*, *Nation*, 28, 22 January 1921, 581–582, 581.

17 Edmund Gosse, 'Nature in poetry', rev. of *Madrigals and chronicles: being newly-found poems by John Clare*, ed. Edmund Blunden (London: Beaumont Press, 1924), *Sunday Times*, 5 October 1924, p. 8, cols. 3–4.

18 John Speirs, rev. of the *The poems of John Clare*, ed. J. W. Tibble, 2 vols. (London: J. M. Dent, 1935), *Scrutiny* (June 1935), 84–86.

19 Rayner Unwin, *The Rural Muse: studies in the peasant poetry of England* (London: George Allen and Unwin, 1954), p. 122.

20 J. G. Fichte, *Science of knowledge (Wissenschaftslehre)*, trans. John Lachs, ed. Peter Heath (New York: Meredith Corporation, 1970; rpt. Cambridge; Cambridge University Press, 1982), p. 15.

21 John Middleton Murray, 'Clare and Wordsworth', rev. of *Madrigals and chronicles*, by John Clare, *Times Literary Supplement*, 21 August 1924, p. 511. Rpt. as 'The case of John Clare', in *John Clare and other studies*, pp. 19–24.

22 Robert Pinsky, 'That sweet man, John Clare', in *The rarer action: essays in honour of Francis Fergusson*, ed. Alan Cheuse and Richard Koffler (New Brunswick NJ: Rutgers University Press, 1970), pp. 258–274, 262.

23 Pinsky, 'That sweet man, John Clare', p. 265, 266.

24 Thomas R. Frosch, 'The descriptive style of John Clare', *Studies in Romanticism*, 10 (Summer 1971), 137–149, 137.

25 Frosch, 'The descriptive style', pp. 139, 141.

26 Frosch, 'The descriptive style', p. 139.

27 Richard Lessa, 'John Clare's voice and two sonnets', *John Clare Society Journal*, 3 July 1984, pp. 26–33, 27.

28 Richard Lessa, 'Time and John Clare's calendar', *Critical Quarterly*, 24: 1 (Spring 1982), 59–71, 59.

29 Richard Lessa, 'John Clare's voice and two sonnets', p. 27.

30 Harold Bloom, 'John Clare: the Wordsworthian shadow', *The visionary company: a reading of English Romantic poetry* (London: Faber and Faber, 1961), pp. 434–445, 434–435.

31 Bloom, 'John Clare', p. 434.

32 Timothy Brownlow, *John Clare and picturesque landscape* (Oxford: Clarendon Press, 1983), p. 1. All references to this text are given parenthetically as Brownlow.

33 L. J. Swingle, 'Stalking the essential John Clare: Clare in relation to his Romantic contemporaries', *Studies in Romanticism*, 14 (Summer 1972), 273–284, 275–276.

34 Murray Krieger, 'Mediation, language and vision in the reading of literature', in *Interpretation: theory and practice*, ed. Charles S. Singleton, pp. 211–242, 215.

35 'I found the poems in the fields', quoted from 'Sighing for Retirement', *The poems of John Clare*, ed. J. W. Tibble and Anne Tibble, 2 vols. (London: J. M. Dent and Sons; New York: E. P. Dutton, 1935), II, 384.

36 Charles Hessey, Letter to John Clare, 3rd November 1824, British Museums MS. Egerton 2246, foll. 405^v–6^v, rpt. in Mark Storey, ed., *Clare: the critical heritage*, pp. 194–195.

37 John Taylor, Letter to John Clare, 4 March 1826, British Museum MS. Egerton 2247, foll. 152, rpt. Storey, ed., *Clare: the critical heritage*, pp. 197–198.

38 Brownlow, p. 39. He quotes from *The prose of John Clare*, ed. J. W. Tibble and Anne Tibble (London: Routledge and Kegan Paul, 1951, rpt. 1970), p. 223.
39 Eric Robinson and Geoffrey Summerfield, eds., *Selected poems and prose of John Clare* (Oxford, London, New York, Toronto: Oxford University Press, 1966, rpt. 1967), p. 66.
40 'To James Augustus Hessey', between 1 and 4 August 1823, *The letters of John Clare*, ed. Mark Storey (Oxford: Clarendon Press, 1985), p. 282.
41 Eric Robinson, ed., *Autobiographical writings* (Oxford, New York: Oxford University Press, 1983), p. 43.
42 *Selected poems and prose of John Clare*, p. 18.
43 *Autobiographical writings*, by John Clare, p. 65, p. 86.
44 'To John Taylor', Helpstone, 20 May 1820, *The letters of John Clare*, p. 70.
45 John Taylor, Introduction, *Poems descriptive of rural life and scenery*, pp. xiv–xv.
46 What's future fame? a melody loud playing
    In crowds where one is wanting, whose esteeming
    Would love to hear it best . . .
    A statue towering over glory's game,
    That cannot feel, while he that was all feeling
    Is past, and gone, and nothing but a name.
    (Tibble, II, 107). See also 'Vanity of Fame', (Tibble, II, 105), 'Sighing for Retirement', II, p. 383, for Clare's criticisms of the vagaries of fame, and sense of posterity.
47 M. H. Abrams, 'Two roads to Wordsworth', in *Wordsworth: a collection of critical essays*, pp. 1–11, 1.
48 Abrams, 'Two roads to Wordsworth', p. 2.
49 Geoffrey Hartman, 'Synopsis: the via naturaliter negativa', *Wordsworth's poetry 1787–1814* (New Haven: Yale University Press, 1964), pp. 33–69, 33.
50 Joseph Warren Beach, *The concept of nature in nineteenth-century English poetry* (New York: Russell and Russell, 1936, rpt. 1966), pp. 25–26.
51 Beach, *The concept of nature*, pp. 26–27. Beach quotes Solomon Francis Gingerich, *Essays in the Romantic poets* (New York, 1929) but gives no page reference.
52 Frederick A. Pottle, 'Eye and object in the poetry of Wordsworth', *Yale Review*, 40 (Autumn 1950), rpt. in *Romanticism and consciousness*, ed. Harold Bloom, pp. 273–287, p. 274. Pottle quotes Wordsworth, 'Preface to the Lyrical Ballads', 1800, *Prose works*, I, 148, 132.
53 Pottle, 'Eye and Object', p. 274.

54 Pottle, 'Eye and Object', p. 276.
55 Pottle, 'Eye and Object', p. 277.
56 Pottle, 'Eye and Object', p. 280.
57 John F. Danby, *The simple Wordsworth: studies in the poems 1797–1807* (London: Routledge and Kegan Paul, 1968, rpt 1971), p. 97.
58 Danby, *The simple Wordsworth*, p. 98.
59 Danby, *The simple Wordsworth*, pp. 102, 107.
60 David Simpson, 'Criticism: politics and style', *Critical Inquiry*, 11 (September 1984), 52–81, 69–70.
61 L. J. Swingle, 'Wordsworth's contrarieties: a prelude to Wordsworthian complexity', *Journal of English Literary History*, 44 (Summer 1977), 337–354, 339.
62 Geoffrey Hartman, 'The use and abuse of structural analysis', *New Literary History*, 7 (Autumn 1975), 165–189, 177.
63 Hartman, 'The via naturaliter negativa', *Wordsworth's poetry*, pp. 37–38.
64 Hartman, 'Romantic nature poetry', *Beyond formalism: literary essays 1958–1970* (New Haven, London: Yale University Press, 1970), pp. 206–230, 222.
65 Hartman, *Wordsworth's poetry*, p. 100.
66 Hartman, *Wordsworth's poetry*, p. 111. For Hartman's Schillerian distinctions, see also 'Wordsworth', *Yale Review*, 58 (June 1969), 507–525. In this article, Hartman says that the poetry of the *Lyrical Ballads*, 'is a reflective, not a naive poetry' (p. 509) and that 'Nature . . . is a haunted house through which we must pass before our spirit can be independent' (507).
67 Bloom, 'William Wordsworth', *The visionary company*, pp. 120–193, 140.
68 Bloom, 'William Wordsworth', *The visionary company*, p. 141.
69 Bloom, *Poetry and repression: revisionism from Blake to Stevens* (New Haven and London: Yale University Press, 1976), p. 72.
70 Bloom, 'The internalization of quest-romance', *Yale Review*, 58 (June 1969), 526–536. In this article Bloom describes how 'Wordsworth's Copernican revolution in poetry is marked by the evanescence of any subject but subjectivity, the loss of what a poem is "about"' (p. 528). This account is close to Schiller's description of the sentimental spirit's self-exaltation beyond any limiting object, to an unlimited subjectivity.
71 Hartman, 'Romanticism and anti-self-consciousness', *Beyond formalism*, pp. 298–310. Hartman explicitly draws the connection with idealism when he says that the idea 'of a return, via knowledge, to naiveté – to a second naiveté – is a commonplace among the German Romantics . . . one can show that the practice of the English

Romantics is involved with a problematical self-consciousness similar to that of the Germans' (p. 300).

72 Abrams, *Natural supernaturalism*, pp. 143–252.
73 de Man, 'The intentional structure', in *Wordsworth: a collection*, p. 134.
74 de Man, 'The intentional structure', p. 137.
75 de Man, 'The intentional structure', pp. 137–138.
76 de Man, 'Symbolic landscape in Wordsworth and Yeats', *The rhetoric of romanticism* (New York: Columbia University Press, 1984), pp. 125–144, p. 132.
77 de Man, 'Symbolic landscape in Wordsworth and Yeats', p. 129.
78 de Man, 'The intentional structure', p. 142.
79 Albert Wlecke, *Wordsworth and the sublime* (Berkeley, LA, London: University of California Press, 1973), p. 2.
80 Cynthia Chase, 'The accidents of disfiguration: limits to literal and rhetorical reading in Book V of *The Prelude*', *Studies in Romanticism*, 18 (Winter 1979), 547–565, 548.
81 Chase, 'The accidents of disfiguration', pp. 561–562.
82 Thomas Weiskel, *The Romantic sublime: studies in the structure and psychology of transcendence* (Baltimore and London: The Johns Hopkins University Press, 1976), p. 59. Weiskel quotes Wordsworth's 'Preface to the Edition of 1815', *Prose Works*, III, 26–29, 33, 36.
83 Weiskel, *The Romantic sublime*, p. 174.
84 J. Hillis Miller, 'The still heart: poetic form in Wordsworth', *New Literary History*, 2 (Winter 1971), 297–310, 305.
85 J. Hillis Miller, 'The still heart', p. 309.
86 J. Hillis Miller, 'The still heart', p. 307.
87 Robert Young, ed., *Untying the text: a post-structuralist reader*, (London: Routledge and Kegan Paul, 1981); Introduction to J. Hillis Miller, 'The stone and the shell: the problem of form in Wordsworth's Dream of the Arab', p. 244.
88 J. Hillis Miller, 'The stone and the shell', in *Untying the text*, pp. 244–265, p. 258.
89 J. Hillis Miller, 'The stone and the shell', p. 258.
90 Frances Ferguson, *Wordsworth: language as counter-spirit* (New Haven and London: Yale University Press, 1977), p. 130.
91 David Simpson, 'Criticism, politics and style', p. 70.
92 Simpson, 'Criticism, politics and style', p. 72.
93 Simpson, 'Criticism, politics and style', p. 77.
94 David Simpson, *Irony and authority in Romantic poetry* (London: Macmillan, 1979), p. 25.
95 David Simpson, *Wordsworth and the figuring of the real* (London: Macmillan, 1982), p. xix.

96 L. J. Swingle, 'Wordsworth's contrarieties', p. 341.
97 Swingle, 'Wordsworth's contrarieties', p. 344.
98 Swingle, 'Wordsworth's contrarieties', p. 351.
99 Swingle, 'Wordsworth's contrarieties', p. 350.

Chapter 4 Ut pictura poesis

1 Cohen, *The art of discrimination*, p. 246.
2 Stephen Land, *From signs to propositions: the concept of form in eighteenth-century semantic theory* (London: Longmans, 1974), pp. 21–22.
3 Joseph Addison, 'Pleasures of the imagination', *The Spectator*, 411 (21 June 1712), rpt. in *Critical essays From 'The Spectator'*, ed. Bond, pp. 175–176.
4 Addison, 'Pleasures of the imagination', in *Critical essays*, p. 176.
5 John Dennis, 'The grounds of criticism in poetry' (1704), *The critical works of John Dennis*, ed. Edward Niles Hooker (Baltimore: Johns Hopkins University Press, 1939), I, iv, 362.
6 Joseph Trapp, Lecture VIII, *Lectures on poetry*, read in Latin at the Schools of Natural Philosophy at Oxford, trans. William Bowyer, (London, 1742, rpt in facsimile, Menston, Yorkshire: Scolar Press, 1973), p. 103.
7 Locke, *An essay concerning human understanding*, II, 12. Locke notes that
> Words . . . came to be made use of by men as the signs of their ideas, not by any natural connexion that there is between particular articulate sounds and certain ideas . . . but by a voluntary imposition.

See also II, 104, where he says that
> the very nature of words makes it almost unavoidable for many of them to be doubtful and uncertain in their significations.

8 Locke, *Essay*, II, 45. Locke says of 'the Names of Mixed Modes and Relations':
> Nobody can doubt but that these ideas of mixed modes are made by a voluntary collection of ideas, put together in the mind, independent of any original patterns in nature, who will but reflect that this sort of complex ideas may be made, abstracted, and have names given them, and so a species be constituted, before any one individual of that species ever existed.

He gives the example of the words, 'sacrilege' and 'adultery', as the kinds of abstracts created in our minds rather than in nature.

9 Locke, *Essay*, II, 122–147, esp. 137:

It is true the names of substances would be much more useful, and propositions made in them much more certain, were the real essence of substances the ideas in our minds which those words signified. And it is for want of those real essences that our words convey so little knowledge or certainty in our discourses about them.

See also p. 143, where Locke emphasizes the need for distinct ideas if language is to be clearly comprehensible.

10 George Berkeley, *Philosophical commentaries, the works of George Berkeley*, ed. A. A. Luce and T. E. Jessop, 9 vols. (London: Thomas Nelson and Sons, 1948, rpt 1967), I, 67.

11 Berkeley, *The principles of human knowledge* (1710), *The principles of human knowledge and three dialogues between Hylas and Philonous* ed. G. J. Warnock (London: Collins, 1962, rpt 1981), p. 60.

12 Berkeley, *Essay towards a new theory of vision and other writings* (1709), ed. Ernest Rhys, Everyman Library 483 (London: J. M. Dent; New York: E. P. Dutton, 1910, rpt 1946), p. 44.

13 Berkeley, *New theory of vision*, pp. 67, 77.

14 Locke, *Essay*, I, 186.

15 Abbé Dubos, *Reflexions critiques sur la poesie et sur la peinture*, 7th ed. (Paris, 1770), I, 294.

16 Hagstrum, *The sister arts*, p. 130. See also, Irving Babbitt, *The new Laokoon: an essay on the confusion of the arts* (London: Constable; Boston and New York: Houghton Mifflin Co, 1910), pp. 30–31, where Babbitt talks of the school of descriptive poetry as 'conceiving of words and phases as pigments to be laid on from without'.

17 Todorov, *Theories of the symbol*, p. 112.

18 Abbé Batteux, 'Les beaux-arts réduits à un même Principe', *Principes de la Litterature*, 15th ed., 5 vols. (Paris: Saillant and Nyon, 1774). Batteux concludes his treatise by insisting on the rules that must govern all the arts, in their imitation of nature:

Tout l'Univers appartient aux beaux Arts. Il peuvent disposer de toutes les richesses de la Nature. Mails ils ne doivent en faire usage que selon les loix de la décence. Toute demeure doit etre l'image de celui qui l'habite, de sa dignité, de sa fortune, de son gout. C'est la régle qui doit guider les Arts dans la construction & dans les ornaments des loeux.   (I. 360).

19 James Harris, 'A discourse on music, painting and poetry', *Three treatises* (London, 1744), p. 58.

20 Addison, 'Pleasures of the imagination', *The Spectator*, 416, (27 June 1712), rpt. in *Critical essays*, p. 191.

21 Alexander Gerard, *An essay on taste*, ed. Walter J. Hipple (Gainsville, Florida: Scholars Facsimiles and Reprints, 1963), p. 53.
22 Richard Hurd, 'A discourse on poetical imitation', in *Q. Horatii Flacci Epistola ad Augustum with an English commentary and notes, to which is added A discourse concerning poetical imitation*, 2nd ed. (London, 1753), II, 133.
23 Hurd, 'A discourse on poetical imitation', p. 122.
24 Joseph Warton, *'An essay in the genius and writings of Pope'*, (London: M. Cooper, 1756), Section 1, (Dedication), pp. iv–v, x–xi; Section 2 ('Of Windsor-Forest, and Lyric Pieces'), pp. 20, 30, 51.
25 Land, *From signs to propositions*, p. 36.
26 Samuel Monk, *The sublime: a study of critical theories in XVIIIth-century England* (New York: MLA of America, 1935), p. 61. See also pp. 235–236, where Monk describes 'the slow and unconscious growth of English art away from the orderly garden of the Augustan age to the open fields . . . of the romantic period', discussing the influence of Longinus and of Burke and the emergence of the sublime.
27 John Dennis, 'The advance and reformation of modern poetry', (1701), *The critical works of John Dennis*, ed. Hooker, I, 202.
28 Dennis, 'The advance and reformation', p. 210.
29 Dennis, 'The advance and reformation', p. 215.
30 Robert Lowth, *Lectures on the sacred poetry of the Hebrews*, trans. from the Latin (London, 1753, rpt 1781), I, 117–118.
31 Lowth, *Lectures on the sacred poetry*, I, 20.
32 See, for example, Stephen Land's remark that
    It was Burke's sublime, rather than that of Dennis or Baillie, which the later eighteenth century adopted and handed down . . . to the Romantics. The establishment of language as the ideal medium for the sublime helped foster an approach to words which was to be cultivated by Wordsworth and Coleridge.   (*From signs to propositions*, p. 40)
33 Edmund Burke, *Inquiry, The works of The Right Honourable Edmund Burke*, The World's Classics, LXXI (London, New York, Toronto: Henry Frowde, Oxford University Press, 1906), p. 211.
34 Burke, *Inquiry*, p. 213.
35 Burke, *Inquiry*, p. 113.
36 Burke, *Inquiry*, p. 215.
37 Burke, *Inquiry*, p. 101.
38 Edward Young, 'A discourse on lyric poetry', *The complete works poetry and prose of the Rev. Edward Young LL.D. to which is prefixed A life of the author by John Doran LL.D.* (London: William Tegg and Co., 1865), I, 415.
39 Joseph Trapp, *Lectures on poetry*, p. 115.
40 Trapp, *Lectures on poetry*, p. 118.

41 Trapp, *Lectures on poetry*, p. 203.
42 K. G. Hamilton, *The two harmonies: poetry and prose in the seventeenth century* (Oxford: Clarendon Press, 1963), p. 191.
43 Sir William Jones, 'On the arts, commonly called imitative', *Poems consisting chiefly of translations from the Asiatick languages to which are added two essays: I. On the poetry of the eastern nations. II. On the arts, commonly called imitative* (Oxford: Clarendon Press, 1772), p. 201.
44 Jones, 'On the arts', p. 210.
45 Jones, 'On the arts', pp. 213–214.
46 Jones, 'On the arts', p. 216.
47 Jones, 'On the arts', pp. 216–217.
48 Hugh Blair, *Lectures on rhetoric and belles lettres*, 2 vols. (London, 1783), p. 93.
49 Blair, *Lectures*, p. 94.
50 Blair, *Lectures*, p. 312.
51 Blair, *Lectures*, p. 353.
52 Blair, *Lectures*, pp. 371–372.
53 Blair, *Lectures*, p. 384.
54 Thomas Twining, 'On poetry considered as an imitative art', *Aristotle's treatise on poetry translated with notes on the translation and on the original and two dissertations on poetical and musical imitation* (London, 1789), pp. 3–43, 3–4.
55 Twining, 'On poetry considered as an imitative art', p. 9, pp. 9–10.
56 Twining, 'On poetry considered', p. 23.
57 Twining, 'On poetry considered', p. 30.
58 Richard Payne Knight, *An analytic inquiry into the principles of taste* (London 1805), 10.95, See also, pp. 382–4 and pp. 105–6, for the non-imitative, expressive powers of poetry.
59 Jonathan Culler, *Saussure*, Fontana Modern Masters (Glasgow: Collins, Fontana Paperbacks, 1976), p. 58.
60 See Abrams, *The mirror and the lamp*, pp. 78–82 for a concise account of the importance of Condillac, Monboddo, Rousseau etc.
61 Culler, *Saussure*, p. 61.
62 Rousseau, 'Essay on the origin of language', trans. John H. Moran in *On the origin of language*, Milestones of Thought (New York: Frederick Ungar Publishing Co., 1966), p. 12.
63 Ernst Cassirer, *The philosophy of symbolic forms*, I, 158.
64 George Steiner, 'After Babel', *Aspects of language and translation* (Oxford: Oxford University Press, 1975, rpt. 1976), p. 81.
65 Wilkinson and Willoughby discuss Schiller's distichs, 'Language' and 'To the Poet' which first appeared in the *Musenalmanach* (1797), under the initials S(chiller) u. G(oethe). Rpt. *Schillers sämtliche Werke*, Sabular-Ausgabe, trans. v. E. v. d. Hellen (Stuttgart and Berlin, 1904–1905), I, 149.

66 Todorov, *Theories of the symbol*, p. 146.
67 'To Schiller', Frankfurt, 17 August 1797, *Correspondence between Schiller and Goethe from 1794 to 1805*, trans. from the 3rd ed. of the German with notes by L. Dora Schmitz (London: George Bell and Sons, 1877), Letter 358, I, 373.
68 Todorov, *Theories of the symbol*, p. 201. See also pp. 201–221 for a detailed account of Romantic theories of the symbol.
69 M. Jadwiga Swiatecka, *The idea of the symbol: some nineteenth-century comparisons with Coleridge* (Cambridge: Cambridge University Press, 1980), p. 44.
70 Coleridge, Appendix A, 'The statesman's manual', *Lay sermons*, p. 79.
71 Coleridge, *Collected letters*, ed. E. L. Griggs (Oxford: Clarendon Press, 1956–1971), I, 626.
72 Goethe 'Introduction to the *Propylaën*', (1790), *Goethe on art*, trans. ed. John Gage (London: Scolar Press, 1980), p. 6.
73 A. W. Schlegel, *A course of lectures*, p. 340.
74 'To Goethe', 1797, *Correspondence between Schiller and Goethe*, Letter 400, I, 455. No month or place given.
75 Friedrich Schlegel, 'Dialogue on poetry', in Behler, p. 75.
76 Schelling, *The philosophy of art: an oration on the relation between the plastic arts and nature*, trans. A. Johnson (London: John Chapman, 1845), p. 2.
77 'To Goethe', Jena, 14 September 1797, *Correspondence between Schiller and Goethe*, Letter 366a, I, 398.
78 Hegel, *Introduction to aesthetics*, pp. 88–89.
79 Hegel, *Introduction to aesthetics*, p. 88.
80 Coleridge, *Notebooks*, ed. Kathleen Coburn (London: Routledge and Kegan Paul, 1957), II, 1963.
81 Hazlitt, 'On poetry in general', *Lectures on the English poets*, Vol. V of *The collected works*, p. 10.
82 'To Thomas Poole', 19 May 1799, *Letters* of S. T. Coleridge, ed. E. L. Griggs, 6 vols. (Oxford: Clarendon Press, 1956–1971), Letter 282, I, 511.
83 Park, *Hazlitt and the spirit of the age*, pp. 124–125. Park quotes Wordsworth, *Prose works*, ed. A. B. Grosart (London, 1876), III, 89.
84 *Coleridge's Shakespearean criticism*, ed. Raysor, II, 174.
85 Coleridge, *Notebooks*, ed. Coburn, I, 132.
86 Schelling, *System of transcendental idealism*, trans. Peter Heath (Charlottesville: University of Virginia Press, 1978), p. 233.
87 Lee McKay Johnson, *The metaphor of painting*, p. 3.
88 Northrop Frye, *Anatomy of criticism: four essays* (Princeton: Princeton University Press, 1957), pp. 4–5.
89 Park, *Hazlitt and the spirit of the age*, p. 135.

90 E. H. Gombrich, *Art and illusion: a study in the psychology of pictorial representation* (Princeton: Princeton University Press, 1960, rpt. 1972), p. 4. All references to this text are given parenthetically as *AI*.

91 Barry Barnes, 'Conceptions of knowledge', *Interests and the growth of knowledge* (London: Routledge and Kegan Paul, 1977), pp. 1–10, rpt. in *Modernism, criticism, realism: alternative contexts for art*, ed. Charles Harrison and Fred Orton (London: Harper and Row, 1984), pp. 101–111, 106. Barnes refers to William McIvins, *Prints and visual communication* (London: Routledge and Kegan Paul, 1953).

92 Barnes, 'Conceptions of knowledge', in *Modernism, criticism and realism*, p. 108.

93 Barnes, 'Conceptions of knowledge', p. 110.

94 Richard Wollheim, 'The work of art as object', *On art and the mind* (Boston, MA: Harvard University Press, 1973), pp. 112–119, rpt. in *Modernism, criticism, realism*, pp. 9–17, 11.

95 Wollheim, *Art and its objects*, (New York: Harper and Row, 1968, rpt. Cambridge: Cambridge University Press, 1980, 1985), p. 18. All references to this text are given parenthetically as Wollheim.

96 Coleridge, 'The statesman's manual', p. 30.

97 Roger Scruton, *Art and imagination: a study in the philosophy of mind* (London: Routledge and Kegan Paul, 1974, rpt. 1982), p. 15.

98 Scruton quotes Wittgenstein, *Philosophical investigations*, trans. G. E. M. Anscombe (Oxford: Basil Blackwell, 1953), p. 216 and Charles Baudelaire, 'Obituary Notice of Eugène Delacroix', rpt. in *L'Art Romantique*, ed. J. Creper (Paris, 1925), no page ref. given.

99 See Kant, *Critique of judgment*, trans. J. H. Bernard, 59, p. 158 for Kant's description of the way abstract words are derived from concrete ones. Kant is talking about the presentational or concrete nature of symbolic language when he says that

the word *ground* (support, basis), *to depend* (to be held up from above), to *flow* from something (instead of, to follow), *substance* (as Locke expresses it, the support of accidents), and countless others are not schematical but symbolical hypotyposes and expressions for concepts, not by means of a direct intuition, but only by analogy with it, i.e. by the transference of reflection upon an object of intuition to a quite different concept to which perhaps an intuition can never directly correspond.

100 Christopher Norris, *The deconstructive turn: essays in the rhetoric of philosophy* (London: Methuen, 1983, rpt 1984), p. 3.

101 See Wittgenstein, *Philosophical investigations*, pp. 193e–204e for 'seeing as'.

102 N. R. Hanson, 'Observation', *Patterns of discovery: an inquiry into*

the conceptual foundations of science (London: Cambridge University Press, 1972), pp. 5–30, rpt in *Modernism, criticism, realism*, pp. 69–84, p. 75.

103 Hanson, 'Observation', *Modernism, criticism, realism*, p. 79.

104 Rudolf Arnheim, 'A plea for visual thinking', *Critical Inquiry*, 6 (Spring 1980), 489–497, rpt in *The language of images*, ed. J. W. T. Mitchell, pp. 171–179, 174.

105 Arnheim, 'A plea for visual thinking', *The language of images*, pp. 176–177.

106 Richard Rorty, *Consequences of pragmatism: essays 1972–1980* (Sussex: Harvester Press, 1982), pp. xiii–xliv, for Rorty's introductory account of the post-philosophical age. Rorty contrasts the pragmatist's lack of interest in absolute values or truths, and understanding of truth as intra-theoretic (p. xxiv) with other philosophical positions: idealism, empiricism, realism. He asks whether it is possible that we can 'see ourselves as never encountering reality *except under a chosen description* – as, in Nelson Goodman's phrase, *making worlds rather than finding them*?' He quotes from Nelson Goodman, *Ways of worldmaking* (Indianapolis: Hackett Publishing Company, 1978) – no specific reference.

Chapter 5 Post-Kantians and post-structuralists

1 Richard Rorty, 'Nineteenth-century idealism and twentieth-century textualism', *The Monist*, 64 (1981), 155–174, rpt. *Consequences of pragmatism*, pp. 139–159. All references to this text are given parenthetically as Rorty.

2 Jacques Derrida, 'The parergon', trans. Craig Owens from part II of *La verité en peinture* (Paris, 1978), *October*, 9 (Summer 1979), 3–40. All subsequent references are given parenthetically as *Parergon*.

3 Warnock, *Imagination*, p. 70.

4 Simpson, *German aesthetic and literary criticism*, p. 7.

5 Claud Sutton, *The German tradition in philosophy* (London: Weidenfeld and Nicolson, 1974), p. 49.

6 Wellek, *The later eighteenth century*, pp. 228–229.

7 Rorty quotes Derrida's statement that 'il n'y a pas de hors-texte', *Of grammatology*, trans. Gayatri Spivak (1967; Baltimore and London: Johns Hopkins University Press, 1974, rpt 1976), p. 158. All references to this text are given parenthetically as *Grammatology*.

8 'For a large class of cases . . . the meaning of a word is its use in the language', Wittgenstein, *Philosophical investigations*, p. 20e.

9 Rorty, *Philosophy and the mirror of nature* (Princeton: Princeton University Press, 1980), p. 168.

10 Vincent B. Leitch, *Deconstructive criticism: an advanced introduction* (London: Hutchinson, 1983), p. 115.

11 Derrida, *Of grammatology*, p. 7.

12 Paul de Man, *Allegories of reading: figural language in Rousseau, Nietzsche, Rilke and Proust* (New Haven and London: Yale University Press, 1979), p. 9.

13 Jonathan Culler, *On deconstruction: theory and criticism after structuralism* (London: Routledge and Kegan Paul, 1983), p. 31.

14 de Man, *Allegories of reading*, p. 10.

15 Derrida, 'Structure, sign and play in the discourse of the human sciences', *Writing and difference*, trans. Alan Bass (1967; Chicago: University of Chicago Press; London: Routledge and Kegan Paul, 1978), pp. 278–293, 278–279.

16 Leitch, *Deconstructive criticism*, pp. 118–119.

17 Leitch, *Deconstructive criticism*, pp. 118.

18 Schelling, *System of transcendental Idealism*, pp. 38–39.

19 Schelling, *System of transcendental Idealism*, p. 41.

20 Schelling, *System of transcendental Idealism*, p. 97.

21 Culler, *On deconstruction*, p. 215.

22 Leitch, *Deconstructive criticism*, p. 160.

23 Culler, *On deconstruction*, p. 26.

24 Leitch, *Deconstructive criticism*, p. 161.

25 'To Goethe', Jena, 24 November 1797, *Correspondence between Schiller and Goethe*, Letter 382, I, 429.

26 Schaper, 'Schiller's Kant', *Studies in Kant's aesthetics*, p. 101.

27 Michael Podro, *The manifold in perception: theories of art from Kant to Hildebrand* (Oxford: Clarendon Press, 1972), p. 9. See also pp. 9–10.

28 David S. Miall, 'Kant's *Critique of judgement*: a biased aesthetics', *British Journal of Aesthetics*, 20 (1980), 135–145, 138.

29 Schaper, 'Epistemological claims of judgments of taste', *Studies in Kant's aesthetics*, pp. 18–52, 51.

30 Podro, *The manifold in perception*, p. 45.

31 Simpson, *German aesthetics and literary criticism*, p. 8.

32 Robert F. Brown, *The later philosophy of Schelling* (Lewisburg: Bucknell University Press; London: Associated University Presses, 1977), p. 24.

33 Frederick Copleston, *Fichte to Nietzsche*, Vol. 7 of *A history of philosophy* (London: Burns and Oates Ltd, 1968), pp. 121–122. Copleston quotes Schelling's *Werke*, ed. M. Schroter, 6 vols (Munich, 1927–28; 2 Supp. vols, Munich 1943–56), III, 402.

34 Schelling, *System of transcendental Idealism*, p. 14.

35 Schelling, *System of transcendental Idealism*, p. 20.

36 Paul Collins Hayner, *Reason and existence: Schelling's philosophy of history* (Leiden: E. J. Brill, 1967), p. 48.

37 Schelling, *System of transcendental Idealism*, p. 9.

38 Charles Taylor, *Hegel* (Cambridge: Cambridge University Press, 1975), pp. 41–42.

39 Frederick Copleston, *Kant*, Vol. VI of *A history of philosophy* (London: Burns and Oates Ltd, 1964), p. 351.

40 Fichte tells us that

> Feeling is entirely *subjective*. To *explain* it, indeed though this is
> an act of theorizing – we require a limiting factor.
>
> (*Science of Knowledge*, p. 255)

acknowledging the need for the 'limit' if we are to articulate theory: a fact borne out by Schiller's need for the 'naive' to articulate sentimentalism. He also tells us, in one of many references to the 'limit' that: 'The self reflects upon itself, as both determinate and indeterminant, and to that extent limits itself' (p. 273), that 'nothing can be an absolute self without at once limiting itself', (p. xii), and that 'the absolute self could not even be real if it were perfectly indeterminate' (p. xvi).

41 Derrida, 'Structure, sign and play', pp. 278–79.

42 Leitch, *Deconstructive criticism*, p. 177.

Chapter 6 The peasant poet

1 'To Isiah Knowles Holland' (mid 1819). *The letters of John Clare*, p. 12.

2 J. W. Tibble and Anne Tibble, *John Clare: his life and poetry* (London: William Heinemann Ltd., 1956), p. 84. No ref. given.

3 John Clare, 'July' (2nd version), *The Shepherds Calendar*, ed. Eric Robinson and Geoffrey Summerfield (London: Oxford University Press, 1964), pp. 132–133.

4 [The Fox], text taken from *John Clare*, Oxford Authors, ed. Eric Robinson and David Powell (Oxford: Oxford University Press, 1984), p. 246.

5 Quotations from *The Prelude* are taken from the Norton Critical Edition text, ed. Wordsworth, Abrams, Gill (see n. 95, ch. 2 above).

6 Clare, 'March', *The Shepherds Calendar*, p. 33.

7 Clare, 'January. A Winters Day', *The Shepherds Calendar*, p. 6.

8 de Man, 'The intentional structure', p. 142.

BIBLIOGRAPHY

Seventeenth- and eighteenth-century works

Addison, Joseph. 'Pleasures of the imagination'. *The Spectator*, 411, 21 June 1712. In *Critical essays from 'The Spectator'*. Ed. Donald F. Bond. Oxford Paperback English Texts. Oxford: Oxford University Press, 1970, pp. 175–177.

'Pleasures of the imagination'. *The Spectator*, 416, 27 June 1712. In *Critical essays from 'The Spectator'*, pp. 190–193.

Aikin, John. *Letters to a young lady on a course of English poetry*. London, 1804.

Batteux, Abbé. 'Les beaux-arts réduits à un même Principe'. In *Principes de la litterature*. 1747, 15th ed. Paris: Saillant and Nyon, 1774.

Berkeley, George. *Essay towards a new theory of vision and other writings*. Ed. Ernest Rhys. Everyman Library 483. London: J. M. Dent; New York: E. P. Dutton, 1910; rpt. 1946.

Philosophical commentaries. In *The works of George Berkeley*. Ed. A. A. Luce and T. E. Jessop. London: Thomas Nelson and Sons, 1948; rpt. 1967. Vol. I.

Blair, Hugh. *Lectures on rhetoric and belles lettres*. 2 vols. London, 1783.

Burke, Edmund. *Inquiry*. In *The works of the Right Honourable Edmund Burke*. The Worlds Classics, LXXI. London, New York, Toronto: Henry Frowde, Oxford University Press, 1906.

Dennis, John. 'The advance and reformation of modern poetry.' In *The critical works of John Dennis*. Ed. Edward Niles Hooker. Baltimore: Johns Hopkins University Press, 1939, Vol. I.

Dubos, Abbé. *Reflexions critiques sur la poesie et sur la peinture*. 7th ed. Paris, 1770.

Gerard, Alexander. *An essay on taste*. Ed. Walter J. Hipple. Gainsville, Florida: Scholars Facsimiles and Reprints, 1963.

Goethe, J. W. von. 'Introduction to the *Propylaen*' (1790). In *Goethe on Art*. Trans., ed. John Gage. London: Scolar Press, 1980.

Harris, James. 'A discourse on music, painting and poetry'. In *Three Treatises*. London, 1744.

Hurd, Richard. 'A discourse on poetical imitation'. In *Q. Horatii Flacci Epistola ad Augustum with an English commentary and notes to which is added A discourse concerning poetical imitation*. 2nd ed. London, 1753. Vol. II.

Jones, Sir William. 'On the arts, commonly called imitative'. In *Poems consisting chiefly of translations from the asiatick languages to which are added two essays: I. On the poetry of the Eastern nations. II. On the arts, commonly called imitative*. Oxford: Clarendon Press, 1772.

Kant, Immanuel. *Critique of judgment*. Trans. J. H. Bernard. The Hafner Library of Classics, 14. New York: Hafner Publishing Company, 1951.

Critique of pure reason. Trans. Norman Kemp-Smith. London: Macmillan, 1929; rpt. 1982.

Knight, Richard Payne. *An analytic inquiry into the principles of taste*. London, 1805.

Locke, John. *An essay concerning human understanding*. Ed. Alexander Campbell Fraser. 2 vols. New York: Dover Publications Inc.: London: Constable & Co., 1959.

Lowth, Robert. *Lectures on the sacred poetry of the Hebrews*. Trans. from the Latin. 2 vols. London 1753; rpt 1781.

Schiller, Friedrich von. *On the aesthetic education of man. In a series of letters*. Trans. Elizabeth Wilkinson and L. A. Willoughby. Oxford: Clarendon Press, 1967; rpt 1982, 1985.

Correspondence between Schiller and Goethe from 1794 to 1805. Trans. from the 3rd ed. of the German with notes by L. Dora Schmitz. 2 vols. London: George Bell and Sons, 1877.

Correspondence of Schiller with Körner. Comprising sketches and anecdotes of Goethe, the Schlegels, Wieland and other contemporaries. London, 1849.

'Language' and 'To the Poet'. *Musenalmanach* (1797). Rpt. *Schillers Samtliche Werke*. Sabular-Ausgabe. Trans. v. E. v. d. Hellen. Stuttgart and Berlin, 1904–1905, Vol. I.

On the naive and sentimental in literature. Trans., ed. Helen Watanabe-O'Kelly. Manchester: Carcanet New Press, 1981.

'On the sublime'. In *Essays Aesthetical and philosophical*. Trans. Anon. Bohn's Standard Library. London: George Bell and Sons, 1875, pp. 128–42.

Shairp, J. C. *On poetic interpretation of nature*. Edinburgh: David Douglas, 1877.

Trapp, Joseph. *Lectures on poetry*. Trans. from the Latin by William Bowyer. London, 1742; rpt. in facsimile, Menston, Yorkshire: Scolar Press, 1973.

Twining, Thomas. 'On poetry considered as an imitative art', in *Aristotle's Treatise on poetry translated with notes on the translation and on the original and two dissertations on poetrical and musical imitation*. London, 1789.

Warton, Joseph. *An essay in the genius and writings of Pope*. London: M. Cooper, 1756.

Young, Edward. 'A discourse on lyric poetry'. In *The complete works poetry and prose of the Rev. Edward Young LL.D* to which is prefixed *A life of the author by John Doran LL.D*. 2 vols. London: William Tegg and Co., 1865.

Nineteenth-century works

Clare, John. *Autobiographical writings*. Ed. Eric Robinson. Oxford: Oxford University Press, 1983.

John Clare: Poems, chiefly from manuscript. Ed. Edmund Blunden and Alan Porter. London: Richard Cobden-Sanderson, 1920.

John Clare. The Oxford Authors. Ed. Eric Robinson and Geoffrey Summerfield. Oxford: Oxford University Press, 1984.

The letters of John Clare. Ed. Mark Storey. Oxford: Clarendon Press, 1985.

Madrigals and chronicles: being newly found poems written by John Clare. Ed. Edmund Blunden. London: The Beaumont Press, 1924.

The Midsummer Cushion. Ed. Anne Tibble. Northumberland: Mid-Northumberland Arts Group, in ass. with Carcanet New Press, 1978.

Poems by John Clare. Ed. Arthur Symons. London: Henry Frowde, 1908.

Poems descriptive of rural life and scenery. London: Taylor and Hessey, 1820.

The poems of John Clare. Ed. J. W. Tibble. 2 vols. London: J. M. Dent, 1935.

The prose of John Clare. Ed. J. W. Tibble and Anne Tibble. London: Routledge and Kegan Paul, 1951; rpt 1971.

The Rural Muse. London: Whittaker, 1835.

Selected poems and prose of John Clare. Ed. Eric Robinson and Geoffrey Summerfield. Oxford: Oxford University Press, 1966; rpt 1970.

The Shepherds Calendar. Ed. Eric Robinson and Geoffrey Summerfield. London: Oxford University Press, 1964.

The Village Minstrel and other poems by John Clare the Northamptonshire peasant. London: Taylor and Hessey, 1821.

Coleridge, Samuel Taylor. *Biographia literaria*. Ed. J. Shawcross. 2 vols. Oxford: Oxford University Press; London: Geoffrey Cumberledge, 1907; rpt 1949.

Collected letters. Ed. E. L. Griggs. 6 vols. Oxford: Clarendon Press, 1956–1971.

Miscellaneous criticism. Ed. T. M. Raysor. Cambridge, Mass., 1936.

Notebooks. Ed. Kathleen Coburn. 3 vols. London: Routledge and Kegan Paul, 1957.

Shakespearean criticism. Ed. T. M. Raysor. 2 vols. London: Constable and Co., 1930.

'The statesman's manual'. In *The collected works of Samuel Taylor Coleridge.* Ed. Kathleen Coburn. Princeton and London, 1971. Vol. 6, *Lay sermons.* Ed. R. J. White. Princeton: Princeton University Press; London: Routledge and Kegan Paul, 1972.

Fichte, J. G. *Science of knowledge.* Trans. John Lachs. Ed. Peter Heath. New York: Meredith Corporation, 1970; rpt. Cambridge: Cambridge University Press, 1982.

Hazlitt, William. *The collected works of William Hazlitt.* Ed. P. P. Howe. 21 vols. London and Toronto: J. M. Dent and Sons, 1930.

Hegel, Georg Wilhelm Friedrich. *Introduction to aesthetics, being the introduction to the Berlin Aesthetics Lectures of the 1820s.* Trans. T. M. Knox. With an interpretative essay by Charles Karelis. Oxford: Oxford University Press, 1979.

Redding, Cyrus. Untitled article. *English Journal,* 22, 29 May 1841, 340–343.

Review of *The Rural Muse* by John Clare. *Druid's Monthly Magazine,* NS 2 (1835), 131–134.

Review of *The Village Minstrel* by John Clare. *Monthly Magazine,* 1 November 1821, pp. 321–325.

Review of *The Village Minstrel* by John Clare. *Eclectic Review,* NS 27 (January–June 1822), 31–45.

Rousseau, J. J. 'Essay on the origin of language'. Trans. John H. Moran. In *On the origin of language.* Milestones of Thought. New York: Frederick Ungar Publishing Co., 1966.

Schelling, F. W. *The philosophy of art: an oration on the relation between the plastic arts and nature* (1807). Trans. A. Johnson. London: John Chapman, 1845.

System of transcendental idealism (1800). Trans. Peter Heath. Charlottesville: University of Virginia Press, 1978.

Schlegel, A. W. *A course of lectures on dramatic art and literature.* Trans. John Black. London: Henry Bohn, 1846.

Schlegel, Friedrich. *Dialogue on poetry and literary aphorisms.* Trans., ed. Ernest Behler and Roman Struc. Pennsylvania State University Park and London: Pennsylvania University Press, 1968.

Wordsworth, William. *Prose works.* Ed. W. J. B. Owen and Jane Worthington Smyser. 3 vols. Oxford: Clarendon Press, 1974.

Twentieth-century works

Abel, Elizabeth. 'Redefining the sister arts: Baudelaire's response to the
    art of Delacroix'. *Critical Inquiry,* 6 (Spring 1980), 363–384. Rpt. in
    The language of images. Ed. J. W. T. Mitchell. Chicago and London:
    University of Chicago Press, 1974, pp. 37–58.
Abrams, M. H. *The mirror and the lamp: Romantic theory and the critical
    tradition.* London: Oxford University Press, 1953; rpt. 1980
    *Natural supernaturalism: tradition and revolution in Romantic litera-
    ture.* New York: W. W. Norton and Co., 1971.
    'Structure and style in the greater Romantic lyric'. In *From sensibility to
    Romanticism: essays presented to Frederick A. Pottle.* Ed. Harold
    Bloom and F. W. Hilles. New York: Oxford University Press, 1965.
    'Two roads to Wordsworth'. In *Wordsworth: a collection of critical
    essays.* Ed. M. H. Abrams. Twentieth-Century Views. Englewood
    Cliffs: Prentice-Hall, 1972.
    Ed. *Wordsworth: a collection of critical essays.* Twentieth-Century
    Views. Englewood Cliffs: Prentice-Hall, 1972.
Ameriks, Karl. 'Kant and the objectivity of taste'. *British Journal of
    Aesthetics,* 23 (1983), 3–17.
Armstrong, Isobel. *Language as living form in nineteenth-century poetry.*
    Sussex: Harvester Press; N.J.: Barnes and Noble, 1982.
Arnheim, Rudolf. 'A plea for visual thinking'. *Critical Inquiry,* 6 (Spring
    1980), 489–497. Rpt. in *The language of images.* Ed. J. W. T.
    Mitchell, pp. 171–179.
Babbitt, Irving. *The new Laokoon: an essay on the confusion of the arts.*
    London: Constable and Co.; Boston and New York: Houghton
    Mifflin Co., 1910.
Barnes, Barry. 'Conception of knowledge'. In *Interests and the growth of
    knowledge.* London: Routledge and Kegan Paul, 1977; rpt. in
    Modernism, criticism, Realism. Ed. Charles Harrison and Fred
    Orton. London: Harper and Row, 1984, pp. 107–111.
Barrell, John. *The idea of landscape and the sense of place 1730–1840: an
    approach to the poetry of John Clare.* Cambridge: Cambridge
    University Press, 1972.
Bate, Walter Jackson. *Coleridge.* London: Weidenfeld and Nicolson,
    1968.
    *From Classic to Romantic: premises of taste in eighteenth-century
    England.* Cambridge, Mass.: Harvard University Press, 1981.
Beach, Joseph Warren. *The concept of nature in nineteenth-century English
    poetry.* New York: Russell and Russell, 1936; rpt. 1966.
Behler, Ernest. 'The origins of the Romantic literary theory'. *Colloquia
    Germanica,* 1–2 (1968), 109–126.

Bloom, Harold. 'The internalization of quest–romance'. *Yale Review*, 58 (June 1969), 526–536.

Poetry and repression: revisionism from Blake to Stevens. New Haven and London: Yale University Press, 1976.

Ed. *Romanticism and consciousness*. New York: W. W. Norton and Co., 1970.

The visionary company: a reading of English Romantic poetry. London: Faber and Faber, 1961.

Bostetter, Edward E. *The Romantic ventriloquists: Wordsworth, Coleridge, Keats, Shelley, Byron*. Seattle: University of Washington Press, 1963.

Brown, Robert F. *The later philosophy of Schelling*. Lewisburg: Bucknell University Press; London: Associated University Presses, 1977.

Brownlow, Timothy. *John Clare and picturesque landscape*. Oxford: Clarendon Press, 1983.

Cassirer, Ernst. *The philosophy of the Enlightenment*. Trans. Fritz C. A. Koelln and James P. Pettegrove. 1932; rpt. Princeton: Princeton University Press, 1951.

Language. Vol. I of *The philosophy of symbolic forms*. Trans. Ralph Manheim. New Haven and London: Yale University Press, 1955; rpt. 1977.

Chase, Cynthia. 'The accidents of disfiguration: limits to literal and rhetorical reading in Book V of *The Prelude*'. *Studies in Romanticism*, 18 (Winter 1979), 547–565.

Cohen, Ralph. *The art of discrimination: Thomson's 'The Seasons' and the language of criticism*. London: Routledge and Kegan Paul, 1964.

Copleston, Frederick. *Kant*. Vol. VI of *A history of philosophy*. London: Burns and Oates Ltd., 1964.

Fichte to Nietzsche. Vol. VII of *A history of philosophy*. London; Burns and Oates Ltd., 1968.

Culler, Jonathan. *On deconstruction: theory and criticism after structuralism*. London: Routledge and Kegan Paul, 1983.

Danby, John. *The simple Wordsworth: studies in the poems 1797–1807*. London: Routledge and Kegan Paul, 1968; rpt. 1971.

Derrida, Jacques. *Of grammatology*. Trans. Gayatri Spivak. 1967; Baltimore and London: Johns Hopkins University Press, 1974; rpt. 1976.

'The Parergon'. Trans. Craig Owens from part II of *La vérité en peinture* (Paris, 1978). *October* 9 (Summer 1979), 3–40.

'Structure, sign and play in the discourse of the human sciences'. In *Writing and difference*. Trans. Alan Bass. 1967; Chicago: University of Chicago Press; London: Routledge and Kegan Paul, 1978, pp. 278–293.

Egan, Rose Frances. 'The genesis of the theory of "art for art's sake" in Germany'. Part I. *Smith College Studies in Modern Languages*, 2 (July 1921).

Engell, James. *The creative imagination: Enlightenment to Romanticism*. Cambridge, Mass.: Harvard University Press, 1981.

Ferguson, Frances. *Wordsworth: language as counter-spirit*. New Haven and London: Yale University Press, 1977.

Firchow, Peter, trans. *Lucinde and the fragments*. By Friedrich Schlegel. Minneapolis: University of Minnesota Press, 1971.

Fish, Stanley. 'How ordinary is ordinary language?' *New Literary History*, 5 (Autumn 1973), 41–54.

Frosch, Thomas R. 'The descriptive style of John Clare'. *Studies in Romanticism*, 10 (Summer 1971), 137–149.

Frye, Northrop. *Antomy of criticism: four essays*. Princeton: Princeton University Press, 1957.

Gadamer, Hans-Georg. *Truth and method*. Trans. William Glen-Doepl from the 2nd (1965) ed. of *Wahrheit und Methode*. Ed. John Cumming and Garret Burdon. London: Sheed and Ward, 1975; rpt. 1979.

Gilbert, Katherine and Helmut Kuhn. *A history of aesthetics*. London: Thames and Hudson, 1956.

Gingerich, Solomon Francis. *Essays in the Romantic poets*. New York, 1929.

Gombrich, E. H. *Art and illusion: a study in the psychology of pictorial representation*. Princeton: Princeton University Press, 1960; rpt. 1972.

Goodman, Nelson. *Languages of art: an approach to a theory of symbols*. Indianapolis: Hackett Publishing Company, 1976.

Ways of worldmaking. Indianapolis: Hackett Publishing Company, 1978.

Gosse, Edmund. 'Nature in poetry'. Rev. of *Madrigals and Chronicles* by John Clare. *Sunday Times*, No. 5295, 5 October 1924, 8, cols. 3–4.

Hagstrum, Jean. *The sister arts: the tradition of literary pictorialism and English poetry from Dryden to Gray*. Chicago: University of Chicago Press, 1958.

Hamilton, K. G. *The two harmonies: poetry and prose in the seventeenth century*. Oxford: Clarendon Press, 1963.

Hamilton, Paul. *Coleridge's poetics*. Cambridge: Cambridge University Press, 1983.

Hanson, N. R. 'Observation'. In *Patterns of discovery: an inquiry into the conceptual foundations of science*. London: Cambridge University Press, 1972. Rpt. in *Modernism, criticism, Realism*. Ed. Harrison and Orton, pp. 69–84.

Harrison, Charles and Fred Orton, eds. *Modernism, criticism, Realism, alternative contexts for art*. London: Harper and Row, 1984.

Hartman, Geoffrey. *Beyond formalism: literary essays 1958–1970*. New Haven and London: Yale University Press, 1970.

'The use and abuse of structural analysis'. *New Literary History*, 7 (Autumn 1975), 165–189.

Wordsworth's poetry 1787–1814. New Haven: Yale University Press, 1964.

Hauser, Arnold. *Rococo, Classicism and Romanticism*. Vol. III of *The social history of art*. London: Routledge and Kegan Paul, 1962; rpt. 1984.

Hayner, Paul Collins. *Reason and existence: Schelling's philosophy of history*. Leiden: E. J. Brill, 1967.

Henrich, Dieter. 'Beauty and freedom: Schiller's struggle with Kant's aesthetics'. *Zeitschrift für philosophische Forschung*, 11 (1957). Rpt. in *Essays in Kant's aesthetics*. Ed. Ted Cohen and Paul Guyer. Chicago: Chicago University Press, 1982, pp. 237–257.

Hinchcliffe, Keith. 'Wordsworth and the kinds of metaphor'. *Studies in Romanticism*, 23 (Spring 1984), 81–100.

Hipple, Walter J. *The beautiful, the sublime and the picturesque in eighteenth-century British aesthetic theory*. Carbondale: Southern Illinois University Press, 1957.

Hirsch, E. D. *Wordsworth and Schelling: a typological study of Romanticism*. New Haven: Yale University Press, 1960.

Hussey, Christopher. *The picturesque: studies in a point of view*. London: Frank Cass and Co., 1967.

Johnson, Lee McKay. *The metaphor of painting: essays on Baudelaire, Ruskin, Proust and Pater*. Studies in the Fine Arts: Criticism 7. Ann Arbor, Michigan: UMI Research Press, 1980.

Kerry, S. S. *Schiller's aesthetics*. Manchester: Manchester University Press, 1961.

Krieger, Murray. 'Mediation, language, and vision in the reading of literature'. In *Interpretation: theory and practice*. Ed. Charles S. Singleton. The Johns Hopkins Humanities Seminars. Baltimore: Johns Hopkins University Press, 1969, pp. 211–242.

Land, Stephen. *From signs to propositions: the concept of form in eighteenth-century semantic theory*. London: Longmans, 1974.

Leavis, F. R. '"Antony and Cleopatra" and "All for Love": a critical exercise'. *Scrutiny* (1931), 158–169.

'English poetry in the eighteenth century'. *Scrutiny* (1936), 13–31.

Leitch, Vincent B. *Deconstructive criticism: an advanced introduction*. London: Hutchinson, 1983.

Lentricchia, Frank. *After the new criticism*. London: The Athlone Press, 1980.

Leppard, David. 'An investigation into the theory and structure of metaphor with special reference to Wordsworth and Yeats'. Unpublished D. Phil thesis, University of Oxford, 1983.

Lessa, Richard. 'John Clare's voice and two sonnets'. *John Clare Society Journal*, 3 July 1984, pp. 26–33.

'Time and John Clare's Calendar'. *Critical Quarterly*, 24 (Spring 1982), 59–71.

Lindenberger, Herbert. 'Images of interaction in *The Prelude*'. In *On Wordsworth's Prelude*. Princeton: Princeton University Press, 1963. Rpt. in *The Prelude. 1799, 1805, 1850*. By Wordsworth. Ed. M. H. Abrams, Stephen Gill, and Jonathan Wordsworth. Norton Critical Editions. London and New York: W. W. Norton and Co., 1979, pp. 642–663.

Looker, Samuel J. 'The life and genius of John Clare'. *Poetry Review*, Sept. Oct. 1920, pp. 263–264.

Lovejoy, Arthur E. 'Schiller and the genesis of German Romanticism'. Part I, *Modern Language Notes*, 35 (January 1920), 1–10. Part 2, *Modern Language Notes*, 35 (March 1920), 136–146.

Lynd, Robert. Unsigned rev. of *Poems, chiefly from manuscript*. By John Clare. *Nation*, 28, 22 January 1921, 581–582.

Man, Paul de. *Allegories of reading: figural language in Rousseau, Nietzsche, Rilke and Proust*. New Haven and London: Yale University Press, 1979.

Blindness and insight: essays in the rhetoric of contemporary criticism. London: Methuen, 1983.

'Structure intentionnelle de l'image romantique'. *Revue internationale de philosophie*, 51 (1960). Rpt. and trans. in *Romanticism and consciousness*. Ed. Harold Bloom, pp. 65–77. Also rpt. in *Wordsworth: a collection of critical essays*. Ed. M. H. Abrams, pp. 133–144.

'The rhetoric of temporality'. In *Interpretation: theory and practice*. Ed. Charles S. Singleton. The Johns Hopkins Humanities Seminars. Baltimore: Johns Hopkins University Press, 1969, pp. 173–209.

'Symbolic landscape in Wordsworth and Yeats'. In *The rhetoric of Romanticism*. New York: Columbia University Press, 1984, pp. 125–144.

McGann, Jerome. *The Romantic ideology: a critical investigation*. Chicago and London: University of Chicago Press, 1983.

McIvins, William. *Prints and visual communication*. London: Routledge and Kegan Paul, 1953.

Massingham, Harold J. Rev. of *John Clare: Poems chiefly from manuscript*. *Athenaeum*. 7, No. 4732, 7 January 1921, pp. 9–10.

Miall, David S. 'Kant's *Critique of judgement*: a biased aesthetics'. *British Journal of Aesthetics*, 20 (1980), 135–145.

Miller, J. Hillis. 'The still heart: poetic form in Wordsworth', *New Literary History*, 2 (Winter 1971), 297–310.

Mitchell, J. W. T., ed. *The language of images*. Chicago and London: University of Chicago Press, 1974, rpt. 1980.

Monk, Samuel. *The sublime: a study of critical theories in XVIIIth-century England*. New York: MLA of America, 1935.

Murry, John Middleton. 'Clare and Wordsworth'. Rev. of *Madrigals and chronicles* by John Clare. Rpt. as 'The case of John Clare'. In *John Clare and other studies*. London, New York: Peter Nevill Ltd., 1950, pp. 19–24.

'The poetry of John Clare'. *Times Literary Supplement*, No. 991, 13 January 1921, pp. 17–18. Rpt. in *Countries of the mind. Essays in Literary Criticism*. London: William Collins, 1922, pp. 103–119. Also rpt. in *John Clare and other studies*, pp. 7–17.

Norris, Christopher. *The deconstructive turn: essays in the rhetoric of philosophy*. London: Methuen, 1983.

Osborne, Harold. *Aesthetics and art theory: an historical introduction*. London: Longmans, 1968.

Park, Roy. *Hazlitt and the spirit of the age: abstraction and critical theory*. Oxford: Clarendon Press, 1971.

Pinsky, Robert. 'That sweet man, John Clare'. In *The rarer action: essays in honour of Francis Fergusson*. Ed. Alan Cheuse and Richard Koffler. New Brunswick, N.J.: Rutgers University Press, 1970, pp. 258–274.

Podro, Michael. *The manifold in perception: theories of art from Kant to Hildebrand*. Oxford: Clarendon Press, 1972.

Pollard, Arthur, ed. *Crabbe: the critical heritage*. London, 1972.

Pottle, Frederick. 'Eye and object in the poetry of Wordsworth'. *Yale Review*, 40 (Autumn 1950). Rpt. in *Romanticism and consciousness*. Ed. Harold Bloom, pp. 273–287.

Praz, Mario. *The Romantic agony*. Trans. Angus Davison. London, New York and Toronto: Geoffrey Cumberlege, Oxford University Press, 1933; 2nd ed. 1951.

Rapf, Joanna. Rev. of *The idea of landscape and the sense of place* by John Barrell and of *John Clare: a life* by J. W. Tibble and Anne Tibble. *Studies in Romanticism*, 13 (Winter 1974), 79–84.

Richards, I. A. *The philosophy of rhetoric*. The Mary Flexner Lectures of the Humanities. February and March 1936. London: Oxford University Press, rpt. 1979.

Rorty, Richard. *Consequences of pragmatism. Essays: 1972–1980*. Sussex: Harvester Press, 1982.

'Nineteenth-century idealism and twentieth-century textualism'. *The Monist*, 64 (1981), 155–174. Rpt. in *Consequences of pragmatism*, pp. 139–159.

Philosophy and the mirror of nature. Princeton: Princeton University Press, 1980.

Savile, Anthony. 'Objectivity in aesthetic judgment: Eva Schaper on Kant'. Rev. of *Studies in Kant's aesthetics* by Eva Schaper. *British Journal of Aesthetics*, 21 (1981), 363–369.

Schaper, Eva. *Studies in Kant's aesthetics.* Edinburgh: Edinburgh University Press, 1979.

Scruton, Roger. *Art and imagination: a study in the philosophy of mind.* London: Routledge and Kegan Paul, 1974; rpt. 1982.

Simpson, David, ed. *German aesthetic and literary criticism: Kant, Fichte, Schelling, Schopenhauer, Hegel.* Cambridge: Cambridge University Press, 1984.

Irony and authority in Romantic poetry. London: Macmillan, 1979.

'Criticism, politics and style'. *Critical Inquiry*, 11 (September 1984), 52–81.

Wordsworth and the figuring of the real. London: Macmillan, 1982.

Spiers, John. Rev. of *The poems of John Clare* ed. J. W. Tibble. *Scrutiny* (June 1935), 84–86.

Steiner, George. *After Babel: aspects of language and translation.* Oxford: Oxford University Press, 1975; rpt. 1976.

Storey, Mark, ed. *Clare: the critical heritage.* London: Routledge and Kegan Paul, 1973.

The poetry of John Clare: a critical introduction. London: Macmillan, 1974.

Sutton, Claud. *The German tradition in philosophy.* London: Weidenfeld and Nicolson, 1974.

Swiatecka, M. Jadwiga. *The idea of the symbol: some nineteenth-century comparisons with Coleridge.* Cambridge: Cambridge University Press, 1980.

Swingle, L. J. 'Stalking the essential John Clare: Clare in relation to his Romantic contemporaries'. *Studies in Romanticism*, 14 (Summer 1972), 273–284.

'Wordsworth's contrarieties: a prelude to Wordsworthian complexity'. *Journal of English Literary History*, 44 (Summer 1977), 337–354.

Taylor, Charles. *Hegel.* Cambridge: Cambridge University Press, 1975.

Tibble, J. W. and Anne Tibble. *John Clare: a life.* London, 1932; Totowa, N.J.: Rouman and Littlefield, 1972.

John Clare: his life and poetry. London: William Heinemann Ltd., 1956.

Todorov, Tzvetan. *Theories of the symbol.* Trans. Catherine Porter. Paris, 1977; Oxford: Basil Blackwell, 1982.

Tuveson, Ernest. 'Shaftesbury and the age of sensibility'. In *Studies in aesthetics and criticism, 1660–1800. Essays in honour of Samuel Holt Monk.* Ed. Howard Anderson and John S. Shea. Minneapolis: University of Minnesota Press, 1967, pp. 73–93.

Unwin, Rayner. *The rural muse: studies in the peasant poetry of England.* London: George Allen and Unwin, 1954.

Warnock, Mary. *Imagination.* London: Faber and Faber, 1976; rpt. 1980.

Wasserman, Earl. 'The English Romantics: the grounds of knowledge'. *Studies in Romanticism,* 4 (Autumn 1964), 17–34.

Wellek, René. *The later eighteenth century.* Vol. 1 of *A history of modern criticism 1750–1950.* London: Jonathan Cape, 1955; rpt. 1966.

The Romantic age. Vol. 2 of *A history of modern criticism 1750–1950.* London: Jonathan Cape 1955; rpt. 1966.

Weiskel, Thomas. *The Romantic sublime: studies in the structure and psychology of transcendence.* Baltimore and London: The Johns Hopkins University Press, 1976.

Wessell, Leonard P. 'The antinomic structure of Friedrich Schlegel's "Romanticism"'. *Studies in Romanticism,* 12 (Summer 1973), 648–669.

'Schiller and the genesis of German Romanticism'. *Studies in Romanticism,* 10 (Summer 1971), 176–198.

Wheeler, Kathleen M., ed. *German aesthetic and literary criticism: the Romantic ironists and Goethe.* Cambridge: Cambridge University Press, 1984.

Wilkinson, Elizabeth. 'Schiller – Poet or Philosopher?' Special Taylorian Lecture, 17 November 1959. Oxford: Clarendon Press, 1961.

Wilkinson, Elizabeth M. and L. A. Willoughby, eds. *On the aesthetic education of Man in a series of letters.* Oxford: Clarendon Press, 1967; rpt. 1982, 1985.

Wimsatt, W. K. 'The structure of Romantic nature imagery'. Rpt. in *The verbal icon: studies in the meaning of poetry.* London: Methuen, 1984, pp. 103–116. Also rpt. in *The age of Johnson: essays presented to Chauncey Brewster Tinker.* Ed. Frederick W. Hilles. New Haven and London: Yale University Press, 1949; rpt. 1964, pp. 291–303.

Wittgenstein, Ludwig. *Philosophical investigations.* Trans. G. E. M. Anscombe. Oxford: Basil Blackwell, 1953; rpt. 1958.

Wlecke, Albert. *Wordsworth and the sublime.* Berkeley, LA, London: University of California Press, 1973.

Wollheim, Richard. *Art and its objects.* New York: Harper and Row, 1968; rpt. Cambridge: Cambridge University Press, 1980, 1985.

'The work of art as object'. In *On art and the mind.* Boston, Mass.: Harvard University Press, 1973, pp. 112–119. Rpt. in *Modernism, criticism, Realism.* Ed. Charles Harrison and Fred Orton, pp. 9–17.

Wright, David, ed. *The Penguin book of English Romantic verse.* Harmondsworth: Penguin, 1968; rpt. 1976.

Young, Robert, ed. *Untying the text: a post-structuralist reader.* London: Routledge and Kegan Paul, 1981.